D0900322

European Revolutions and the American Literary Renaissance

European Revolutions
and the
American Literary
Renaissance

Larry J. Reynolds

Yale University Press
New Haven and London

PS
217
E87
R49
1988

11/1988
Lit Lane

Designed by James J. Johnson
and set in Caledonia types.
Printed in the United States of America by Murray
Printing Co., Westford, Massachusetts.

Library of Congress Cataloging-in-Publication Data

Reynolds, Larry J.
    European revolutions and the American literary Renais-
sance / Larry J. Reynolds.
        p.   cm.
    Bibliography: p.
    Includes index.
    ISBN 0-300-04242-6 (alk. paper)
    1. American literature—19th century—History and crit-
icism. 2. American literature—European influences.
3. Europe in literature. 4. Revolutions in literature.
5. Revolutionary literature, American—History and criticism. 6. Literature and revolutions—History—19th century. I. Title.
PS217.E87R49   1988
810'.9'003—dc19   88-3784
                                                    CIP

The paper in this book meets the guidelines for perma-
nence and durability of the Committee on Production
Guidelines for Book Longevity of the Council on Library
Resources.

10 9 8 7 6 5 4 3 2 1

For Carol

Contents

	List of Illustrations	ix
	Preface	xi
1	Revolution and Response	1
2	Emerson and "The Movement"	25
3	The "Red Revolution"	44
4	The "Cause" and Fuller's *Tribune* Letters	54
5	*The Scarlet Letter* and Revolutions Abroad	79
6	*Moby-Dick* and the Matter of France	97
7	Revolution, Martyrdom, and *Leaves of Grass*	125
8	Kossuth "Fever" and the Serenity of *Walden*	153
	Epilogue	171
	Notes	175
	Index	201

Illustrations

Students at the Pont de la Concorde.   7

Barricade in the Rue St. Martin.   8

The People in the Throne-Room of the Tuileries.   9

Headlines of the New York *Tribune*, 22 April 1848.   13

Engraving of Lamartine on Front Page of the New York *Herald*,
29 March 1848.   20

Lamartine Addressing the Mob in Front of the Hôtel de Ville.   23

National Workshop (Tailors) in the Prison of Clichy, at Paris.   33

A Paris Club in 1848.   34

The June Days—Place Maubert, Paris.   47

Women on a Barricade Near the Porte St. Denis, Paris, during the
June Days.   56

Battle at the Porta San Pancrazio.   70

Garibaldi and His Men.   73

The Princess Belgiojoso.   75

Woodcut in the Boston *Post*, 14 June 1849.   83

The Execution of Charles I.   85

The Death of Louis XVI.   89

Hester Standing on the Scaffold.   90

French Men-of-War in Typee Bay.   102

"Pêche de la Baleine" (detail) by Ambroise Louis Garneray.   112

"Battle of Marengo, 1800" (detail) by L. F. Lejeune.   112

Engraved Bust of Napoleon Owned by Herman Melville.   115

Illustration from the *Working Man's Advocate,* 15 March 1845.   120

The People of Paris during the February Revolution.   121

Lamartine and the Red Flag.   122

The End of *Moby-Dick.*   123

The Sower (1850) by Jean-François Millet.   129

Kossuth's Entrance into Central Park, New York.   146

The Hungarian War.   155

The Freeman's Defence in *Uncle Tom's Cabin.*   156

Portrait of Louis Kossuth.   158

Preface

This book is about the influence of the European revolutions of 1848–49 upon American literature of the mid–nineteenth century, a period often referred to as the American literary renaissance. F. O. Matthiessen, in the preface to his seminal *American Renaissance*, explained that his study began with the realization of "how great a number of our past masterpieces were produced in one extraordinarily concentrated moment of expression." The moment was 1850–55, and the masterpieces were Emerson's *Representative Men* (1850), Hawthorne's *The Scarlet Letter* (1850), Melville's *Moby-Dick* (1851), Thoreau's *Walden* (1854), and Whitman's *Leaves of Grass* (1855). Matthiessen chose not to explore the questions of how or why these works all appeared at just this point in time, focusing his attention instead upon "their fusions of form and content."[1] Subsequent critics and scholars, however, have offered a variety of persuasive answers, all emphasizing the importance of national developments.

In 1850, of course, the spirit of nationalism was peaking in the United States. During 1845–49, President Polk, "Young Hickory," had taken Jacksonian Democracy, with its boisterous, bumptious celebration of the "People," to new limits with his aggressive foreign policies. By the end of his term, the Oregon Territory belonged to the United States south of forty-nine degrees latitude, the Mexican War had been won, and not only Texas but present-day California, Arizona, Nevada, Utah, and parts of New Mexico, Colorado, and Wyoming would soon belong to the Union. With the discovery of gold in California in January 1848, America seemed more than ever a promised land inhabited by a chosen people. By midcentury, the growing literate public had acquired an appreciation of novels and poems that celebrated American settings and American ideals; and, as literary

Young America reached its climax with Melville's orgasmic review "Haw-thorne and His Mosses" (1850), a national literature of considerable value flowered. Not surprisingly, to twentieth-century scholars its roots seemed to go deep into American soil.

As this study intends to show, however, historic international develop-ments, especially the European revolutions of 1848–49, helped effect this flowering. Although now long forgotten, European revolutionary heroes, imagery, and issues quickened the American literary imagination and shaped the characters, plots, and themes of American writings. To under-stand the ideological forces impelling *The Scarlet Letter* or *Moby-Dick*, or lesser achievements such as Lowell's *Biglow Papers* (1848) or Stowe's *Uncle Tom's Cabin* (1852), one must first recognize that these works were written during a revolutionary age, at a time when King Louis Philippe had been overthrown in France, Prince Metternich driven from Vienna, King William IV from Berlin, the pope from Rome. At midcentury republicanism and absolutism had fought and were fighting a desperate battle for the future of Europe, or so it seemed to Americans, and the shifts in political power caused by radical action and conservative reaction deeply engaged the American literary mind and acted as a catalyst upon it.

The reader deserves here some credible explanation of why, if my the-sis is valid, it has never been put forward before. The first of several likely answers is that the revolutions of 1848–49, unlike the famous American Revolution of 1776 and French Revolution of 1789, came to naught; with just a few exceptions, the overthrown rulers regained authority, making the revolutions appear inconsequential in retrospect. In addition, the excite-ment they generated in America, while intense, lasted only about four years; after 1852, national attention turned to the growing tensions of the slavery issue, with the Civil War eventually eclipsing Europe's role as the previous focus of this attention. Moreover, studies of the literature of the period by modern academics have tended to focus on native topics and themes, such as American Puritanism, Jacksonian Democracy, westward expansion, American transcendentalism, the myth of the American Adam, and the American frontier. Concomitantly, reference works have provided chronol-ogies that correlate American history with the lives and works of American authors. In other words, the critical tradition in American literary studies has emphasized the national features of the literature it has treated, thus obscuring the substantial international influences upon American writers at midcentury.

Two patterns of organization shape the discussion of this book. Within each chapter, the progress is from context to text, from general description of relevant historical materials to an examination of specific literary works, with the focus upon how these works were inspired, informed, and shaped by the European revolutionary scene. Between chapters, the progress is roughly chronological. Chapter 1 attempts to recapture the spirit of the times in America during the first half of 1848. Drawing upon contemporary American newspapers, magazines, journals, diaries, and letters, I summarize events in Europe and document the intense response to them by members of the American literati. The first major author I discuss at length is Emerson, who was in England and Paris in the spring of 1848 and, as I show in Chapter 2, was challenged and stimulated by the revolutionary events he witnessed, especially the clamor about socialism in the clubs and streets of Paris. My third chapter discusses the Bloody June Days that occurred in Paris following Emerson's departure and briefly examines their effect upon the American public and American writers. The subject of my fourth chapter is Margaret Fuller, who served as a foreign correspondent for the New York *Tribune* during the revolutions and became a Roman revolutionary herself during the spring and summer of 1849. After comparing Emerson's and Fuller's responses to Revolutionary Europe, I focus on Fuller's *Tribune* dispatches from Italy and demonstrate how they constitute a coherent historical narrative of unrecognized artistry and value. Chapter 5 examines Hawthorne's relationship with Fuller and shows how *The Scarlet Letter*, written in the fall of 1849, was influenced by the revolutions abroad and by Fuller's revolutionary activities. Chapter 6 examines Melville's lifelong obsession with revolution in France and indicates how this obsession shaped *Moby-Dick*, written during 1850–51, following Melville's return from France and England in the winter of 1849. My seventh chapter shows how Whitman was inspired by the European revolutionary scene he covered as editor of the New Orleans *Crescent* and describes the process by which, in response to the revolutions, he reconceived himself as a poet of insurrection and revolt. Focusing upon his tribute to the European revolutionaries in the poem "Resurgemus," published in the 21 June 1850 *Tribune*, I discuss how that work served as the chronological, stylistic, and thematic beginning of *Leaves of Grass* (1855). Chapter 8 treats the events that occurred in the wake of the revolutions, especially Kossuth's visit of 1851–52 to the United States, and shows how these informed the action of *Uncle Tom's Cabin* and precipitated the reshaping of *Walden* into a spiritual autobiography emphasizing purity and serenity. The Epilogue offers some general conclusions and discusses their implications with regard to recent scholarship on the literature of the period.

Acknowledgments

In the course of writing this study, I have received much help, and I take pleasure in acknowledging it here. Texas A&M University provided me with both a summer research grant and an academic study leave to work on the book. My dean, Daniel Fallon, and my former department head, David H.

Stewart, have been generous in their support. I am grateful to my current department head, Hamlin Hill, and to my colleagues Harrison T. Meserole and Dale T. Knobel, who were kind enough to read the completed manuscript and to offer helpful responses to it. For permission to use an earlier version of my Hawthorne chapter and a portion of my Whitman chapter, I am grateful to the editors of *American Literature* and *American Transcendental Quarterly,* respectively.[2] Six scholars at other institutions—Merton M. Sealts, Jr., Robert N. Hudspeth, Buford Jones, Lawrence Buell, Milton R. Stern, and Anthony O'Keeffe—read versions of one or more chapters and gave me valuable criticism and encouragement. At Texas A&M, the Fellows of the Interdisciplinary Group for Historical Literary Study have created a genial and stimulating intellectual community that I have benefited from greatly. I am particularly indebted to Jeffrey N. Cox, Pamela Mathews, and Dennis A. Berthold, who gave me helpful responses to portions of the manuscript, and to Paul A. Parrish, Kenneth M. Price, Mark B. Busby, and David R. Anderson, who read all of the chapters in early drafts and provided reliable and valuable suggestions for revision. To my friend and colleague Katherine O'Brien O'Keeffe I am especially indebted, for not only reading my work but also talking with me often about it and helping me discover what I thought and knew. My debt to my wife, Carol, exceeds all others; through her goodness and vitality she has shown me what is valuable about life and literature.

European Revolutions and the American Literary Renaissance

1

Revolution and Response

> If there is any period one would desire to be born in, is it not the age of Revolution: when the old and the new stand side by side and admit of being compared; when the energies of all men are searched by fear and hope; when the historic glories of the old can be compensated by the rich possibilities of the new era?
>
> —EMERSON, "The American Scholar" (1837)

Unlike the other major writers of the American renaissance, Henry David Thoreau struggled not to take an interest in the European upheavals that engaged the attention of all around him. Nevertheless, on the evening of 26 January 1848, when he stood before the Concord Lyceum and spoke to his neighbors about tyranny and revolution, he gave expression to the spirit of revolution peaking in intensity across the Atlantic. "All men recognize the right of revolution," Thoreau declared, "that is, the right to refuse allegiance to and to resist the government, when its tyranny or its inefficiency are great and unendurable. . . . I think that it is not too soon for honest men to rebel and revolutionize."[1] Thoreau's quarrel, of course, was with the American government because of its toleration of slavery and its imperialism in Mexico, but his talk, "The Relation of the Individual to the State" (later to be published and known as "Civil Disobedience"), provided counsel for conscientious men everywhere and coincided with radical sentiments abroad that his friends Emerson and Fuller were then encountering and that would soon lead to an unprecedented series of riots, insurrections, and revolutions across the Continent.

For several years revolution in Europe had been anticipated, and by the beginning of 1848, it seemed imminent to the perceptive. In her essay "First of January" (1846), Margaret Fuller had observed that "the caldron simmers, and so great is the fire that we expect it soon to boil over, and new fates appear for Europe." During the next two years, the caldron grew hotter, and three days before Thoreau's talk, Friedrich Engels summarized the events that had made 1847 the "most agitated" year "for a long time." A constitution and United Diet in Prussia, a political awakening in Italy and a call to arms against Austria, a civil war in Switzerland, a new, radical parliament in England, scandals and reform banquets in France, the conquest of

Mexico by the United States—"this," said Engels, "is a sequence of changes and movements such as we have not seen in recent years."[2]

The sequence presaged even more dramatic changes in the coming months, as Engels and his friend Marx well knew, which is why the latter, in Brussels, was hurriedly trying to complete the *Communist Manifesto* before the 1 February deadline set by the Communist League. Marx met the deadline, and the *Manifesto*'s strutting conclusion, urging workers to unite in the "forcible overthrow of all existing social conditions,"[3] seemed to make him and his colleagues leaders of the parade of coming events. Written in German and read at first only by leaders of the European communes, the *Manifesto* actually had little effect upon the revolutions that occurred within weeks; however, the radicalism it expressed did, for the socialist and communist doctrines of Saint-Simon, Fourier, Owen, Cabet, and Proudhon (all of whom Marx rejected in the *Manifesto* as bourgeois or insufficiently revolutionary) had been gaining adherents and advocates among workers and intellectuals in the major cities of Europe. In addition, the Social-Democrats in France, whom Marx claimed as allies of the communists, had formulated ideas about the right to work and the organization of labor that had become familiar to the Paris working class and would become slogans during their uprisings.[4]

The growing influence and import of radical doctrines had not been lost on one astute social observer, Alexis de Tocqueville, author of the brilliant *Democracy in America* (1835). At the same moment that Thoreau in Concord was addressing the Lyceum audience and Marx in Brussels was completing the *Manifesto*, Tocqueville in Paris was preparing a prophetic speech to be delivered to his colleagues in the French Chamber of Deputies. On 27 January, he warned this group that the Paris working classes were acquiring opinions and ideas that tended not simply to the overthrow of laws, ministers, or governments, "but rather to the overthrow of society, breaking down the bases on which it now rests." After referring to the "most terrifying of revolutions" that these opinions would "bring in their train," he declared, "Gentlemen, my profound conviction is that we are lulling ourselves to sleep over an active volcano."[5] Although most of Tocqueville's colleagues responded to his words with insulting laughter, revolution was indeed at hand and, in fact, in one part of Europe had already erupted.

On 12 January, the people of Palermo had risen in revolt against Ferdinand II, the tyrant king of Naples and Sicily. The king's troops had been defeated and driven from the city and a provisional government established. Other towns in Sicily had followed suit, riots had broken out in Naples, and Austria was threatening to intervene on behalf of the beleaguered Bourbon king.[6] On the same day Tocqueville voiced concern to his colleagues, Margaret Fuller wrote to her *Tribune* readers from Rome, "There is news that the revolution has now broken out in Naples; that neither Sicilians nor Neapolitans will trust the king, but demand his abdication. . . . Aggressions on the part of the Austrians continue in the North. . . . Every day the cloud swells, and the next fortnight is likely to bring important tidings."[7] From the south news soon came that on the day of Fuller's dispatch, 27 January, the frightened King Ferdinand II had granted Naples and Sicily a popular constitution. Within a month, the more imposing monarchy of France fell.

On 22–24 February, the subjects of King Louis Philippe, inspired by events in Italy, fulfilled Tocqueville's prophecy. Barricades were erected in the streets of Paris; mobs of workers joined by students and members of the National Guard converged on the Tuileries; the king abdicated; and a provisional government, led by the poet-statesman Alphonse de Lamartine, quickly formed and declared France a republic. Thoreau in his lecture had asserted that "when the subject has refused allegiance, and the officer has resigned his office, then the revolution is accomplished,"[8] and in the case of the French revolution of 1848, he was right. It was almost that simple.

The success of the revolution in France and the ease with which it was accomplished initiated a wave of upheavals across Europe; within months more than fifty revolutions broke out in the cities and towns of Austria, Prussia, Italy, and the lesser German states, with peripheral uprisings in Spain, Ireland, Denmark, and Rumania. Prince Metternich of Austria, who for more than fifty years had been the most powerful despot in Europe, fled to England. King Frederick William IV of Prussia, after revolutions had progressed from Munich northward through Frankfurt, Nassau, Cologne, and Solingen, finally reaching Berlin on 18 March, withdrew his troops from the city after eight hours of fierce street fighting and agreed to the election of a constituent assembly. In London, the Chartists planned a massive and potentially revolutionary demonstration on 10 April, but the government intimidated participants and defused the demonstration through the use of thousands of special constables and army troops. In Russia, Czar Nicholas's iron rule likewise maintained law and order (the torture and imprisonment in 1849 of Dostoyevski and others in the Petraskevski circle, who had been inspired by the French revolution, exemplify his methods). "Que reste-t-il encore debout en Europe?" [What remains standing in Europe?] the czar wrote to Queen Victoria on 3 April 1848. "La Grande Bretagne et la Russie!"[9] And at the time, his boast was accurate. The lands between those two powers had indeed been swept by a revolutionary whirlwind.

The causes of the revolutions were many and complex. In Italy and Hungary, the nationalist movements led by Joseph Mazzini and Louis Kossuth played major roles in inspiring the revolutions. In France, socialist and communist doctrines eventually seemed the major causes of the revolution to American observers. Two popular French books, Louis Blanc's *History of the Ten Years, 1830–1840* (1841–44) (a scathing analysis of Louis Philippe's reign) and Lamartine's *History of the Girondists* (1847) (a stirring narrative of the French Revolution of 1789), were also credited with encouraging the people to stage a revolution and providing them a script for doing so.

Ironically, Emerson, who viewed the French revolution of 1848 with skepticism, had, unbeknownst to himself, contributed to its outbreak. Three famous professors at the Collège de France—Jules Michelet, Edgar Quinet, and Adam Mickiewicz—became during the early forties great admirers of Emerson, and they in turn through their lectures cultivated revolutionary impulses in their students. Michelet, historian of the great French Revolution, apparently appreciated Emerson's apology for subjectivism in history, which seemed to justify the republican biases in his own lectures and writings. Quinet, a reformer and philosopher, was attracted to Emerson's ethical ideas and incorporated striking phrases from Emerson's works into his lectures. Mickiewicz, the Polish poet and mystic who would become the godfather of Margaret Fuller's child, enthusiastically accepted Emerson's idealism as his own, and he too quoted Emerson frequently in his lectures.[10] Together, these three, because they opposed the materialistic spirit of the age and advocated a democratic idealism associated with the 1789 French Revolution, posed a threat to Louis Philippe's government, which canceled their lectures—Mickiewicz's in 1844, Quinet's in 1846, and Michelet's in 1848. Not before their influence had been felt, however. As Daniel Stern (the comtesse d'Agoult) put it in her *Histoire de la Révolution de 1848*, "At the College of France, the courses of Michelet, Quinet and Mickiewicz gave life to the republican traditions of the colleges, spread among the youth a sense of love for the people, of contempt for the church and 'official' society, and thus prepared the union of students and workers that was destined to manifest itself on the barricades."[11]

Although the advocacy by intellectuals of abstractions such as nationalism, communism, and socialism, or liberté, egalité, and fraternité, indeed generated much of the charged political atmosphere in Europe, the facts of starvation, unemployment, and oppression among the masses can be seen as more immediate causes for the revolutions that occurred. At the beginning of 1848, the poor and the desperate crowded the cities of Europe. The potato blight of 1846–1847 had caused widespread famine. Poor wheat harvests, the high price of bread, and a slump in manufacturing had also inflicted hunger and unemployment upon thousands. In the search for food and work, masses of people moved to the cities, where most found only increasing crime, misery, and social injustice, all aggravated by the suppression of dissent. As peasants, laborers, and especially urban artisans grew daily more restless,[12] the rising middle class, or bourgeoisie, who in France especially had prospered financially in the recent decades, started demanding greater political representation, especially when their governments failed to solve the financial crisis of 1847. In the spring of 1848, then, an unhappy bourgeoisie, along with militant students and intellectuals, was ready to encourage the laboring poor as they resorted to popular violence to protest their plight, and although the changes sought by the middle class were political and those sought by the workers social, this difference in goals was initially ignored by both.

The fact and spirit of revolution that permeated Europe during the years 1848–49 engaged the attention of the American people and stirred the imaginations of American writers. A long list of American authors either visited or lived in Europe during these two years, including Emerson, Fuller, Melville, Bryant, Caroline Kirkland, George William Curtis, George S. Hillard, Frederick Hedge, Joel T. Headley, Charles A. Dana, Charles G. Leland, George Bancroft, William H. Prescott, James Freeman Clarke, William Ware, Donald Mitchell (Ik Marvel), George Kendall, James Jackson Jarves, George Duyckinck, Samuel Goodrich, Christopher Cranch, William Wetmore Story, and Henry Greenough. The degree of their involvement in political events varied, of course. Some, such as Bryant and Kirkland, merely saw and reported on the aftermath of the revolutions in letters to friends and American periodicals.[13] Some, such as Cranch and Story, wrote poetry about the revolutions;[14] others, such as the Unitarian ministers Clarke and Ware, wrote travel books that discussed the European political scene.[15] Of those who witnessed revolutionary events at first hand, Margaret Fuller, of course, was the most deeply and seriously engaged in the revolutionary struggle. For others the revolutions provided youthful adventure. Curtis, for example, the gentle Brook Farmer who later became editor of *Harper's Magazine*, came to the aid of an officer of the King's Guards during the street fighting in Berlin.[16] More dramatically, Leland, a Philadelphia poet who would gain prominence as editor of *Vanity Fair* and the *Knickerbocker Magazine*, fought with the republicans in Paris, armed with a pistol and dirk and decked out in a rakish student cap and a dashing red waist sash.[17] The more subdued Henry Greenough, writer and architect, was arrested, along with his famous brother Horatio, by Austrian troops and accused of being an Italian spy; he later incorporated this and other adventures of the times into his novel *Ernest Carroll, or Artist-Life in Italy* (1858).[18] As for the major writers Emerson and Melville, the revolutions affected their works in more subtle and substantial ways, and the same was true for Whitman and Hawthorne, who observed the European scene from the distance of America.

The French Revolution of February 1848

Of all the revolutions that occurred in 1848, the French revolution made the greatest impression upon both the American public and American writers. The monarchical government of Louis Philippe, the "Broker King," who had come to power in 1830, was perceived, accurately, as corrupt and repressive, and his overthrow became a cause for celebration as soon as it was learned that the revolution had been relatively bloodless and joyously republican. The British press, for the most part, provided unsympathetic coverage, describing the revolution as mob violence. Americans in Paris, however, sent home enthusiastic accounts that interpreted the revolution in terms of American democratic ideals. Two students, George Sumner and Charles Leland, wrote lively letters that were published in the Boston *Advertiser* and the Philadelphia *North American,* respectively. Samuel Goodrich, Hawthorne's former editor at the *Token* and the author of the popular Peter Parley books, wrote perhaps the most widely read account, which appeared in both the Boston *Courier* and the New York *Herald.* On the first day of the revolution, 22 February, Goodrich saw the thousands of workmen from the faubourgs converging on the square of the Madeleine to protest the government's prohibition of a scheduled reform banquet. Standing on one of the pillars of the Pont de la Concorde, he watched as the crowd of workers, students, and street urchins challenged the king's troops and dispersed themselves through the Champs-Elysées, building barricades across it. Some of the rioters set fire to several guardhouses, but no one was injured. With the soldiers watching, according to Goodrich, "the people fed the fire with fuel from the surrounding trees and fences, sang their songs, cracked their jokes, and cried, *'Down with Guizot!—Vive la Réforme!'* &c. . . . A remarkable air of fun and frolic characterized the mob—wit flew as freely on all sides as stones and sticks; every missile seemed winged with a joke."[19]

According to all accounts, riots occurred throughout the city during the day, and on the twenty-third the National Guard was called out to reenforce the troops, but they refused to fire on the crowds when ordered to. "In one instance," Goodrich reported, "four hundred National Guards were seen marching, in uniform, but without arms. It became evident that the soldiers generally were taking part with the people." After learning of this development, the king dismissed the unpopular ministry of François Guizot, which elated everyone. "An immense population—men, women and children— poured into the Boulevards, to share in the jubilation," Goodrich wrote. "Large parties of the National Guard paraded the streets, the officers and men shouting, 'Vive la Réforme!' and the crowd cheering loudly."[20]

Late that night a squad of troops guarding the ministry of foreign affairs, made nervous by a rowdy crowd that fronted them, reacted to the sound of a gunshot and opened fire, killing some fifty people and wounding many others. "From this moment the doom of the monarchy was sealed," Goodrich correctly observed.[21] As a torchlight procession with the bodies of the dead wound its way through the streets, outraged spectators reacted. More than a thousand barricades were built that night, some more than ten feet

Students at the Pont de la Concorde. (From Daniel Stern, *Histoire de la Révolution de 1848*. 3d Edition. Paris, 1869.)

high, yet most of the inhabitants of Paris thought that the crisis was over and that they would awake to a peaceful city.

One of these inhabitants was George Duyckinck, a New Yorker living and attending lectures in Paris. In a long letter home telling of his adventures, he provided a stirring description of the events of the twenty-fourth, and, like Goodrich, he celebrated the revolution as a triumph of democracy over despotism. Writing not for the papers, but for his brother Evert and their circle of friends, which included the very interested Herman Melville, George related that upon awaking on the morning of the twenty-fourth he was amazed. "It was a mournful sight," he wrote.

> Every shop was shut and in the [R]ue [B]ivienne and other streets the pavement was torn up at every corner and formidable barricades formed. I suppose that I scrambled over a score in the course of my walk. Doors, boards, car-

Barricade in the Rue St. Martin during the 1848 French Revolution. (From *Illustrated London News*, 12 (4 March 1848), 181.)

riages, whatever came to hand was pressed into the Barricade service. In many the stones were as regularly arranged as in a wall. Men were mustered about them armed with rusty old swords, spits, hatchets and iron bars from the railings of the nearest church. The boulevards were completely rased, trees, omnibus stands, benches and even the columns swept into barricades.[22]

As he wandered about the streets, Duyckinck missed the battle between an armed crowd and the municipal guards at the Château d'Eau as well as the attack on the Palais Royal led by a woman affecting the dishabille of Delacroix's *Liberty Leading the People* (1830), complete with bare shoulders, arms, and breast.[23] Duyckinck arrived at the Place de la Concorde shortly after Louis Philippe in disguise had precipitously fled in a carriage. "The people drove off monarchy in the most humiliating manner," the historian George Bancroft would soon report with Jacksonian contempt, "shorn of its crown, its wig, its whiskers, its clothes, its purse, leaving it to land as a beggar on the shores of England."[24]

The People in the Throne-Room of the Tuileries. (From *Illustrated London News*, 12 [4 March 1848], 138.)

After the king's flight, the crowds poured into the Tuileries Palace. "It was a magnificent sight though a savage one," reported Duyckinck, who could not resist entering the palace to witness the sacking. There he saw "rich furniture" in which "begrimed blouses" [workingmen] were "ensconced . . . kicking up their legs in immense glee." There he also heard the deafening "din of the shouting and cheering" and the occasional "discharge of a musket" which "would set the lustres of the chandeliers (which were almost within reach of the hands of the mob) in vibration." "It is impossible," he explained, "to give an idea of the uproar and the contrast with the repose of every thing around—the deeply carved oak ceilings[,] the gilding dimmed by age[,] the rich hangings of the walls, the curtains and pictures." Making his way to the throne room, he discovered "the most terrific scene" and declared that "there the mob were in a perfect phrensy—it was the 1792 of Scott and Carlyle realised."[25]

The crowd took the throne outside, and Duyckinck saw it being carried through the streets, "the embroidered seat and gilt legs tilted up in the air like any commonplace arm chair on May day."[26] At the Palais Royal, he also witnessed "two great bonfires in the court" being fed with articles thrown from the windows of the palace. "I saw a large portfolio of prints," Duyckinck related, "with its contents showered down in the haste but parts of these were burnt and many were scattered over the pavement. I was tempted to pick some up—they were leaves of the finest quality but much as I love prints I would not run the risk of being shot to possess them and such was the fate of many who carried off things, a terrible justice commendible [sic] as the circumstances." Bringing his twenty-page account to a close, Duyckinck declared, "I expect to hear of great excitement at home and great celebrations. It is a proud thing now to be an American in Europe for our country leads the world."[27]

Duyckinck got his wish, for indeed a wave of great excitement and great celebrations swept across America. On March 18, his brother Evert, the distinguished editor and leader of literary Young America (the group of New York writers and critics calling for a new, democratic, and Democratic American literature), described for George, whose letter he awaited, the initial response to the revolution by New Yorkers:

> A walk in Broadway to-day is a thing for excitement, the news of the Revolution in Paris having imparted to every one that vivacity of eye, quickness of intelligence and general exhilaration which great public events extend to private ones. I have heard one rather quiet man say he would give a thousand dollars to have been there. What a happy man then must you have been on the spot tingling all over with revolutionary imaginations, roused by authentic cannon which echo those of '89, a listener to the suitable Marseilles, *rechappo* allonsing it yourself and mayhap pledging a bumper to liberty in the Royal wine of the Tuilleries . . . You have fairly shaken hands with History.

At six o'clock that evening, Evert continued, "the letter *has* arrived. Bravo! You are an able hand at a reconnoitre, here there and everywhere over the map of Paris with just that best information which puts me alongside of you throughout. I am fairly *en rapport* with the Revolution."[28]

The American public, with important exceptions such as Melville and Hawthorne, shared Evert's feelings. They overlooked the social dimensions of the revolution and celebrated the liberty and human rights the French had gained by extending suffrage and instituting a republic. Songs, poetry, meetings, marches, proclamations, speeches, and toasts proliferated across the United States. In Pennsylvania the poetaster Thomas Buchanan Read penned "France is Free," which appeared in numerous periodicals and revealed how revolutionary events quickly became literary material: "The rough shod foot of the people tramps," wrote Read,

> Through the silken rooms of royalty,
> And over the floor the mirrors and lamps

> Lie like the shattered monarchy!
> They have grasped the throne in their irony,
> And have borne it aloft in mockery.
> . . . .
> They dash it to earth, and trample it down,
> Shivered to dust, with the Orleans crown.
> And shout with a voice that rends the air,
> "*France, France is free!*"[29]

Although not found in Read's poem, the words "great," "glorious," and especially "sublime" were on almost everyone's lips as they celebrated France's freedom and attributed it to America's example.

The cities on the East Coast, of course, were the first to respond to the news from France. In Washington, several torchlight processions were held, complete with speeches, and President Polk sent a message to Congress declaring that "the world has seldom witnessed a more interesting spectacle than the peaceful rising of the French people, resolved to secure themselves enlarged liberty, and to assert, in the majesty of their strength, the great truth, that, in this enlightened age, man is capable of governing himself."[30] In New York, William Cullen Bryant praised France's new government and its "reverent recognition of human rights" while Horace Greeley rejoiced in his *Tribune* that "the Emancipation of Europe has begun in earnest" and accurately predicted that "the news from Paris shall thrill the hearts of Milan, of Venice, of Rome and of Naples," stirring them to overthrow despotism.[31] With less seriousness, the southern novelist John Pendleton Kennedy wrote from Baltimore to a friend in England that the revolution "is a great, gorgeous, crashing, thundering and volcanic opera, apparently got up after full rehearsal in private, with the programme, scenery and decorations carefully prepared. . . . Is it not the most comical and the most sublime pageant,—take it altogether—that the world ever saw?"[32]

At a great meeting in City Hall Park on 3 April, thousands of New Yorkers, many of them immigrants recently arrived from Europe, celebrated the French revolution. Mayor William Brady presided over the festivities, which began at noon. Speeches, shouting, singing filled the afternoon, with Dingle's Brass Band playing patriotic airs. At seven o'clock, City Hall, Tammany Hall, and the block of adjoining buildings were illuminated with more than fifteen hundred candles, and then at eight, signal rockets were set off from the balcony of City Hall, and fires of first blue and then red burned at the ends of the esplanade. Meanwhile the band played "Hail Columbia," the "Marseilles Hymn," the "Star Spangled Banner," and "Yankee Doodle."

Herman Melville missed the festivities, for he was visiting his uncle Robert and cousin Priscilla in the Berkshires at the time. His friend Duyckinck, though, spent the day at the park, sharing in the excitement while maintaining a gentlemanly distance from what he called the mob. The best collection of flags flew over the French stand, and these, according to Duyckinck, "a new company of Red breeches militia dipped down in the mob with a waving motion, as if stirring up the political caldron."[33] As Duyckinck would soon discover, the spirit of nationalism that his Young America had expressed would soon renew itself in response to the European scene. (Melville in *Redburn, White-Jacket,* and *Moby-Dick* would be one spokesman for this nationalism, although he maintained reservations about American democracy.) The sentiments of the young poet and travel writer Bayard Taylor, who stood on the French stand in the park, reveal this renewed spirit in its most enthusiastic, unthinking form. Writing to his fiancée Mary Agnew, Taylor related,

> We had one of the most sublime meetings I ever beheld, on Monday. One hundred thousand people—French, Italians, Swiss, Poles, Irish, Scotch, Spanish—all united in one grand national congress, as it were, to rejoice over the freedom of France. I was on the stand with the French and Italian speakers. The banners of all nations hung above us, and were waved to the grand chorus of the Marseillaise, sung by thousands! Our own banner was over my head, and sometimes, when the wind blew, I was wrapped in its folds. I clasped them in my arms, and thrilled with patriotic excitement to think that under their protection *alone*, on the wide earth, could such a scene have been presented. I never beheld such enthusiasm as was manifested on the occasion.[34]

Taylor, who would soon celebrate the revolution in Italy in his poem "A Voice from Piedmont," managed the literary department for Greeley's *Tribune,* and his paper, like all the others in the city, gave the meeting in the park extensive coverage and credited America with being a political messiah to the world.

For weeks, the entire country echoed with this "universal babblement,"[35] as John Pendleton Kennedy put it, which swelled with the arrival of each steamer. Newspapers vied with one another to obtain the most up-to-date information, and their front pages overflowed with reports from the Old World. One front-page column of the 22 April 1848 *Tribune,* for example, enticed readers with a promise of the latest news from France, Prussia, and Italy and of reports of revolutions in Holstein and Warsaw as well as uprisings in Lombardy, Belgium, and Spain.

Such headlines and the coverage that accompanied them, although now forgotten, became commonplace during 1848–49, and they illustrate the importance Americans attached to international events of the day. Ole Munch Raeder, a Norwegian scholar and traveler, has left us another reminder of contemporary interests in the letters he sent back to Norway. In May 1848, Raeder related that whenever word came by telegraph that a ship was in sight off Boston Harbor or had arrived in New York, people filled the streets to learn the latest news. "All flock to the newspaper offices," he

Headlines of the New York *Tribune*, 22 April 1848.

added, "and there is great competition among the various papers as to which one shall reap the profits of satisfying the public. An army of little boys waits impatiently outside the newspaper offices. As soon as the papers are out they rush off in every direction noisily crying their wares. Posters are put up here and there, giving brief summaries of the most important news in huge letters painted with brush and ink."[36]

It was such unrestrained curiosity and the self-congratulatory glee that accompanied it which inspired Melville to satirize his fellow Americans. Melville at the time was living with his bride of seven months (along with five other members of his family) in their new home at 103 Fourth Avenue. As a regular participant in the genial conversations over Roman punch and cigars in the basement of Evert Duyckinck's Clinton Street house and as an avid reader of the newspapers at the New York Society Library, he was well informed about contemporary events; moreover, he found them so engaging that he felt compelled to add a treatment of them to the book he was struggling to finish, *Mardi*. In the political allegory he added (thus extending his completion date from May 1848 to January 1849),[37] his Mardian travelers arrive in the land of Vivenza (the United States) after having seen a "violent eruption" in Franko (France) which "kindled new flames in the distant valleys of Porpheero" (Europe). In Vivenza the people call themselves "sovereign-kings," and they run to the beaches every day and greet the news from arriving canoes. "Hurrah!" they cry out, "another kingdom is burnt down to the earth's edge; another demi-god is unhelmed; another republic is dawning. . . . all Porpheero's volcanoes are bursting! Who may withstand the people?"[38]

Melville, of course, could have traveled to cities other than New York and found the same behavior he satirized. In New Orleans, where Walt Whitman was editing the *Crescent*, the response to the revolutions in Europe was equally enthusiastic, and Whitman himself could have posed for a representative Vivenzan. The city, with its large French and German population, many of whom had fled despotism in Europe,[39] was kept "in a perfect ferment" by the news brought by arriving ships or the telegraph from Mobile. "One's blood rushes and grows hot within him," Whitman wrote, "the more he learns or thinks of this news from the continent of Europe! Is it not glorious? *This* time, the advent of Human Rights, though amid unavoidable agitation, is also amid comparative peace."[40]

Demonstrations in the square and the Exchange, banquets, toasts, military salutes, patriotic songs were some of the ways New Orleans celebrated the news from Europe, with the figure of Liberty often at the center of things. During a lavish grand banquet held at the Orleans Ball Room, "the assemblage was thrown into a state of the most intense excitement by the entrance of a gentleman, leading by the hand a most beautiful dark-eyed maiden, dressed to impersonate the Goddess of Liberty. The enthusiasm created by the advent of this beautiful creature, was indescribable—as if swayed by an involuntary and spontaneous feeling, every person arose, and the band struck up *la Marseillaise*, which was reechoed by the voice of almost the entire company."[41] Before he left New Orleans on May 26, Whitman wrote numerous editorials in support of the republican movement in Europe, and he selected for publication poetic works celebrating its spirit and leaders. The Irish "Fall, Flag of Tyrants!," the "Marseilles Hymn," "Vive le Tricolor," the "New Song of German Liberty," Bryant's translation of the "Italian Patriot Song," Eliza Cook's "To Alphonse de Lamartine," and Read's "France is Free" all appeared in the pages of the *Crescent* in April and May.[42] Given his exposure to this literary atmosphere, it is not surprising that Whitman himself soon tried his hand at political poetry, which became the foundation for the remarkable first edition of *Leaves of Grass*.

Of all the major cities in the United States, Boston, with its strong conservative and commercial tradition, was most noticeably tepid in its response to the French revolution. Many Bostonians worried about the financial consequences of European upheaval. On 12 April a sympathy meeting was held at Tremont Temple, Mayor Josiah Quincy, Jr., presiding, and the participants drafted a series of resolutions offering congratulations to the French people, but only after several protests and considerable wrangling. ("Somewhat of an eccentric meeting," the *Crescent* called it.) Boston did supply a typically civilized response to the revolution, however: the play *The Last of the Kings, or the French Revolution*, on which, according to the announcement of the Boston Museum, "all the artists of the establishment, aided by a powerful force of auxiliaries, have been employed day and night, and which is to be produced with all the splendid adjuncts that the nature of the incidents demand." The play, which dramatized the "three days" of the February revolution, was indeed hastily put together, taking only eight days to create, complete with scenery and music, but it proved popular; by 8 April, it had been performed sixteen times before large audiences.[43]

The literati of Boston, with a few exceptions such as the ultraconservative George Ticknor, responded to the French revolution with an enthusiasm similar to Whitman's. Longfellow, basking in the warm critical reception of *Evangeline* (1847), rejoiced at the "glorious tidings from Europe" and told his friend George Hillard, then in London, "We hope by the next steamer to hear that the King of Naples and one or two more kings have followed Louis Philippe to England;—in a word, that the wretched juggle and puppet-show of monarchies is about played out, and is to give place to something better!"[44] From London the Bostonian George Bancroft, serving as minister to Great Britain (and host to Emerson), celebrated the "wonderful times" in Paris and asked Secretary of State James Buchanan, "Has the echo of American Democracy which you now hear from France, and Austria, and Prussia and all Old Germany, no power to stir up the hearts of the American people to new achievements?" Bancroft found it impossible to repress his enthusiasm for the revolutions, even though the aristocracy in his court circle were "overwhelmed with gloom" and dismayed at his outspoken "love for the rule of the people."[45]

Whittier and Lowell were especially euphoric about the French revolution, because one of the acts of the new government abolished slavery in France's colonies. "What glorious changes in the Old World!" Whittier wrote to Charles Sumner in March 1848. "I feel, almost like going to France myself, and would if I could do anything more than gratify my feelings by so doing. The position of Lamartine, Arago and their colleagues is a sublime one, but its responsibility is terrible." Whittier, having learned that "they are determined to put an end to Slavery at once," told Sumner, who fully agreed, that "the sympathies of all friends of Liberty should be with them." In a number of his poems in *Songs of Labor* (1850), Whittier expressed his sympathies as he attacked European rulers such as Pope Pius IX and Ferdinand II and criticized his own countrymen who refused to follow France's example. In "The Crisis," written on learning the terms of the treaty with Mexico, he asks, "as the Old World rolls in light, shall ours in shadow turn?" Using imagery that jarringly alludes to sowing and reaping, he makes his question more specific:

> Is this, O countrymen of mine! a day for us to sow
> The soil of new-gained empire with slavery's seeds of woe?
> To feed with our fresh life-blood the Old World's cast-off crime,
> Dropped, like some monstrous early birth, from the tired lap of Time?[46]

Lowell, who published the finest works of his career in 1848, was editing the *Anti-Slavery Standard* when he learned of the French revolution, and like Whittier, he incorporated his response into his poetry. His longest treatment is his "Ode to France," where he focuses upon Freedom and traces her steps through history. Refusing to condemn the "savagery of the Oppressed," he writes that during the great French Revolution,

> They reared to thee such symbol as they knew,
> And worshipped it with flame and blood,
> A Vengeance, axe in hand, that stood
> Holding a tyrant's head up by the clotted hair.

Freedom as she appeared in the recent revolution, however, he sees in a new form:

> I have learned to love thee now
> Without the helm upon thy gleaming brow,
> A maiden mild and undefiled
> Like her who bore the world's redeeming child;
> And surely never did thine altars glance
> With purer fires than now in France;[47]

Throughout the summer of 1848, Lowell used his *Biglow Papers* and his editorials for the *Standard* to criticize American conservatives who showed sympathy for Louis Philippe or expressed reservations about the revolution.[48] Two groups of Americans fell into this category: the defenders of slavery and the wealthy, both of whom saw in the revolution a frightening threat to property.[49] The former were disturbed by the provisional government's abolishing slavery in France's colonies, and the latter by the establishment of national workshops which seemed to them the beginning of a socialist state.

Whereas the majority of Americans supported the revolution openly and wholeheartedly, these two groups opposed it surreptitiously and cautiously. When John Calhoun spoke against the Senate bill extending congratulations to the French, for example, he did not mention slavery. Instead, he called the revolution "a wonderful event—the most striking, in my opinion, in history," and then added that because it might become "a mighty evil," congratulations were "premature." "We must look to the consequences and the end," Calhoun urged. "We must await the termination of the movement." Whitman angrily responded in the *Crescent*, "Had France reasoned thus, at the time of our revolution, we might still have been colonies of England."[50] The sixty-nine-year-old Knickerbocker writer James Kirke Paulding, however, sympathized with Calhoun and clearly understood the unstated concern about France's emancipation of slaves. In a letter to the senator, Paulding praised his speech and lamented seeing "among the first acts of the Provisional Government . . . the robbing of the West India Planters and an interference in the relations of the Labourer and Employer— savouring of the worst Species of Despotism."[51] Southern periodicals that supported Calhoun's position likewise spoke with more candor than he. William Gilmore Simms's *Southern Quarterly Review*, for example, termed the decree abolishing slavery a "mad experiment in philanthropy" and declared that "as an assertion of the right of government to confiscate private property at its pleasure, it was without justification; and it was still more out of character with the position of the Provisional Government, as it had no connection with the necessities that created that government and clothed it with power."[52]

In "The Pious Editor's Creed," the sixth of his *Biglow Papers*, Lowell satirized such arguments by referring again to Freedom, a fairly obvious "connection," it would seem, between the rights of all men, including blacks. "I DU believe in Freedom's cause," his pious editor asserts,

> Ez fur away ez Payris is;
> I love to see her stick her claws
> In them infarnal Phayrisees;
> It's wal enough agin a king
> To dror resolves an' triggers,—
> But libbaty's a kind o' thing
> Thet don't agree with niggers.

Lowell's *Biglow Paper* No. V, "The Debate in the Sennit," also alludes to European developments in order to satirize the views of eight southern and three northern senators, all supporters of slavery:

> "Jest look wut is doin', wut annyky's brewin'
> In the beautiful clime o' the olive an' vine,
> All the wise aristoxy's atumblin' to ruin,
> An' the sankylots drorin' an' drinkin' their wine,"
> Sez John C. Calhoun sez he;—
> "Yes," sez Johnson, "in France
> They're beginnin' to dance
> Beelzebub's own rigadoon," sez he.[53]

Southern detractors of the French revolution were joined by conservative New England Whigs who worried about the financial consequences of the revolution and felt considerable hostility toward the socialists and communists influencing the new government. The main spokesman of the Whigs, Daniel Webster, dismissed the new leaders of France as "poets, editors, pretenders to literature, and idealists."[54] He did not speak out publicly against the new government, but his views were well known. Charles Sumner, writing to his brother George in the spring of 1848, related that "the rich and the commercial classes feel that property is rendered insecure, and with many of these the pocket is the chief sensorium. Mr. Webster, I am told, condemns this revolution, saying it is a movement of communists and socialists. . . . Lamartine's position is one of incalculable influence, not only over the destinies of France, but the progress of civilization."[55] Both the *North American Review* and the *American Whig Review* in a series of articles in the spring and summer of 1848 lamented the financial situation in France—the loss of public credit, the depression of funds, the commercial failures, the check to manufacturing—all caused, so it was claimed, by the revolution and the pernicious socialist doctrines preached by the journals and agents of the red republicans.[56]

Lamartine and Moderation

The matter of radical social thought absorbed the attention of English and American observers throughout the years of the European revolutions and made its way into the literature of the period. "Red Republicanism," "Socialism," "Communism" were ubiquitous words in the contemporary periodicals, most of which used the terms as synonymous with each other and with "anarchism," "terrorism," and "Jacobinism."[57] This phenomenon, a nineteenth-century Red Scare, began soon after the French revolution when it was learned that the provisional government included among its members the radical democrat Ledru-Rollin, the socialist Louis Blanc, and an unknown worker named Albert. The political newspapers and clubs of Paris, which sprang up by the hundreds following the February revolution, were also perceived, accurately, as seedbeds of radicalism. Karl Marx, in Paris from 5 March to 11 April before going to Germany to promote the revolutions there, was just one of many propagandists using the clubs to indoctrinate workers (in his case, German workers) and to plot the overthrow of bourgeoisie rule.[58] The most notorious club leaders were Louis Auguste Blanqui and Armand Barbès, professional revolutionaries released from prison following the February revolution. Blanqui, a small, bitter man who inspired devout loyalty among the Paris workers, termed the existing social order "nothing more than organized cannibalism" and called for "the dictatorship of the proletariat." The dark, handsome Barbès, Blanqui's cellmate and hated enemy, conspired with Ledru-Rollin and George Sand to rid the new government of its conservative members.[59]

When Americans initially celebrated the liberty gained by the French people as a result of the February revolution, they ignored the fact that the revolution was initiated by only a portion of the French populace—the Paris workers—and that these men wanted not just political freedom, but a change in their social condition; not just the vote, but work, an income, and food for themselves and their families—all of which the provisional government promised them. Because socialism (in the form of common ownership of property, designed to free men from economic oppression and material want) was so foreign to the experience of most Americans, they failed at first to see the attraction it held for many Frenchmen, and when they did, they reacted with suspicion and fear.

American moderates as well as conservatives firmly believed that bloodshed and anarchy would result if the socialists gained control of the government in France, and they thus watched with interest the leadership provided by the moderate republican Lamartine. "LAMARTINE is the ruling spirit in the new order of things in France," proclaimed the New York *Morning Courier and Enquirer*, "—and he has explored the whole theory of Socialism, in all its forms, and proclaimed its hollowness and the evils which it involves. He, more than any other man in France, has the command of that multitude who are most likely to be imposed upon by Socialist demagogues; and we have great confidence in his ability to avert the danger which threatens the new Republic from this source." During an April 1848 visit to Paris, Bancroft reported that Lamartine "spoke warmly and most explicitly on the subject of property. He is resolved that all interests be respected and secured. . . . The power he has shown in moderating selfish passions and swaying the people is something unexampled."[60]

During the spring of 1848, Lamartine became one of the most celebrated figures in the world, and his idealism, courage, and eloquence received much praise in America. An engraved portrait of him appeared on the front page of the New York *Herald.* Biographical sketches of him appeared in numerous periodicals, including *Sartain's Union Magazine,* the *Southern Literary Messenger,* the *Tribune,* and the New York *Evening Post.* Translations of his poetry, by Whittier and others, became commonplace. A large painting of him proclaiming the French Republic became one of the notable attractions at P. T. Barnum's American Museum. And one New York speculator, trying to dignify a venture, even named a street of sixpenny shanties Lamartine's Row.[61]

Lamartine's *History of the Girondists,* which had established his credentials as a republican and inspired the revolution that he struggled to lead and moderate, was widely read in America and greatly influenced American writers. "We doubt whether this is not already the most popular *book,* as its

Engraving of Lamartine on Front Page of the New York *Herald*.

author is the most popular *man* of the day," a reviewer for the New York *Courier and Enquirer* proclaimed, when the English translation appeared.[62] Whitman reviewed it twice, once for the Brooklyn *Daily Eagle* and again for the New Orleans *Crescent*, calling it "the most dramatic work" he had ever read and, as a history of the great French Revolution, "beyond comparison, the best book yet written." As he began *Leaves of Grass*, Whitman identified with the revolutionary leaders of 1848, especially Lamartine, in whom he perceived "a wondrous union of physical and moral courage."[63] Fuller, who shared Whitman's impulse to pay tribute to the foiled European revolutionaries, studied Lamartine's *Girondists* in preparation for her history of the Roman Republic; Hawthorne, who saw himself as a political martyr such as Lamartine became, read and borrowed from the *Girondists* as he wrote *The Scarlet Letter;* and Melville, like Whitman, came to view Lamartine as an alter ego of sorts, especially in the poet–statesman's later years, after the people had turned their backs upon him.

Tall, handsome, aristocratic, Lamartine had captured the hearts of his countrymen as a romantic poet long before he came to American attention as historian and revolutionary. Born into a family of minor nobility, he led a life of leisure in his youth, enjoying a number of love affairs. Eventually he married an English woman of means and began a career as a diplomat, writing and publishing his verses as an avocation, in the manner of Byron, with whom he was often compared. While his poetry collections enthralled thousands of romantic readers, his eloquence and independence in the Chamber of Deputies, where he took a seat in 1833, earned him a large political following, which grew in size and influence with the publication of his *Histoire des Girondins*. In April 1847, Bancroft described a visit to Lamartine, then nearing the height of his career: "He is a tall man, with the manners of the world. His work just published has the greatest success of almost anything that has yet appeared. The third volume was on a table, and is to appear on Monday." A year later, Bancroft was back in Paris, and in a letter to his wife left a record of his friend's ascendance. At the theater, where Bancroft saw him arrive, Lamartine's "reception was magnificent; such as becomes a man who had just united nearly three hundred thousand suffrages in his favour in a single city. All eyes were on him, all voices raised to bless him. Again and again, the warm salutation burst from the immense crowd that absolutely filled the theatre; and to perfect the exuberant expression or opinion, the orchestra must play 'The Marseillaise.'" Tocqueville, who was probably a bit jealous, characterized Lamartine as an unscrupulous egoist. Yet he qualified this criticism by conceding that his colleague was "capable of anything except a cowardly act or vulgar phrase."[64]

During the February revolution, Lamartine had two moments of greatness that won him the admiration of American observers. The first occurred during the meeting of the Chamber of Deputies following the king's flight from Paris. The beautiful duchess of Orléans had arrived with her nine-year-old son, the count of Paris, who was heir apparent, and she was seeking to be named regent. An armed mob had invaded the building and was becoming increasingly hostile. The new form of the French government needed to be decided, but confusion reigned. It was at this moment that Lamartine rose to speak and soon had the attention of the crowd. He first praised the courage of the duchess, saying that he was deeply moved "at beholding the most touching sight that human annals can present, that of a princess, august in her misfortune, shielding herself by the innocence of her child, and coming from the heart of an invaded and abandoned palace, to throw herself into the bosom of the asylum of popular representation." To these words, the monarchists responded with cheers and hope. But then Lamartine, sensing that the moment was critical, declared that a regency could not unite the nation. "I demand, therefore," he said, "the instant establishment of the right of public peace, the right of blood yet flowing, the right of this people,

exhausted by the glorious work it has accomplished in three days. I demand
the institution of a provisional government."[65] As he concluded, Lamartine
saw insurgents pouring into the building. One rioter leveled a gun at him,
but he maintained his composure and, after the provisional government was
named, made his way to the Hôtel de Ville (Paris's palatial city hall), where
he and his colleagues proclaimed France a republic.

In America, the drama in the chamber received much attention, and
the most famous female poet in the country, Lydia Sigourney, made it into
one of her typically sentimental poems. Having been presented to Louis
Philippe at the French court in 1840, Mrs. Sigourney apparently felt grateful to the royal family, for in her poem, entitled "Too Late," they become
the central figures. After describing the "tumultuous scene" in the chamber,
she writes,

> A mournful woman came;
> The widow's sable wrapped her form,
>   As one estranged from joy,
> Yet graceful, with a mother's care
>   She led a princely boy.
>
> Bright was his sunny brow,
>   Though bearded warriors frowned,
> And strong in childhood's innocence
>   He fearless gazed around,—

The poem continues in this vein all the way through to its last pathetic
stanza, where the cry "too late" becomes "the knell of life for ever lost" for
mother and child.[66]

Although Sigourney, the precursor of Twain's Emmeline Grangerford,
found nothing worthy of tears in Lamartine's other moment of greatness,
when he quieted the mobs swarming the Hôtel de Ville, it too became a
world-famous event, of interest to American writers. Some seven times on
25 February as the provisional government was meeting in the city hall,
portions of the crowd of sixty thousand outside in the Place de Grève forced
their way into the building, challenging the provisional government's right
to rule for the people. Armed workers wearing red sashes demanded a Paris
commune and the flying of the red flag of socialism in place of the tricolor.
Although the situation was fraught with danger, Lamartine went out to
speak to the mobs time and again, to the point of exhaustion. His purpose
was to dissuade them from violence and terrorism, and to this end he urged
them to reject the symbols associated with the bloodshed of the great revolution of 1789. As Whitman reported in the *Crescent*, Lamartine said of the
red flag, "For my part, citizens, I will never adopt it, and in a few words I
will tell you why I oppose it with all the energy of my patriotism. It is that
the tri-color, citizens, has floated in every quarter of the world, over the

Lamartine Addressing the Mob in Front of the Hôtel de Ville. (Courtesy of Bildarchiv Preussischer Kulturbesitz, Berlin.)

republic and the empire, over our liberties and our glory, and that the red flag has but traversed the C[h]amp de Mars, dragged through rivers of the people's blood." "At this spirit-stirring address," reported the Paris paper *La Presse*, which was widely quoted in America, "every man was in a moment subdued: they clapped their hands, shed tears, and finished by embracing him, clasping his hands, and carrying him in triumph." Responding to Lamartine's "humane and generous principles," Whitman commented, "A man who in the very heat and turmoil of a revolution, can proclaim such sentiments in the ears of an exasperated multitude, on whose forbearance and good will his very life depends, requires no farther eulogy."[67]

During the early days of the 1848 French revolution, the 1789 Revolution with its horrifying Reign of Terror was always at the forefront of people's minds—thus the importance Lamartine and everyone else attached to symbols such as the red flag. With no sense of hyperbole, *Blackwood's,* in an article entitled "Sentiments and Symbols of the French Republic,"

could declare that when Lamartine rejected "the blood-red banner of terror"
and defended the tricolor flag "as the true standard of peace and order," "he
consummated a deed upon which the destiny of France, perhaps of the
whole world, for the moment depended."[68] Because a renewed interest in
the symbols of 1789 accompanied and followed the 1848 revolution, writers
and painters drew upon them, especially the figure of Liberty, the barricade, the *bonnet rouge* (red liberty cap), the pike, the scaffold, and the
guillotine.[69] Images of the arm and hammer were also adapted as symbols of
revolution, because like the workingmen they represented, they became
politicized during the turmoil of 1848.

It is not coincidental that some of the finest works in American literature contain this revolutionary imagery of the day. When Ahab flies the red
flag on the mainmast of the *Pequod*, when Steelkilt and his mob of desperadoes become "sea-Parisians" on the *Town-Ho* and entrench themselves "behind the barricade," when Hester Prynne or Arthur Dimmesdale ascend the
scaffold, when Surveyor Hawthorne talks about being guillotined, or even
when Thoreau's neighboring ants become red republicans and black imperialists engaged in internecine war, they reveal their creators' indebtedness
to contemporary events and iconography. All the major writers of the period, Thoreau included, found themselves stirred by the French revolution
of 1848 and the revolutionary turmoil it brought in its wake.

2

Emerson and "The Movement"

I fancied, when I heard that the times were anxious & political, that there is to be a Chartist revolution on Monday next, and an Irish revolution in the following week, that the right scholar would feel,—now was the hour to test his genius. His kingdom is at once over & under these perturbed regions. Let him produce its Charter now, & try whether it cannot win a hearing, & make felt its infinite superiority today, even today.

—EMERSON, Journal Entry (April 1848)

Some American writers, such as Hawthorne, Whitman, and Thoreau, journeyed to the scenes of the European revolutions only in their imaginations; others, including Emerson, Fuller, and Melville, went there in person. Emerson, who visited London and Paris in the spring of 1848, found himself surrounded by revolutionary turmoil and stimulated by it. The evident impact of French socialism directly challenged his belief in individualism and stirred him to reassert with new vigor the personal idealism that had recently been receding from his writings. During his lecture tour throughout England before the revolutions, Emerson became enthralled with the power, wealth, and character of that nation and almost unconsciously more pragmatic and conservative in his opinions; his trip to revolutionary France in May, however, shifted his outlook back toward the left and gave him a new perspective on England, allowing him to view that nation more clearly and critically. The acclaimed balance of *English Traits* owes much to his experiences in Paris; the more immediate literary result of his encounter with revolutionary events, however, was the lecture series of June 1848 entitled "Mind and Manners in the Nineteenth Century," which returned to the visionary themes of his early addresses and glorified the inspired individual, aloof from the political strife of the times.

When Emerson arrived in England in October 1847, his mind and baggage were filled with ideas and lectures on "the Uses of Great Men" (one title given to his "Representative Men" series on Plato, Swedenborg, Montaigne, Shakespeare, Napoleon, and Goethe). This series provided most of the sixty-four lectures he delivered throughout England and Scotland between 2 November 1847 and 24 February 1848. His lecture "Napoleon," for example, he read on fourteen occasions.[1] While engaged in this enterprise, he heard the growing clamor about socialism on the Continent, but at first he belittled it. He was convinced that only great individuals, not groups or associations, could provide leadership to an age, and having witnessed the failure of the absurd experiment at Fruitlands and the recent bankruptcy and dispersal of Brook Farm, he found it easy to ridicule the talk about socialism, communism, and Fourierism he now heard in the air. "Individualism has never been tried," he wrote in his journal late in 1847. "All history[,] all poetry deal with it only & because now it was in the minds of men to go alone and now before it was tried, now, when a few began to think of the celestial Enterprise, sounds this tin trumpet of a French Phalanstery and the newsboys throw up their caps & cry, Egotism is exploded; now for Communism! But all that is valuable in the Phalanstery comes of individualism. You may settle it in your hearts that when you get a great man, he will be hard to keep step with."[2] Although Emerson often wavered in his attitude toward socialism ("On no subject was he more undecided," John C. Gerber has observed),[3] he characteristically admired its goals but questioned its actual benefits. His enthusiasm for individualism, on the other hand, remained constant and unqualified; whenever he gave his lectures "The Spirit of the Times" or "The Spirit of the Age" during the thirties, forties, and fifties, he asserted that the entire hope and vigor of a historical period radiates from the importance of the individual man.[4]

Although Emerson discounted the "tin trumpet" being sounded in France, it irritated him enough to provoke an indirect response in a new lecture he decided to write. On 10 February, he informed his wife that he had spent the last fortnight in Manchester, "where I have written a lecture on Natural Aristocracy, which I am to read in Edinburgh tomorrow." Composed of "some old webs with patches of new tapestry,"[5] the lecture defended social inequality, especially the "natural" superiority of the "man of honour—accomplished in all arts & generosities." It also put contemporary levelers in their place. "The young adventurer finds," Emerson declared, "that the relations of society, the position of classes irk & sting him, and he lends himself to each malignant party that assails what is eminent. He will one day know, that this is not removable, but a distinction in the nature of things; that neither the caucus nor the newspaper, nor the congress, nor the mob, nor the guillotine, nor fire, nor all together, can avail to outlaw, cut out, burn, or destroy the offence of superiority in persons." As for the apparent injustice that one person's elevation or another's suffering often results from the workings of fortune, he argued that opportunity eventually comes round to all, and when it does, those who deserve better, achieve it.[6]

Emerson completed his lecture tour just as the barricades went up in Paris, and he proceeded to London on 3 March, "through all these wondrous French news which all tongues & telegraphs discuss."[7] There he learned that the tin trumpet had heralded one of the greatest political upheavals of his age, the February French revolution, and that when the masses revolted, eminent individuals such as Lamartine did not lead, but instead "let themselves go without resistance whither the explosion was hurling them." The new influence of the masses in Paris and the apparent fact that a socialist restructuring of French society was occurring left Emerson temporarily perplexed. "For the matter of Socialism," he wrote in his journal, "there are no oracles. The oracle is dumb. When we would pronounce anything truly of man, we retreat instantly on the individual. We are authorized to say much on the destinies of one, nothing on those of many."[8]

During the two months he spent in London before going to Paris, Emerson circulated among the "best" society in that city (thanks to his friendship with the Bancrofts), meeting the talented, the rich, and the wellborn. And while in London, he came up with two ways to deal with the apparent potency of socialism on the Continent (later, he would attribute the French revolution to the inspiration of "great" individuals such as Owen and Fourier). First, he denigrated events in France as a mere scramble for property and money. He declared that greed, not principle, powered the revolution, and that the masses wanted to take by force what individuals had earned through talent and industry. "In the question of socialism, which now proposes the confiscation of France[,]" he wrote, "one has only this guidance. You shall not so arrange property as to remove the motive to industry. If you refuse rent & interest, you make all men idle & immoral. As to the poor a vast proportion have made themselves so, and in any new arrangement will only prove a burden on the state." Returning to the central theme of "Natural Aristocracy," he asserted in his journal, "When men feel & say, 'Those men occupy my place,' the revolution is near. But I never feel that any men occupy my place; but that the reason I do not have what I wish, is, that I want the faculty which entitles. All spiritual or real power makes its own place. Revolutions of violence then are scrambles merely."[9]

Even when he acknowledged that humanitarianism might lie behind developments in France, Emerson was able to dismiss the importance of socialism a second way, by declaring that it concerned itself with the body, not the soul, and it failed to recognize the spiritual necessity of poverty and pain. When he took this view, however, he experienced some guilt and doubt, as can be seen in the following journal entry written at the same time as the others above:

> It seems cruel that every man should be in false position, &, that, scholar & saint though he be, he should find himself in this most awkward relation to loaves of bread. And the promise of Socialism is to redress this disturbed balance. But I think it needs that we must have the substance in purity which we will analyze, and not only cling to individuals but to angels. We must consider

the condition of a youthful soul sent for its education into this University of
Nature, and perhaps it must have this drastic treatment of famine & plenty,
insult & rapture, wisdom & tragedy, infernal & supernal society, in order to
secure that breadth of culture so longlived a destiny needs.[10]

Obviously ill at ease with his "false position," Emerson here attempts to
relocate the area of concern from the material to the spiritual, but his ratio-
nale, as he surely knew, offers little solace to those suffering famine, insult,
and the infernal, instead of merely studying them. The Puritan background
of his thinking, with its notions of election and predestination, looms large
here, and at the center of his thought is the belief that some divine necessity,
benevolent of course, renders good works irrelevant.

In England, the most sympathetic response to the revolution in Paris
came from the Chartists, who were encouraged to renew their calls for political and social reform in their own country. At the suggestion of Carlyle,[11]
Emerson attended a Chartist meeting in London on 7 March and was unimpressed. Those assembled welcomed home the deputation sent to Paris
to congratulate the new French Republic, and Emerson listened to the Marseillaise "sung by a party of men & women on the platform, & chorused by
the whole assembly," and he heard among the crowd whispers about the
English soldiers, "that 'they would catch it,' i.e. the contagion of chartism &
rebellion." Although the Chartist leaders tried to maintain "order & moral
tone," Emerson noticed that "the great body of the meeting liked best the
sentiment, 'Every man a ballot & every man a musket'[.]"[12] In general, the
Chartists repelled him, and in notes for a lecture on Chartism, which he
never completed, he declared, "Chartist meetings are pathetic. You can see
how badly supported they are by a constituency that cannot read & are
drunk with gin."[13]

Although Emerson saw the Chartists with his own eyes, he tended to
view "French politics & English mobs" through the colored lens of the conservative London *Times*, a paper he admired greatly. On 8 March, he wrote
to George Bradford that "every one now is full of this astounding French
Revolution, and I read the Times newspaper through day by day. The Times,
since the first days, has taken the best tone on the subject. . . . London has
a mob of 'sympathizers' & there are dangerous mobs in Glasgow & in Lan-
cashire."[14] While he recognized that the *Times* had an arrogant tone, he
found this as it should be. "Who would care for it, if it 'surmised,'" he asked,
"or 'dared to confess,' or 'ventured to predict,' etc.?"[15] He visited the *Times*'s
offices, speculated on the identities of its contributors, and sent copies home
to his wife, Lidian, that she might see "what we all read every day, the best
newspaper of the world." He even proposed to Bradford that at home they
"have a little club of neighbours who should take the Times newspaper. Ever
since I have been here, I read that, & think it the best English literature by
far."[16] The *Times* heaped contempt on the Chartists in England and the so-

cialists in France, a response that Emerson supported, and, in *English Traits*, based for the most part upon his trip abroad, he devotes an entire chapter to the paper and credits it with preventing a revolution in England in 1848.

This revolution was anticipated for 10 April, the date the Chartists, led by Feargus O'Connor, were to hold a "monster meeting" in London and then march to Parliament to present a gigantic petition on behalf of the "People's Charter." The government, fearful that mobs of unemployed workers would stage a revolution as they had in Paris, deployed 4,000 policemen to guard the bridges crossing the Thames, placed the duke of Wellington in command of 8,000 soldiers to protect strategic points between the Tower and Millbank, and swore in 150,000 constables to protect property within the city. Meanwhile, Queen Victoria and Prince Albert left London for the security of the Isle of Wight. Not surprisingly, when the meeting took place, a much smaller crowd than anticipated showed up, and when the chief commissioner of police told O'Connor to send the Chartists home peacefully, he complied, thus betraying the cause in the eyes of many and signaling the end of the Chartist movement. (The petition, later ridiculed, was taken to Parliament in three taxi cabs.)

In the *Times*'s columns, many of which were reprinted in American papers, the demonstrators were described as intent upon revolution—their liberty caps, pikes, and banners were duly noted—and the demonstration was interpreted as "the signal of unconstitutional menace, of violence, of insurrection, of revolution," which was put down by "a peaceful, prudent, and loyal metropolis." The crowd, which did not challenge the 150,000 constables, was estimated at only 10,000 by the *Times*, a number that led the paper to crow: "There you have the proportions of the day, 150,000 to 10,000—15 to 1. To every man or boy in London yesterday, disposed to bully and intimidate the Legislature, and ready to carry a pike against it, there were *fifteen* picked and trustworthy men who could procure vouchers to their respectability, who took an oath to defend the Queen's peace, and were ready to wield a truncheon in her defence."[17] In *English Traits*, Emerson would claim that the Chartists had felt the power of the *Times*: "It denounced and discredited the French Republic of 1848, and checked every sympathy with it in England, until it had enrolled 200,000 special constables to watch the Chartists and make them ridiculous on the 10th April."[18]

This is typical Emersonian overstatement, of course, for the *Times* reflected the attitudes of the British more than it generated them, as Emerson well knew; nevertheless, the *Times* and other London papers did wield great influence, and some of Emerson's admirers, unlike him, considered this influence pernicious. "The great journals of the Empire—the London morning papers—studiously cater for the middle and upper classes and allow them to read nothing but what they would wish to be true," Garth Wilkinson the Fourierist reported from London. "Their version of the movement is a thoroughly expurgated edition of contemporary history; the desires of these classes are made the grounds of a Censorship as stringent as anything which exists in St. Petersburg."[19] From New Orleans, Whitman, who called the government of Great Britain "the mainstay of tyranny and oppression all over the earth," sympathized with the Chartists and observed that the *Times*, the *Chronicle*, and *Willmer & Smith's* paper "never utter the truth while any thing else will answer their purpose." With less patience, Margaret Fuller complained from Rome that articles on the revolutionary movement were copied from the *Times* with "perfect good faith" in the American papers. "There exists not in Europe a paper more violently opposed to the cause of freedom than the *Times*," she wrote, "and neither its leaders nor its foreign correspondence [*sic*] are to be depended upon."[20]

One American writer who shared Emerson's and the *Times's* view of the Chartists was Herman Melville, who drew upon what he read in the New York papers to satirize the abortive demonstration of 10 April in *Mardi*. Although inclined to sympathize with the lowly and oppressed, Melville nevertheless harbored a lifelong skepticism toward violent popular uprisings, and the developments in Europe in 1848, especially the French revolution, acted as a catalyst upon his political thought, bringing its conservative side to the fore. In chapter 6, I discuss why revolution in France affected Melville so strongly. Here I want to suggest that Melville's own firsthand encounter with Chartism during his visit to England in 1839 contributed to his treatment of the events of 1848.

As a seaman of nineteen and the son of a gentleman, Melville had spent six weeks in Liverpool during Chartism's most violent period of activity. From 2 July to 13 August 1839, the period he spent ashore waiting for the departure of his ship, the Chartists staged riots at Birmingham and Newcastle-upon-Tyne and, according to the *Times* of 1839, scared "the whole north of England with hourly threats of plunging into utter desolation the most affluent and prosperous of our manufacturing cities."[21] After being in the midst of this turmoil and encountering Chartist revolutionary oratory in the streets of Liverpool,[22] Melville, upon his return to the United States, doubtless read reports of the climactic Newport Insurrection of November 1839, when a regiment of British troops battled some 7,000 Chartist marchers, killing at least 22 of them and wounding scores of others (an event which remains the most deadly clash between civilians and the British authorities in the nineteenth and twentieth centuries). The celebrated mass trial of more than 250 for treason followed.[23]

Writing about current events with comparable past ones in mind, Melville in *Mardi* has his Mardian travelers wander through the country of Dominora (England), where they encounter "a riotous red-bonneted mob," who race by carrying a "crimson banner" and shouting, "Mardi is man's!"

"Down with landholders!" "Bread! Bread!" "Take the tide, ere it turns!" (479). Melville's association of the Chartists with revolutionary extremism becomes even more cutting as he describes their behavior. "Waving their banners," he writes, "and flourishing aloft clubs, hammers, and sickles, with fierce yells the crowd ran on toward the palace of Bello (the King). Foremost, and inciting the rest by mad outcries and gestures, were six masks" (479). (These masks, probably suggested by Shelley's *Masque of Anarchy*, apparently represent the six points of the charter: adult manhood suffrage, vote by ballot, annual parliaments, payment of members, abolition of property qualifications, and equal electoral districts.) In *Mardi*, the masks lead the mob into a dark wood, where many of them fall into "a long covered trench." The remainder are confronted by Bello's imposing "spears": "A crash as of icicles against icebergs round Zembla, and down went the hammers and sickles." Meanwhile heralds in the service of Bello reward those leading the mob for betraying "their kith and their kin" (479–80). Showing no great regard for the rapacious, robust King Bello, Melville shows even less for the rioting mob, and the least for their treacherous leaders.

Emerson, like Melville, reserved his greatest contempt for the Chartists' "miserable fustian swindling leaders," whom he also called "gross & bloody."[24] After he went to France in May 1848, he continued to reflect upon the Chartists as he observed their kindred spirits, the socialists and communists; however, in Paris, the icy elitism he felt and expressed in London thawed. In Paris, he began to sound less like a social Darwinist and more like a democratic idealist. The distance he placed between himself and the English upper and middle classes probably contributed to, or at least allowed for, this development. His new "angle of vision"[25] also altered his estimates of both nations.

Paris in May

Before he went to France, Emerson was reminded of the prevailing English attitude toward the Paris political scene when Tennyson jokingly warned him he "should never come back alive."[26] Another acquaintance, however, Wilkinson, tried to bias him in favor of the socialist movement. The two of them had talked about "Association," Wilkinson reported for the *Harbinger* (a Brook Farm product), and he had tried to persuade Emerson that "that individuality which he would maintain so inviolate" meant nothing during the present revolutionary time but "would come forth with power and great splendor under the new social *regime*." According to Wilkinson, Emerson was "quite willing to see whatever there is in this same Association, and I am sure to help it with his own earnest soul. He goes to Paris in a few days and will take a letter to Hugh Doherty."[27] In Paris, Emerson (unimpressed with Doherty, an Irish socialist who had fled England) did experience a shift in his attitude toward socialism as he observed the energy and sincerity of its French proponents, whose discussions about getting food to the starving and work to the unemployed especially impressed him. His response was tempered, however, by reservations about the French character, which he accurately perceived as volatile and contentious at this time.

When Emerson arrived on 7 May, Lamartine was engaged in a losing struggle to steer the new republic on a moderate course acceptable to both radicals and conservatives. The former, as members of the National Assembly and leaders of the Paris clubs, were becoming more threatening in their demands for radical social reform and an aggressive foreign policy actively supporting the liberation movements in Hungary, Italy, and especially Poland. The radicals felt particularly frustrated because the new universal suffrage, which extended the vote to the conservative peasantry (troglodytes, Marx called them), had resulted, ironically but typically, in the radicals' overwhelming defeat in the elections of 23 April. Of the nine hundred seats in the Constituent Assembly, they won only one hundred. Although the radicals felt they controlled Paris, moderates and conservatives controlled France.

The national workshops, which had enrolled 70,000 workers by April and 100,000 by May, had aggravated the tension between conservatives and radicals, both of whom found them outrageous. While the workshops masqueraded as socialist cooperatives similar to those advocated by Louis Blanc, they were actually large-scale charities, where little work was done and men showed up merely to receive their two francs a day. Conservatives questioned why thousands of "loafers" should be paid to do nothing, except menace the public order, while "respectable" citizens were forced to pay higher taxes to save the country from bankruptcy. Radicals, on the other hand, felt that the Republic had not kept its promise to provide bread and work to all its citizens. Among members of the workshops, guilt, confusion, and anger reigned.

The question of what should be done about these thousands of men was addressed constantly during the spring of 1848 by speakers in the Assembly, the streets, the journals, and especially the clubs of Paris. Emerson stayed in the city until 2 June, using his time as might be expected: touring the Louvre, attending lectures at the Sorbonne, going to performances starring the famous actress Rachel, watching and hearing Lamartine speak to the National Assembly, spending an evening at the Tocquevilles', paying a visit to Comtesse d'Agoult, and working on the lectures he was scheduled to give on his return to London. With the exception of his lectures, however, it was the clubs that engaged his interest more than anything else. There he found deadly earnest radicalism, as opposed to flaccid Brook Farm utopianism, and there the explosive energy of the sessions challenged the cool aloofness with which he had been regarding the poor and the hungry.

National Workshop (Tailors) in the Prison of Clichy, at Paris. (From *Illustrated London News*, 12 (17 June 1848), 386.)

After attending the fairly tame Free Trade Club on 9 May, he went the following evening to Barbès' club with Mrs. Paulet and the Reverend Mr. Forster, friends from England. The meeting was held in a large, low concert room containing a number of pillars which made listening difficult. From a side box Emerson and his friends had a good view of the room, which was crowded. "They were a fierce, wild-looking set," Forster recorded in his journal, "but mostly well dressed. Few blouses, chiefly, I suppose, students, *hommes de lettres,* and artists, moustachiod [*sic*] and bearded in all possible varieties. Barbès himself, a tall, handsome, soldier-like man, with resolute lips and commanding air. I was much struck with the audience's intense rage at any, even friendly, interruptions, as though they feared they own excitability." "A most stormy affair it was," Forster observed, "even disturbing Emerson's equanimity."[28]

Anyone familiar with Emerson's habitual serenity and imperturbability (which the volcanic Carlyle found irritating) will realize how unusual and memorable the scene must have been for him. "The fire & fury of the people, when they are interrupted or thwarted," he wrote home, "are inconceivable to New England." Their clothing too struck him as "formidable," with everyone "in some kind of uniform [—] red sash, red cap, blouse perhaps bound by red sash, brass helmet, & sword, and every body supposed to have a pistol in his pocket." Despite this pent up "fire and fury," or per-

A Paris Club in 1848. (From Stern, *Histoire de la Révolution de 1848*.)

haps because of it, Emerson's sympathies were engaged. In a letter to his wife, he declared that "the deep sincerity of the speakers who are agitating social not political questions, and who are studying how to secure a fair share of bread to every man, and to get the God's justice done through the land, is very good to hear."[29] His perception of this desire for fairness and justice dispelled his earlier, London belief that the socialists were engaged in the "confiscation of France."

On the evenings of 13 May and 14 May, Emerson went to the other notorious Paris club, Blanqui's, and there he probably saw, although he did not realize it at the time, secret arrangements being made by this revolutionary and his Montagnards to overthrow the government the next day, using as a pretext a massive demonstration on behalf of Poland. At about noon on 15 May, thousands of demonstrators, mostly workers, invaded the National Assembly, and, after listening to harangues by Barbès and Blanqui, declared the Assembly dissolved. They then went to the Hôtel de Ville, where a new provisional government was proclaimed. This time, however, the National Guard, "the shopkeepers" Emerson called them, chose not to join the workers in their revolt; instead, they responded to the government's call to arms. They marched to the Assembly to secure it, and they preceded Lamartine to the Hôtel de Ville, where he arrested the ringleaders of the rebellion and had them imprisoned.

During the midday excitement, Emerson was attending a lecture of Michelet's at the Sorbonne and was oblivious to unfolding events, but as he was dining with the Paulets and Forster at the Palais Royal, he heard the blood-stirring *rappel* and rushed outside. "I saw the sudden & immense display of arms when the rappel was beaten on Monday afternoon," he wrote home, "the streets full of bayonets, and the furious driving of the horses dragging cannon towards the National Assembly; the rapid succession of proclamations proceeding from the Government, & pasted on the walls at the corners of all streets, eagerly read by crowds of people." That evening he wrote in his journal, "I have seen Barbé's role in his *Club de la Revolution*, & Blanqui in his *Club des Droits de l'homme*, and today they are both in the dungeon of Vincennes."[30]

Even though he was "heartily glad of the Shopkeepers' victory," Emerson retained his newfound sympathy for the socialists. A few of them had confirmed his previous cynicism, such as the wag at Blanqui's Club who pretended to reassure the rich about their property by declaring, "We shall guard it with the utmost care, in the belief that it will soon be our own."[31] As a whole, however, they acquired his respect, and he would soon be telling a London audience, "truly I honour the generous ideas of the socialists, the magnificence of their theories, & the enthusiasm with which they have been urged. They are the inspired men of the time."[32] During his stay in Paris, he confided in his journal, "I have been exaggerating the English merits all winter, & disparaging the French. Now I am correcting my judgment of both, & the French have risen very fast." He noticed, for example, that "the French have greatly more influence in Europe than the English. What influence the English have is by brute force of wealth; that of the French, by affinity & talent." From France he also saw, as *English Traits* would emphasize, England's arrogance, its materialism, and its overwhelming emphasis upon utility. By the end of his stay in Paris, when he attended the national fête in the Champs de Mars along with more than a million other people, he sensed what was possible when the spirit of brotherhood replaced dogged class consciousness. "It was like an immense family the perfect good humour & fellowship is so habitual to them all," he wrote home. "The skill with [which] festal chandeliers were hung all up & down a mile of avenue gave it all the appearance of an immense ballroom in which the countless crowds of men & women walked with ease & pleasure. It was easy to see that France is far nearer to Socialism than England & it would be a short step to convert Paris into a phalanstery."[33]

Before he left France, Emerson reconsidered the Chartists along with the socialists and realized that his previous recoil from them had been wrong. As he pondered their revolutionary behavior, he saw that it served the "Movement party," to which he, as a democratic idealist, had long before declared allegiance. Using a revealing progression of pronouns, he made the following journal entry:

> The writers are bold & democratic. The moment revolution comes, are they Chartists & Montagnards? No, but they talk & sit with the rich, & sympathize with them. Should they go with the Chartists? Alas they cannot: These have such gross & bloody chiefs to mislead them, and are so full of hatred & murder, that the scholar recoils;—and joins the rich. That he should not do. He should accept as necessary the position of armed neutrality abhorring the crimes of the Chartist, yet more abhorring the oppression & hopeless selfishness of the rich, &, still *writing the truth*, say, the time will come when these poor enfans perdus of revolution will have instructed their party, if only by their fate, & wiser counsels will prevail, & the music & the dance of liberty will take me in also. Then I shall not have forefeited my right to speak & act for the Movement party. Shame to the fop of philosophy who suffers a little vulgarity of speech & of character to hide from him the true current of Tendency, & who abandons his true position of being priest & poet of those impious & unpoetic doers of God's work.[34]

The way Emerson in this passage uses first "they" then "he" then "I" then "his"/"him" again suggests a high degree of self-instruction. He seems resolved now to extend sympathy to the revolutionaries (though in a patronizing manner), rather than disdain them as he had previously done. This development represents a change in attitude, however, not in philosophy. For Emerson, the scholar, like the priest and poet, concerned himself with eternity, not the times, and thus the new "true position" he has in mind exists in an ideal kingdom far above the day-to-day workings of "French politics & English mobs."

The London Lectures

In "Mind and Manners in the Nineteenth Century," the course of six lectures Emerson gave upon his return to London, he responded to the revolutionary turmoil of the day by rising above it, or rather, by encouraging his audience to do so. Secluded in his rooms, he gave time and thought to metaphysics while the world outside quaked with revolution. He began writing on this project in London during the spring of 1848, and on 25 April, he informed Margaret Fuller, "I am working away in these mornings at some papers, which, if I do not, as I suppose I shall not, get ready for lectures here, will serve me in a better capacity as a kind of Book of Metaphysics to print at home." His papers served immediate purposes after Carlyle, Dickens, and others signed a petition asking him to give a course of lectures in London. He agreed to do so, thinking the time was propitious "to test his genius," as he put it.[35] The test, however, required more of his time and energy than he had anticipated. On 31 May, he wrote to Fuller from Paris that he had "spoiled" his visit to that city "by bringing my portfolio of papers to prepare lectures for London, which I go back tomorrow to read, the first on 6th June." After giving his second lecture on 8 June, he informed his wife that he had "been writing all day . . . & must work all tomorrow on my third for Saturday P.M."[36] Both the complexity of his subject and its vital importance to him contributed to his struggle to treat it. The first three lectures, which he grouped under the heading "Natural History of the Intellect," were his new ones on metaphysics, and he entitled them "Powers and Laws of Thought," "Relation of Intellect to Natural Science," and "Tendencies and Duties of Men of Thought."[37] The second three were updated versions of "Politics and Socialism," "Poetry and Eloquence," and "Natural Aristocracy." The entire six-lecture course, delivered before the Literary and Scientific Institution at Portman Square in London, 6–17 June,[38] drew upon contemporary revolutionary events but used them to argue that the scholar should remain aloof from the times. "I write 'Mind & Manners in the XIX Century,'" Emerson declared in his journal, "and my rede is to make the student independent of the century, to show him that his class offer one immutable front in all times & countries, cannot hear the drums of Paris, cannot read the London journals, they are the Wandering Jew or the Eternal Angel that survives all, & stands in the same fraternal relation to all."[39]

This entry seems slightly ironic, coming as it does from one who had pored over the London *Times* and been stirred by the *rappel* in Paris, but Emerson's teaching often opposed his behavior.[40] During his travels before the revolutions, he had been fascinated by the technological power of England, and, as Phyllis Cole has shown, his observations turned his thoughts toward the concept of fate and led to its use in his later social analyses.[41] Nevertheless, the revolutions of 1848 temporarily arrested this development by evoking the persona of the transcendental prophet, the teacher who had spoken so earnestly in "The American Scholar" and "The Divinity School Address" to young men in need of spiritual guidance. Because the times were obviously exerting such a strong attraction upon the minds of so many—including and especially his own—Emerson felt stimulated to become advocate of the ideal. In January his aunt Mary had expressed delight at reports that her nephew was getting "beyond the mists & rainbow visions of transcendental philosophy" and instead mingling "with the woes & cares of *practical* life,"[42] but her delight was premature. Surrounded by political

turmoil and by young men eager to hear his thoughts, Emerson the seer
rather than Emerson the observer spoke.

The "student" whom Emerson envisioned as his audience for "Mind
and Manners" certainly resembled the undergraduates at Oxford whom he
had recently met. During his visit to Oxford at the end of March he came
to admire "the very earnest, faithful, affectionate" fellows of the university,
"some of them highly gifted men; some of them, too, prepared & decided
to make great sacrifices for conscience sake."[43] They looked to him for inspiration, and one of them, Arthur Hugh Clough, followed him to Paris and
dined with him there daily, assuming the role of a disciple. Clough's desire
to absorb Emersonian thought was typical of his class. As Matthew Arnold
recalled in his famous lecture of 1883, Emerson enthralled the young men
at Oxford during the 1840s; his was, said Arnold, "a clear and pure voice,
which for my ear, at any rate, brought a strain as new, and moving, and
unforgettable, as the strain of Newman, or Carlyle, or Goethe."[44]

The "Mind and Manners" lectures were written in the voice Arnold
remembered, the "Orphic voice" of Emerson's early addresses[45]—radical,
visionary, exhortatory. The standard account of Emerson's career, of course,
is that the ardent personal idealism which characterizes his writings of the
late 1830s and early 1840s evolved into the restrained social realism of *Representative Men* (1850), *English Traits* (1856), and *The Conduct of Life*
(1860). The unpublished "Mind and Manners" lectures, however, represent
an anomaly in this development.[46] Written after the "Representative Men"
series yet before the lectures that would become *English Traits*, they have
a transcendental emphasis and expansiveness linking them closely to his
early work. This is especially true of the first three in the series, "Natural
History of the Intellect." These were to become, as Gay Wilson Allen has
said, his "most ambitious undertaking,"[47] but he was unable to complete the
book he envisioned. He reworked the lectures for a course he gave at Harvard in 1870–71, but his mental powers by then were failing, and the papers
published posthumously in *Natural History of Intellect* (1893) are but fragments. Because Emerson excelled as a poetic perceiver of truth but not as
maker of philosophical systems, his failure to write his great work on metaphysics is understandable. The task did not suit him.

As their titles suggest, Emerson's first three London lectures are meant
to elaborate his theory that the laws governing the workings of the mind
could be specified and described just as those governing the operations of
nature. In notes he made in 1835, he called these laws "the First Philosophy" and declared that "their enunciation awakens the feeling of the moral
sublime, and *great men* are they who believe in them."[48] In 1848 his attendance at lectures by eminent scientists in London and Paris renewed his interest in the task of "enunciation," and he asked in his first lecture, "Why
cannot the laws and powers of the mind be stated as simply and as attrac-

tively as the physical laws are stated by Owen and Faraday?" What Emerson was struggling toward with his metaphysics, at a time when no plausible theory of cognitive psychology existed, was an explanation, other than the conventional religious one, of those moments of mystical insight he had experienced in his life, those moments when the world seemed to become transparent before his eyes and he saw, or rather felt, the divine flowing through himself and all of creation. Because he was an idealist who believed that the physical world was a projection of the mind, he naturally looked to nature for means to "unfold" and make visible the laws which governed the mind and its heightened states. He recognized the monumental nature of the task. "The Natural History of the Intellect," he declared at the beginning of his first lecture, "would be an enumeration of the laws of the world,— laws common to chemistry, anatomy, geometry, moral and social life. In the human brain the universe is reproduced with all its opulence of relations; it is high time that is should be humanly and popularly unfolded, that the Decalogue of the Intellect should be written."[49] However, neither in his first lecture nor in any of them did he attempt or achieve this task. Rather, he penned what he called "sketches" for the complete "natural history."

In the first lecture, "Powers and Laws of Thought," Emerson offered a dark rendering of the conspiracy against the intellect and a glowing account of the intellect's power. Recent events and the contemporary world provided him with somber foreground details. "The very scale according to which the popular voice ranges the employments of men; the dignity of political employment; the general consent that Lamartine, in leaving the profession of poet for the business of statesman has risen, only show how ill the office of intellectual man is served," he claimed. Both the French and the English, he argued, were failing to engage the intellect; the former were wasting their energy "playing soldier or playing at politics" while the latter labored to acquire power and wealth. "The demands of the practical faculty were never carried to such a height as at this day," he declared, "in the predominance of the English race with their prodigious power of performance in all parts of the globe. It was inevitable that a people with such admirable hands should overvalue the hand." (The compliment, of course, reduces the sting to his hosts.) The mind, Emerson went on to claim, could easily take control of the corporeal; it "absorbs so much vital power" when rightly engaged "that it kills or suspends the senses." Using rhetoric reminiscent of the famous transparent eyeball passage of *Nature*, he asked, "How can a man of any inwardness not feel the inwardness of the Universe? If he is capable of sincere Moral Sentiment, the masses of nature undulate & flow; and in his hour of thought the world[,] the galaxy[,] is a scrap before the metaphysical power. In the words of the Koran, 'Verily worlds upon worlds can add nothing to it.'"[50]

Emerson's second and third lectures continued in this vein, contem-

porary and transcendental. "The Relation of Intellect to Natural Science"
argued the identity of intellect and nature, especially in their organicism.
He explained that every truth leads to another; every idea is a power that
can inspire other minds, make revolutions, and shape an age.[51] The lecture
"Tendencies and Duties of Men of Thought" tried to make palpable, through
the use of striking metaphors, the distinguishing features of the inspired and
inspiring individual: "He is a man as other men, has come into new circu-
lations, the marrow of the world is in his bones, the opulence of forms begins to pour into his intellect, & he is permitted to dip his brush into the
old paint pot with which birds, flowers, the human cheek, the living rock,
the ocean, the broad landscape, & the eternal sky were painted. It is this
employment of new means, of means not mechanical but spontaneous—by
appeasing for the new need, and as good as the end, that denotes the inspired man." Addressing the issue of the struggle by English Chartists and
French workers to better their lot, Emerson advised, "Each must be rich
but not only in money or land but he may have instead the riches of riches
[—] creative supplying power. He must be armed not necessarily with muskets & pikes—Better, if seeing these; he can feel, that he has better muskets
& pikes in his energy & constancy. . . . The way to mend the bad world is
to create the right world."[52]

In two of his last three lectures Emerson again alluded to the contemporary political scene as he exhorted his auditors to seek inspiration and
create a new world. The fourth lecture, "Politics and Socialism," drew upon
his recent journal entries as it praised the efforts of the socialists yet subor-
dinated them to the workings of the divine through the self. The socialists
"are not the creators they believe themselves," he declared, "but they are
unconscious prophets of a true state of society; one which the tendencies of
nature lead unto; one which always establishes itself for the same soul."[53]
(Upon hearing Emerson's reservations about the socialists, Wilkinson whis-
pered to a friend in the audience, "All lies.")[54] Emerson's fifth lecture, "Poetry and Eloquence," was an old standby containing little that was new or
contemporary; however, his sixth and last lecture, "Natural Aristocracy,"
which he had given in Edinburgh, swept close with its fiery rhetoric to the
explosive issues of the day. In the discourse, he still defended the notion of
the superior individual, the "natural aristocrat," but he also attacked "the
dressed & perfumed trifler who serves the people in no wise, and adorns
them not, is not even *not-afraid-of-them*." Apparently echoing rhetoric he
had recently heard, Emerson asked, "If such an one go about to set ill examples, dishonour, swindle, & corrupt them, who shall blame them if they
burn his barns, insult his children, assault his person, & express, in every
manner, their unequivocal indignation & contempt?—He eats their bread;
he does not scorn to live by their labour; and, after breakfast, he cannot
remember that there are human beings! To live without duties, is ob-

scene."[55] Drifting momentarily into the perturbed regions of the times, Emerson may have thought he was fulfilling his resolution to be "priest and poet" to the Chartists and Montagnards, but he had gone too far for some in his audience. Lord Morpeth, apparently distressed, visited Emerson's rooms that night and asked him to remove the passage if he ever again delivered the lecture. (According to Edward Emerson, who edited his father's works, the passage "still stands" in the printed essay,[56] and although this is indeed the case for Edward's edition, an examination of the lecture in manuscript shows that Emerson himself removed the last sentence and then the entire passage from the lecture.)[57] He complied with the request, for it would have been ill-mannered not to have.

The six London lectures constituted Emerson's personal "Charter," which he had urged himself to produce and make others feel its "infinite superiority today, even today."[58] Whether he succeeded or not, whether any in his audience were awakened to the overwhelming importance of the inspired mind aloof from the times remains an open question. He himself had the grace to scorn his performance. "We have a very moderate audience," he wrote to his wife, "& I was right of course in not wishing to undertake it for I spoil my work by giving it this too rapid casting."[59] The three new lectures were especially unstructured and fluid, and although they contain arresting passages, as wholes they lack coherence and force. Older members of the audience noticed this. Henry Crabb Robinson, who habitually fell asleep during such presentations, described the first as "one of those rhapsodical exercises of mind like those of Coleridge in his table talk that [sic] & of Carlyle in his lectures which leave a dreamy sense of pleasure, not easy to analyse or render an account of." The fourth, Robinson said, "was full of brilliant thoughts, but I was unable to connect them." Carlyle himself, whose respect for Emerson was waning, attended all six lectures but dismissed them in a letter to his sister as "pleasant *moonshiny* discourses, delivered to a rather vapid miscellany of persons (friends of humanity, chiefly)," and added that he "was not much grieved at the ending of them."[60] On the other hand, some members of the audience may have been impressed; Townsend Scudder III has labored to show that the "very earnest" young men of the day were inspired, men such as Clough, J. A. Froude, and James Hutchinson Sterling, all of whom later distinguished themselves as writers and thinkers.[61] Although Scudder tends to overstate, there is support for his case. "These lectures had important results," the Manchester *Guardian* claimed in 1882 following Emerson's death; "they were wonderfully stimulative to the young and fresh intellects to whom they were perhaps mainly addressed." Similarly, the *Pall Mall Gazette* of 1 May 1882 recalled that during his British lectures Emerson "really dealt with things of tremendous import to the people before him. His pictures of the fairer society, where love breathed through life, and justice organized the State . . . were as in-

cidental sketches made on the wayside; but they seemed to come from a
region where the dreams of many slow-climbing ages had expanded in at
least ideal realization."[62]

From one point of view, Emerson's "Mind and Manners" lectures were
conservative, in the sense that they belittled the importance of political and
social change. From another point of view, however, Emerson's own, they
advocated a radicalism far more profound than any being voiced by his European contemporaries, including Marx, Blanqui, and Proudhon. At the
heart of Emerson's idealism is the call for spiritual regeneration, for new
men, not new social orders. And it was on this basis that he criticized the
French socialists for being superficial. "All these orators in blouse or broad-
cloth seem to me to treat the matter quite literarily, & with the ends of the
fingers," he wrote Lidian from Paris. "They are earnest & furious but about
patent methods, and ingenious machines." In his lecture "Politics and Socialism," he repeated this sentiment and asserted, "In this age of mutations
every little while people become alarmed at the masses in society, & expect
a revolution. There will be no revolution, none that deserves to be called
so. . . . There will be no revolution until there are revolutionists." Emerson's definition of a revolutionist was an inspired individual whose right action could redeem the state. "Forever we must say, the hope of the world
depends on private independence & sanctity," he declared, and his thinking
matched that of his friend Thoreau, who several months earlier had declared
in "Civil Disobedience" that "the perception and the performance of
right,—changes things and relations; it is essentially revolutionary."[63]

A major consequence of Emerson's experiences in Europe during its
period of upheaval was a new appreciation of Thoreau as revolutionist. Although he had dismissed as quixotic Thoreau's stand that led to his night in
jail, his esteem for his friend's radicalism grew when he compared it to the
forms of radicalism he had encountered in Europe, for the latter seemed
not only more violent and materialistic, but also less bold. Just before he
departed from England for America, Emerson spoke with Arthur Helps and
Carlyle and responded to their query whether there were any Americans
"who had an American idea?" by assuring "them there were such monsters
hard by the setting sun, who believed in a future such as was never a past,
but if I should show it to them, they would think French communism solid
and practicable in comparison."[64] When he incorporated this exchange into
English Traits, he elaborated by saying that "'those who hold [the theory of
the right future] are fanatics of a dream which I should hardly care to relate
to your English ears, to which it might be only ridiculous,—and yet it is the
only true.' So I opened the dogma of no-government and non-resistance,
and anticipated the objections and the fun, and procured a kind of hearing
for it." Carlyle, as Wilkinson told Emerson, had adopted "Musketworship"
in reaction to the revolutions, and Emerson placed himself in direct oppo-

sition to this old friend when he added, "I can easily see the bankruptcy of
the vulgar musket-worship,—though great men be musket-worshippers;—
and 't is certain as God liveth, the gun that does not need another gun, the
law of love and justice alone, can effect a clean revolution."[65] This wisdom,
or folly if you will, Emerson had come to share with Thoreau at midcentury.

After returning to the United States, Emerson lectured on England and
France and became even more convinced of the superficiality of the recent
upheavals abroad. His lectures on England, of course, evolved into *English
Traits*, but he never developed his lecture on France, probably because he
lost respect for that nation during the months following his return home.
His unpublished lecture "France, or Urbanity," which he read during 1854–
56, praises the French slightly and charges them with thoughtlessness, vanity, lack of moral character, inconstancy, and ferocity. In *English Traits*, he
treats the French in passing even more harshly, claiming at one point that
"in France 'fraternity,' 'equality,' and 'indivisible unity' are names for assassination."[66] To understand his antipathy, which was shared by many Americans of his day, one must know about the Bloody June Days of 1848 and the
accounts of them that appeared in the American press.

3

The "Red Revolution"

Revolution is   "lord of the visionary eye whose lid
Once raised, remains aghast, & will not fall."
[Wordsworth, "Dion," 11 92–93]

—EMERSON, Journal Entry (August 1849)

Emerson referred to Lamartine in his first "Mind and Manners" lecture to make the point that the public valued the statesman more than the poet, but within three weeks of the reference, Lamartine had fallen from public favor and his country was in turmoil. On the afternoon of 23 June, as Emerson listened to Chopin play the piano at the residence of Mrs. Sartoris in London, Lamartine was greeted by gunfire in the streets of Paris as he tried to approach recently erected barricades. His influence with both the workers and members of the National Assembly had become negligible, and the insurrection that began at dawn that day would last for three more, leaving over four thousand Frenchmen dead, including Lamartine's two colleagues, shot while accompanying him on his futile peace-keeping mission.

The "Bloody June Days"

After the abortive uprising of 15 May that Emerson had witnessed, the moderates and conservatives who controlled France's Constituent Assembly had felt compelled to rid Paris of the thousands of restless workers swelling the workshops by day and the streets by night. Before the government took action, however, it placed an experienced army general, Louis Cavaignac, the former governor of Algeria, in charge of the army and National Guard. On 22 June a decree abolishing the national workshops was published in the government newspaper. Young members were called up for the army, and old members were told to go to the provinces to be on public work crews.

The workers' reaction was expected and immediate. On the morning of 23 June, the barricades went up throughout the working-class districts of eastern Paris, as some fifty thousand workers rebelled. Although Lamartine argued that lives could be saved by attacking each barricade as it went up, his voice went unheard as Cavaignac, soon given dictatorial powers by the National Assembly, held back for a major onslaught and treated the situation

44

as a war. He prepared battle plans, secured four-days' provisions for his soldiers, and declared Paris to be in a state of siege. On the twenty-fourth Cavaignac trained his artillery on buildings and barricades, and the insurgents fought desperately, using homemade weapons and munitions to kill the government troops. By Sunday 25 June, it was apparent that the attempted revolution would fail, for thousands of guardsmen were pouring in from the provinces; however, the small groups of remaining insurgents fought fiercely. The archbishop of Paris was killed while trying to negotiate a cease-fire, a number of attrocities were committed, and after the government's victory, thousands of insurgents were hunted down and shot without trial. On the morning of the twenty-sixth, fighting broke out again briefly, but by 11:00 A.M. Paris was quiet. The forces of law and order had prevailed. Czar Nicholas extended his congratulations.

Twelve thousand suspects were arrested and tried, and of these four thousand were sentenced to prison or deported to Algerian labor camps. The number of people killed during the June Days was estimated at the time to be ten thousand to thirty thousand, but historians now set the figure at about forty-five hundred.[1] The actual total will never be known, for as George Bourgin has pointed out, "No one could ever count those who died in hospitals, or were buried on the spot, or crept away to die in the cornfields and were not found till the harvest. No one ever recorded the reprisals: the summary executions and the prisoners herded into the cellars of public buildings, of which Flaubert paints so horrifying a picture in *Education Sentimentale*."[2]

The coverage that filled the American papers on 13 and 14 July, because it was compiled from the London papers and the press releases of the French government, was especially sensational and biased. "In one word it was the Blue and Red Republicans which have just been in conflict," a typical dispatch related. "Communism, Socialism, Pillage, Murder, Anarchy the Guillotine vs. Law and Order, Family and Property—these were the parties in presence."[3] The follow-up reports had almost the same tone and content, except there now appeared letters from reputable foreign correspondents paid to analyze as well as narrate events.

During March and April, when interest in the upheavals in Europe boomed, a number of editors had recognized the need to have their own reporters on the scene, and a group of writers, some of them distinguished, responded to the need. Margaret Fuller, of course, was already in Italy, writing letters to the *Tribune* that stand out from all others, containing as they do a coherent work of art, a history of the rise and fall of the Roman Republic. Samuel Goodrich, George William Curtis, Caroline Kirkland, Donald Mitchell, and Charles A. Dana were other literary figures who supplied letters for publication from Europe, with Mitchell and Dana reporting on the June Days as eyewitnesses.

46 THE "RED REVOLUTION"

Mitchell, who was to become famous as the author of the best-selling *Reveries of a Bachelor* (1850), explains in his *The Battle Summer* (1849) how he was studying law when news of the February revolution arrived. Unable to concentrate, he wondered whether the French labor organizations and barricades did not represent "a set of ideas about Constitutional Liberty, and Right to Property, . . . wider, and newer, and richer than all preached about" in his law books. After a moment's reflection, he supposedly threw his lawbook into the corner and declared, "I will go and see!"[4] Before he went, though, Mitchell made arrangements with James Watson Webb's Whig newspaper, the New York *Courier and Enquirer*, to supply them with the "Marvel Letters from Abroad," and he arrived in Paris several days before the Bloody June Days began.

Because he was observant, literate, and cultured, Mitchell was able to provide lively, colorful accounts of the Paris he encountered upon his arrival. He also saw and related the mounting tension between what he called "the people and the bourgeoisie," and he accurately predicted the bloodshed that would result if the workshops were dissolved. Because he was also sniveling, immature, and elitist, however, Mitchell, once the fighting began, holed up in his room, scared to death, and sent home letters that merely tell what he saw from his window and relay the government propaganda he picked up from the papers (Cavaignac, of course, had suppressed the radical press).

Dana, a former Brook Farmer, was working as city editor of Greeley's *Tribune* in the spring of 1848 when he, like Mitchell, proposed to go to Europe and report on events there. He later recalled, "Greeley said that would be no use, as I did not know anything about European matters, and would have to learn everything before I could write anything worth while. Then I asked him how much he would give me for a letter a week. He said ten dollars."[5] Deciding he could supplement this income by writing letters for other papers, Dana left for Paris, arriving there in time to witness the June Days and file what at the time was an insightful minority report, with which Greeley could not agree.

A bold, energetic reporter, Dana, who would later be known as Dana of the *Sun* and set new standards for nineteenth-century journalism, arrived in Paris at 5:00 A.M. on 25 June at the Gare St. Lazare. Leaving his bags at the train station, he set out to the other side of the city, in the direction of the hardest fighting. While Mitchell was "imprisoned," as he called it, in his chamber on the Boulevard des Italiens, Dana, passing close by, made his way around blockades and guarded streets to the Place de la Concorde (which was an army camp), then through the Champs-Elysées, over an unguarded bridge to the Left Bank, where he procured a guide who took him to the eastern section of the city. There he observed the fighting from a

The June Days—Place Maubert, Paris. (From *Illustrated London News*, 12 (1 July 1848), 436.)

distance and apparently made contact with friends sympathetic to the socialist movement.[6]

Mitchell, in his account of the fighting, which he never saw, emphasizes the unholy, demonic behavior of the workers; and in his analysis of the causes of the insurrection, he claims that communist extremists had crazed the workers and made them greedy and dangerous. On 25 June, with the sound of cannon coming in his window, he writes that the insurgents' "violence is equalled by their cruelty; in defiance of all civil usage, they have murdered their prisoners either beheaded them with such rude implements as were at hand, or hanging them to the window bars. Such is the action of the advocates, of what they call a *Social Republic!* God forbid that it should triumph!" Writing the next day, he adds details to his account of the "horrible excesses" of the insurgents: "In the Poissonnoiere, a soldier is said to have been impaled and disembowelled in the presence of his comrades!

Another, an officer of the line, had both hands cut off.—another, a dragoon, had both feet cut off, after which he was put upon his horse and in this horrible condition suffered to die. Several women were arrested who had sold poisoned brandy to the soldiers. But enough of these frightful details." After raising the question of why all this happened, he declares, "Socialism gives us an answer. That shameless doctrine which instructs us that all the systems of Public Liberty now current throughout the civilized world are spurious and ill founded; . . . this is the doctrine which has set on the workmen of Paris to their revolt, and barbarity, and happily, to their utter discomfiture."[7]

Dana, who still subscribed to the socialist ideals of Brook Farm and showed no inkling of the cynicism and reactionary spirit he was later famous for, interpreted the June Days as a class struggle and thus anticipated the later analyses of Marx and Tocqueville. For Dana, the crisis could be traced to events in February, when the leaders of the provisional government would not make the revolution a social as well as a political one. To him it was obvious that the government should have made the workmen their own employers and arranged for them to secure food, clothing, and shelter at minimum cost. Instead, the government did nothing. According to Dana, Lamartine, "a man of noble aspiration, a poet, a splendid writer, the very man in fact for the first days of the Revolution, was no more equal to the great practical work which was its duty, than were his compeers." As for the recent insurrection, Dana posits that it was almost spontaneous and leaderless, an opinion shared by modern historians.[8] He admits that the workers were "no doubt operated on by the agents of the various factions," but he accurately observes that "most of them have not thought out the idea which animates their movements into any definite systematic form. They are not Communists any more than they are Socialists of any other particular school. They only cherish a conviction, which they carry to fanaticism, that justice is not and cannot be done by the existing relation of employed and employer."[9]

Reaction

Dana's analysis carried little weight, especially when American public opinion rested on the side of the bourgeoisie. It was Mitchell's interpretation of events that was most in accord with the dominant American ideology and thus most credible. Even Dana's friend and employer Greeley found it difficult to extend sympathy to the Paris insurgents, and he published alongside of Dana's report editorials criticizing them and arguing that they were opposed by the French Fourierists. (Greeley, of course, was a Fourierist, and the rival New York papers, to abuse the *Tribune*, habitually referred to the Paris radicals as communists, socialists, and Fourierists.) The Democrat

Bryant similarly felt compelled to insist that the insurgents were not little "d" democrats, or even "ultra-democrats," as the English papers called them. "Such men as these," he wrote, "are not democrats in any sense— they have learned their practices in the school of absolutism, and so far from carrying their democracy to an extreme length, they have not yet acquired its first rudiments."[10] Americans who greeted the February revolution of the Paris workers as "sublime" thus devised rhetorical ways of distancing themselves from these wretched men, now that they were dead or defeated.

For Emerson, the June Days seemed to confirm his original skepticism shaped by the London *Times:* "perhaps the French Revolution of 1848 was not worth the trees it cut down on the Boulevards of Paris," he wrote in his journal.[11] In his lectures, he likewise spoke critically of events in France, and in a revised version of "Natural Aristocracy," he told his auditors that the "Chartist and outlaw" had "been dragged in their ignorance by furious chiefs to the Red Revolution."[12] This view of recent events accorded with Melville's, and it is not surprising that when he heard Emerson deliver what was probably this lecture,[13] he wrote his friend Duyckinck, "Say what they will, he's a great man."[14] The two writers differed in fundamental ways, of course, yet they shared an admiration for the idea of man and a dislike for the masses of actual men. The Bloody June Days in Paris strengthened the latter sentiment because of the accounts of mob violence that appeared in the American press.

In *Mardi*, Melville dealt with the June Days by using a mysterious scroll to express a number of Burkean reflections. This scroll, read to a crowd of Vivenzans, challenges the belief that monarchies are "utterly evil" and that republics are preferable forms of government. "Better, on all hands," it asserts, "that peace should rule with a scepter, than the tribunes of the people should brandish their broadswords. Better be the subject of a king, upright and just; than a freeman in Franko, with the executioner's ax at every corner" (527). The violence and bloodshed in France also form the basis for the scroll's assertion that "freedom is more social than political." "Better to be secure under one king," it declares, "than exposed to violence from twenty millions of monarchs, though oneself be of the number" (529).

The cry for *egalité*, as it was used by the Paris radicals, became another of Melville's topics in the scroll, which points out that multitudinous "organic causes" "inevitably divide mankind into brigades and battalions, with captains at their head" (527). Furthermore, violence only brings harm, the scroll maintains. Although "great reforms, of a verity, be needed; nowhere are bloody revolutions required. Though it be the most certain of remedies, no prudent invalid opens his veins, to let out his disease with his life" (529). Sounding much like Emerson in his London journals (or Hawthorne in "Earth's Holocaust"), the scroll declares that a faith in the efficacy of revolutions is unfounded, for "though all evils may be assuaged; all evils can not be done away. For evil is the chronic malady of the universe; and checked in one place, breaks forth in another" (529).

After the June Days, the Red Scare that had arisen in the spring of 1848 appeared amply justified, and soon a firm reaction set in. In France, freedom of speech, freedom of the press, the right to assembly, all were dramatically curtailed, and the popularity of Louis Napoleon (the emperor's ambitious nephew, who presented himself as the champion of order) grew rapidly. Some French conservatives, as they sought means to counter the enthusiasm for socialism among the people, turned to Emerson's writings. Émile Montégut, who published thirteen essays of Emerson in 1851 under the title "Essais de Philosophie américaine par Ralph Emerson," accurately credited Emerson with teaching the importance of reserve, of remaining aloof from all extreme opinions and extravagant beliefs. Emerson's "suprême indifférence," argued Montégut, was the answer to the "contagious fanaticism" of the socialists and to their "false democratic endeavors and demagoguery."[15]

In America, the June Days changed not laws or leaders, but attitudes. Whereas previously various social theories could be tolerated as the innocuous brainchildren of humanitarian reformers such as Greeley, Brisbane, and Ripley, now they provoked fear and hostility. To set up a utopian community at Brook Farm or to publish the theories of Fourier on the front page of the *Tribune* was one thing; to overthrow the government of France, to provoke four days of bloodletting in the streets of Paris, to oust Metternich from Vienna and the pope from Rome, however, was another. During the year 1848, radical and speculative thought acquired more fearful potency in the American consciousness than it had had since the days of Anne Hutchinson, and as a result, the next several years saw opprobrium cast upon radicals of every sort, who were usually charged with red republicanism, communism, or socialism. A reviewer of Thoreau's "Civil Disobedience," for example, suggested that the author "become a better subject in time, or else take a trip to France, and preach his doctrine of 'Resistance to Civil Government' to the red republicans." George Templeton Strong, the conservative New York lawyer, running short of funds, wrote sarcastically in his diary, "I shall turn Socialist, Fourierite, Free-Soiler, and Red Republican." Elizabeth Barrett Browning wrote a friend that Margaret Fuller, before she left Italy, had become "one of the out & out *Reds.*" And because of prevailing attitudes, the eminently respectable radical Henry James, Sr., when asked by Emerson to speak before the Town and Country Club in the summer of 1849, felt obliged to reply, "I should greatly like to consider socialism from the highest point of view, but the name is a stench in the nostrils of all the devout and honourable, and I would not willingly outrage your kindness in introducing me by *obtruding* the topic upon my audience."[16]

Even Walt Whitman, who, as chapter 7 will show, was stirred by the

revolutions to assume the role of political radical in his poetry, came to regard communism and socialism with contempt. While editor of the Brooklyn
Daily Eagle in 1846–47, before the revolutions, Whitman had criticized
utopian socialism generally, asserting that "it is utterly chimerical . . . to
attempt remodelling the world on an unalloyed basis of purity and perfec-
tion. God did not see fit to do so, and we hardly expect the thing will be
accomplished by Mr Robert Owen." Whitman's belief in Jefferson's motto
that "the best government is that which governs least" kept him from sym-
pathizing with any attempt to achieve social justice by political means, and
with the onset of the 1848 French revolution and the Red Scare, his resistance to socialism hardened. In the New Orleans *Crescent*, as he praised
Lamartine's provisional government, he warned against its socialist tendencies. "That the Government should have taken into consideration the condition of the laboring classes, was right and proper," he wrote; "it was a thing
absolutely demanded. But that it should attempt, by direct decrees, to fix
the hours of labor, the rate of wages, the price of food, or to furnish all the
unemployed with work in national workshops, was but to continue the
kingly system of interference with the laws of nature; interference . . .
equally pernicious in its immediate and remote consequences."[17] Whitman
and his friend Dana obviously disagreed on this issue. Whitman loved the
people, at least in the abstract; he hated kings and priests; he encouraged
revolution, even violent revolution, if the cause was liberty; but he would
have no truck with reformers, activists, and others who wanted to tinker
with government for the sake of society. Some nine years after the events of
1848, he editorialized on the violence between nativists and Irish immigrants and declared, "Educate, Educate,—it is the only true remedy for
mobs, emeutes, wild communistic theories, and red-republican ravings."[18]
Although some critics believe that Whitman adopted a conservative stance
in his editorials in order to satisfy his readers, the truth is that the private
Whitman held the same views as Whitman the editor. "He believed in the
old ways," his close friend of the 1860s Charles W. Eldridge recalled, "had
no faith in any 'reforms' as such, and thought that no change could be made
in the condition of mankind except by the most gradual evolution. . . .
He was likewise very hostile to anything like anarchy, communism or socialism."[19]

The most explicit and fierce literary reaction to the revolutionary socialist movement of 1848–49 was written by Orestes Brownson, the former
transcendental socialist turned Catholic reactionary. In a series of articles
that appeared in *Brownson's Quarterly Review*, he portrayed the European
radicals as blind and vicious: "Your modern reformers, socialists, communists, Red Republicans and radical democrats," he wrote in April 1850, "are
a stupid race of mortals, and as blind as they are destructive. They all undertake to obtain from unmitigated selfishness the results, which, in the

nature of things, can be obtained only from the severest and most self-denying virtue." For Brownson, only "the will of God," proclaimed "through the voice of his Church," could improve man's earthly condition. In his review of Hawthorne's *Blithedale Romance* (1852), Brownson not surprisingly hailed it as an antidote to the dangerous radicalism at large in the world. Praising the novel, he declared that "perhaps nothing has been written among us better calculated to bring modern philanthropists into deserved disrepute, and to cure the young and enthusiastic of their socialistic tendencies and dreams of world reform." [20]

In *Uncle Tom's Cabin*, which also appeared in 1852, Harriet Beecher Stowe used the prevailing fear of and hostility toward the "Red Revolution" in Europe to dramatize her antislavery themes. Knowing that her readers anticipated future uprisings of the masses abroad, she played upon their fears to get them to consider the possibility of similar events in the United States if the Negroes were not freed. Her first reference to the revolutionary socialist movement occurs in chapter 19 as Augustine St. Clare explains to his northern cousin Ophelia his feelings about slavery. When she asks what he thinks the future holds, he replies, "I don't know. One thing is certain,—that there is a mustering among the masses, the world over; and there is a *dies irae* coming on, sooner or later. The same thing is working in Europe, in England, and in this country. My mother used to tell me of a millennium that was coming, when Christ should reign, and all men should be free and happy. . . . Sometimes I think all this sighing, and groaning, and stirring among the dry bones foretells what she used to tell me was coming." [21] Some four chapters later, Stowe returns to this historical context in the debate between Augustine St. Clare and his twin brother, Alfred. In their exchange, which is central to the elitist-egalitarian debate about humanity in general and Negro slaves in particular, Alfred argues that all men are not born equal and that "it is the educated, the intelligent, the wealthy, the refined, who ought to have equal rights and not the canaille." Augustine, the respectable southern gentleman, does not challenge this assertion, but he predicts that if slaves get the upper hand, they will act like the beasts their owners have made them. When Alfred boasts that he is "not afraid to sit on the escape-valve, as long as the boilers are strong, and the machinery works well," Augustine warns, "The nobles in Louis XVI's time thought just so; and Austria and Pius IX think so now; and, some pleasant morning you may all be caught up to meet each other in the air, *when the boilers burst.*" "I tell you," he adds, "if there is anything that is revealed with the strength of a divine law in our times, it is that the masses are to rise, and the under class become the upper one" (324–25).

Although Alfred dismisses this prediction as "one of your red republican humbugs," Stowe's and the reader's sympathies reside with Augustine, so his assessment of the power and relevance of the European socialist movement is meant to be credited. The Red Scare serves Stowe's purposes by adding emotional appeal to the lengthy polemic that is her novel, and in her peroration, she uses it again to add a sense of urgency to her argument against slavery. Under the heading "Concluding Remarks," she declares, "This is an age of the world when nations are trembling and convulsed. A mighty influence is abroad, surging and heaving the world, as with an earth-quake. And is America safe? Every nation that carries in its bosom great and unredressed injustice has in it the elements of this last convulsion" (510).[22] From such a point of view (which has much to recommend it), one can re-gard the Civil War (which Stowe's novel helped precipitate) as the final dis-turbance of the earthquake that convulsed Europe in 1848–49.

Stowe's references to socialism in *Uncle Tom's Cabin* lead one to think that she regarded it sympathetically, but her *Key to Uncle Tom's Cabin* (1853) reveals her fundamental conservatism. As she discusses the philanthropy of a Boston merchant-prince, Amos Lawrence, she explains, "This is the *true* socialism, which comes from the spirit of Christ, and without breaking down existing orders of society, *by love* makes the property and possessions of the higher class the property of the lower. . . . Men would break up all ranks of society, and throw all property into common stock; but Christ would inspire the higher class with that Divine Spirit by which all the wealth, and means, and advantages of their position are used for the good of the lower."[23] Like Whitman and Emerson, Stowe was an optimistic evolutionist. She alludes to the uprising of the masses in *Uncle Tom's Cabin* to inspire peaceful re-form, not to make bullets fly or blood flow.

The international background of *Uncle Tom's Cabin* was shared, of course, by all contemporary literature. The February French revolution, the Red Scare, the Bloody June Days, the Reaction created a charged political atmosphere in which the entire American literary renaissance occurred. When Francis Bowen in an October 1849 article in the *North American Review* asserted that "the fatal disease under which the people of France, especially the inhabitants of Paris, have long been laboring, is speculative fanaticism," when he referred to "the false and pernicious theories which [have] betrayed the populace . . . and made shipwreck of the cause of re-publicanism in France,"[24] he not merely expressed a widely shared percep-tion, he also described the background of the times, out of which literary figures such as Hester Prynne and Captain Ahab would emerge. That *The Scarlet Letter*, written in the fall and winter of 1849, contains a brief against speculative thought and the overthrow of governments is not accidental; that *Moby-Dick*, written during 1850, contains within it a damning commentary on French political radicalism is not accidental. Hawthorne, Melville, Whit-man, Thoreau, and especially Margaret Fuller, all responded to the revolu-tionary spirit of the times and incorporated their responses into their finest works.

4

The "Cause" and Fuller's *Tribune* Letters

Leave this hypocritical prating about the masses. Masses are rude, lame, unmade, pernicious in their demands and influence, and need not to be flattered but to be schooled. I wish not to concede anything to them, but to tame, drill, divide and break them all up, and draw individuals out of them. The worst of charity is that the lives you are asked to preserve are not worth preserving.

—EMERSON, The Conduct of Life (1860)

On 19–20 July 1848, one week after America learned about the Bloody June Days in Paris, the first Women's Rights Convention was held in Seneca Falls, New York. Although the declaration, resolutions, and speeches of this historic meeting overflowed with revolutionary rhetoric, the convention's organizers, Lucretia Mott, Elizabeth Cady Stanton, Martha C. Wright, and Mary Ann McClintock—upstanding citizens all—took care to disassociate themselves from the European scene and to place their cause at the center of the American political tradition. They claimed Jefferson, not Marx or Fourier, as their guide and used as their manifesto a revised version of the Declaration of Independence, asserting the "self-evident truth" that "all men and women are created equal."[1]

By thus appealing to "principles cherished by all Americans," Stanton and company participated in what Sacvan Bercovitch has termed the American "ritual of consensus," that is, the assertion of independence having as its goal national coherence as opposed to social upheaval. In an illuminating study of the ideological context of the American renaissance, Bercovitch has argued that revolution in America has meant "the unfolding of a redemptive plan," in contrast to revolution elsewhere, which has meant "a threat to social order." In his view, the militant feminists of 1848 "were conforming, like most American radicals of the time, to a ritual of consensus that not only allowed for but actually elicited social criticism." Whereas in Europe at this time "revolution bared the dialectics of historical change," in America "the summons to dissent, because it was grounded in prescribed ritual forms, ruled out the threat of radical alternatives."[2]

But in fact this threat was not ruled out entirely, because an antagonistic press, by alluding to the European upheavals, insisted on its presence. In the summer of 1848, the militant feminists, despite their patriotic rhetoric, were compared to the female "Reds" of Europe, whose recent behavior in Paris, as reported by Ik Marvel and others, had appalled the American public. James Gordon Bennett, for example, dealt with the Seneca Falls convention as follows in his influential New York *Herald:*

> This is the age of revolutions. To whatever part of the world the attention is directed, the political and social fabric of the world is crumbling to pieces; and changes which far exceed the wildest dreams of the enthusiastic Utopians of the last generation, are now pursued with ardor and perseverance. The principal agent, however, that has hitherto taken part in these movements has been the rougher sex. It was by man the flame of liberty, now burning with such fury on the continent of Europe, was first kindled; and though it is asserted that no inconsiderable assistance was contributed by the gentler sex to the late sanguinary carnage at Paris, we are disposed to believe that such a revolting imputation proceeds from base calumniators, and is a libel upon woman.
>
> By the intelligence, however, which we have lately received, the work of revolution is no longer confined to the Old World, nor to the masculine gender. The flag of independence has been hoisted, for the second time, on this side of the Atlantic; and a solemn league and covenant has just been entered into by a Convention of women at Seneca Falls. . . . Little did we expect this new element to be thrown into the cauldron of agitation which is now bubbling around us with such fury. . . . Though we have the most perfect confidence in the courage and daring of Miss Lucretia Mott and several others of our lady acquaintances, we confess it would go to our hearts to see them putting on the panoply of war, and mixing in scenes like those at which, it is said, the fair sex in Paris lately took prominent part.[3]

After a second convention was held in Rochester on 2 August, the Rochester *Democrat* patronized the participants in a similar fashion, calling the convention "a regular *emeute* of a congregation of females gathered from various quarters, who seem to be really in earnest in their aim at revolution, and who evince entire confidence that 'the day of their deliverance is at hand.' Verily, this is a progressive era!"[4]

There is a smugness in these editorials, of course, common among those who take power for granted, and the yoking of the women's rights conventions to the revolutions in Europe seems contrived for the purposes of mockery. The participants at the conventions, moreover, certainly did not see, or rather wish to see, the relationship between their struggle for liberation and that of the oppressed of Europe. Ironically, though, the woman most responsible for pioneering the American feminist movement, the woman whose writings and teachings had inspired many of America's most prominent women, had just become an advocate of foreign radical thought and would soon be mixing in scenes of revolutionary violence in the streets of Rome.

At the time of the Seneca Falls convention, Margaret Fuller, whose Boston "Conversations" held in Elizabeth Peabody's parlor had liberated the

Women on a Barricade near the Porte St. Denis, Paris, during the June Days. (From *Illustrated London News*, 12 (1 July 1848), 426.)

minds of many women and whose feminist work *Woman in the Nineteenth Century* (1845) had generated widespread discussion and agitation, was secluded in the small Italian village of Rieti, writing a narrative of her European experiences and waiting to bear a child. Interrupted in her writing not only by the birth of her son, but also by her subsequent involvement in the Italian Revolution and the Siege of Rome, she returned to her book in the winter of 1849–50, intending to make it a history of the Roman Republic told from a radical socialist's point of view. "Believe that in thought I am more radical than ever,"[5] Fuller warned one of her friends in Italy, and she must have sensed that her radicalism would provoke the hostility of conservative readers everywhere once her history appeared. According to Elizabeth Barrett Browning, who befriended Fuller in Florence during the later stages of the history's composition, the book when published could not "have been otherwise than deeply coloured by those blood-colours of Socialistic views, which would have drawn the wolves on her, with a still more howling enmity, both in England & America."[6] Such a development never occurred, however, because on 19 July 1850, the manuscript was lost in the shipwreck of the *Elizabeth*, which took the lives of Fuller, her husband, and child.

Many biographers have lamented the loss of the "History of the Roman Republic," believing, as Fuller did, that it was her magnum opus, the work that would have at last established her reputation as a major American author. Fortunately, Fuller prepared a complete set of sketches for the history, sketches that have certainly more immediacy, and probably more fidelity and force because of their immediacy, than the history itself possessed. I am referring to her twenty-four dispatches from Italy published in the New York *Tribune* during 1847–50. These letters, which have received little critical attention, can be seen as a coherent and powerful rhetorical construct, and as such they represent not only Fuller's finest work but also a worthy addition to the canon of the American renaissance.

Fuller, Emerson, and Associationism

Fuller's achievement in her Italian dispatches resulted directly from her radicalization, a process that began about 1844 and culminated five years later during her immersion in the European revolutionary scene.[7] Before Fuller left for Europe in the summer of 1846, the greatest living influence upon her thought and work had been, of course, Emerson. As a guest in his house, a visitor to his study, a reader of his journal, she achieved an intimacy with him that no other person, with the exception of his first wife, Ellen, equalled. From 1836, the year they met, until 1844, when she moved to New York City, Emerson's intellectual brilliance and spiritual integrity stirred Fuller profoundly. Through his public lectures especially, he taught her to value the life of the mind and to challenge the social conventions limiting her personal development.[8] More significant, he also convinced her of the primacy of individualism and the ineffectiveness of cooperative reform efforts, two convictions she would eventually reject in Europe.

Fuller's work as columnist and literary critic for the *Tribune* from 1844 to 1846 essentially ended her reliance upon Emerson for intellectual and spiritual guidance. After she moved in with the Greeleys and became absorbed in her newspaper work, she found herself more engaged by social problems than ever before. Responding to the reform-minded Greeley's editorial preferences, she used her *Tribune* articles to discuss the injustices faced by women, Irish immigrants, blacks, prisoners, prostitutes, and the mentally ill; however, she held back from advocating any *-ism* designed to change the existing social order. As Margaret V. Allen has pointed out, "Her columns show that she implicitly believed that knowledge of wrongs or evils led to their correction: her readers had only to be told of injustice and suffering and inevitably these ills would be eradicated."[9]

Although Fuller's years in New York City enhanced her social aware-

ness, it was her experiences in Europe during 1846–49 that led her farthest
away from Emersonian individualism and gave her new values, new concerns, and new forms of expression. In the spring of 1848, as Fuller was
making plans to leave Rome to conceal her pregnancy, she received an affectionate letter from Emerson (then in Manchester) asking her to meet him
in Paris in May "if bullets have ceased to sing on the Boulevards." He had
originally planned to ask her to come home with him and live in his house,
but before he could extend the invitation, he heard from his wife, Lidian,
who vetoed the idea. After mentioning "poor exhausted Lidian's tragic letters," Emerson told Fuller, "but I mean yet to coax you into Mrs Brown's
little house opposite to my gate."[10] The invitation was sincere, but it was
extended in complete ignorance of Fuller's lover (the handsome, proud, devoted Count Ossoli), of her pregnancy, and of her newly acquired radicalism, all of which placed a distance between the two friends far greater than
that separating Manchester and Rome.

To compare Fuller's and Emerson's responses to contemporary Europe
can reveal the magnitude of this distance and the intellectual poles between
which it lay. Their trips to Europe began just fifteen months apart: Fuller
arrived in England in August of 1846, Emerson in October of 1847. Although their paths never crossed, their itineraries were similar; they traveled to many of the same places (Liverpool, Manchester, Edinburgh, Glasgow, London, and Paris) and saw many of the same people (Alexander
Ireland, Garth Wilkinson, James Martineau, De Quincey, Harriet Martineau, Wordsworth, Carlyle, and Chopin, among others). For both Americans, socialism and revolution moved to the center of their thoughts while
they were abroad, yet their responses to these issues and to all they encountered were strikingly at odds.

During Emerson's stay in England, that country's power, its wealth, its
rapid growth, its vast machinery, all fascinated and impressed him, as did
its people, especially its liberal industrialists and well-mannered aristocrats.
"There is a sort of people here," he wrote Elizabeth Hoar, "whom we hardly
have the like of in New England,—great manufacturers who exercise a paternal patronage & providence over their district. Such are the Brights at
Rochdale, whom I visited, and the Schwanns at Huddersfield;—best of their
sort. And England will stand many a day & year yet, and tis all idle the talk
of revolution & decay, for they have the energy now which made all these
things."[11] After Emerson arrived in London in March, following his lecture
tour throughout the north of Britain, he continued to be impressed by what
he saw. For him London was not Blake's with its cries and woe, or even
Dickens's bleak city, but rather an inspiring show. The dehumanizing effects
of the industrial revolution touched him little, and he informed Lidian that
"the most wonderful thing I see is this London at once seen to be the centre
of the world the 'nation in brick'; the immense masses of life of power of

wealth, and the effect upon the men running in & out amidst the play of the vast machinery, the effect to keep them tense & silent, and to mind every man his own,—it is all very entertaining, I assure you. . . . I have many good thoughts, many insights, as I go up & down."[12]

Emerson had sailed to England on the *Washington Irving*, which was fitting; for like Irving, he became an Anglophile, especially in his response to the British upper classes. Visiting London "in season," he met many aristocrats, which led to a luncheon invitation from the duchess of Sutherland, who showed him around Stafford House. He found it seductive. "I have seen nothing so sumptuous as was all this," he wrote. "One would so gladly forget that there was anything else in England than these golden chambers & the high & gentle people who walk in them! May the grim Revolution, with his iron hand, if come he must, come slowly & late to Stafford House & deal softly with its inmates!"[13]

While Emerson was captivated by England's power and wealth, Fuller was appalled by its poverty and "shocking inhumanity of exclusiveness." "To the horrors and sorrows of the streets in such places as Liverpool, Glasgow, and, above all, London, one has to grow insensible or die daily," she reported. The plight of the poor, especially women, struck her as more terrible than anything she had dreamed of in the United States. "I saw here in Glasgow," she told her *Tribune* readers, "persons, especially women, dressed in dirty, wretched tatters, worse than none, and with an expression of listless, unexpecting woe upon their faces, far more tragic than the inscription over the gate of Dante's *Inferno*." When she arrived in London, it was "out of season," but she claimed to be glad that the aristocracy were still on their country estates so that she was not faced with "all that pomp and parade of wealth and luxury in contrast with the misery, squalid, agonizing, ruffianly, which stares out in the face in every street of London." She did see Carlyle, however, and at his house Joseph Mazzini, the leader of the Italian nationalist movement, who shared her belief that "there can be no genuine happiness, no salvation for any, unless the same can be secured for all."[14]

How and why Fuller and Emerson had such different responses to England can be traced to a number of causes. First, of course, was the different purposes of their travel. Emerson went to England to give his series of lectures, to renew old acquaintances, and to gather material and insights for future writings. In many respects, the lecture circuit, with its obligatory dinners and social gatherings and hectic travel schedule, made him its captive. When he was not traveling or being lionized by his hosts, he spent his time in his rooms, preparing his lectures, studying the *Times*, writing entries in his journals and letters to friends. Both his isolation and his delight with England's progress can be seen in the following description of his travels: "I ride everywhere as on a cannonball," he wrote to his wife, "(though cushioned & comforted in every manner) high & low over rivers & towns through mountains in tunnels of 3 miles & more at twice the speed & with half the motion of our cars & read quietly the Times Newspaper which seems to have machinized the world, for my occasions."[15]

Fuller, on the other hand, disdained the railroad as "that convenient but most unprofitable and stupid way of travelling"[16] and rode in the open air on the top of a stagecoach, seeking out landscapes and people that Emerson ignored. Traveling with her Quaker friends Marcus and Rebecca Spring, wealthy supporters of various socialist enterprises, including the North American Phalanx, Fuller studied British society closely. She descended into a Newcastle coal mine, observed "the sooty servitors tending their furnaces" at Sheffield, toured a model prison at Pentonville, and visited Mazzini's school for poor Italian boys in London.[17] Similarly, in France, Fuller evidenced sociological interests that contrasted with Emerson's metaphysical ones. Whereas he spent much of his time in Paris working on his "Mind and Manners" lectures, which would celebrate detachment and transcendence, she became absorbed in the practical application of French socialism. She visited a progressive school for idiots, observed the *crèches* (child care centers for working mothers), and talked with writers and intellectuals concerned with reforming European society.

Exactly when and where Fuller acquired the socialism that became such a firm and intense part of her thought have never been determined, but the evidence points to Paris in the winter of 1846–47. We know that she went to Europe predisposed to admire and support the work being done by socialists to institute reforms; her friendships with William H. Channing, Greeley, and the Springs made that certain. The poverty and misery of England stirred her to express admiration toward those searching for remedies, and in a letter written from Glasgow on 30 September 1846, she defended the Associationists "for their attempt to find prevention against such misery and wickedness in our land."[18] It was in Paris, however, that intellectual discussion of Associationism was flourishing, and it was there that the Fourierists apparently made a convert of her. Her meetings with George Sand, the French novelist who would turn out socialist-republican propaganda during the revolution a year later, and Adam Mickiewicz, the Polish poet and exiled revolutionary leader, affected her personal life most profoundly, giving her the courage to take a lover and enlarge the scope of her experiences; however, her discussion with other notable Parisian intellectuals gave her the belief in a new social system, which she took to Italy with her. According to a notebook Emerson compiled on Fuller after her death, among those she saw in Paris were Victor Considérant, the well-known disciple of Fourier and France's leading socialist; Hugh Doherty, the Irish socialist and editor of the London *Phalanx;* Clarisse Vigoureux, an early follower of Fourier; and Félicité Robert de Lamennais, a French abbé and socialist philosopher.[19] She also met the socialist Pierre Leroux, the founder of *La Revue Indépendente*, who published a translation of her essay on American literature and invited her to write additional pieces.[20] Although she found some of the Fourierists wearisome, their ideas inspired her. Several months after leaving France, Fuller informed Mary Rotch, "Paris is the very focus of the intellectual activity of Europe, there I found every topic intensified, clarified, reduced to portable dimensions: there is the cream of all the milk."[21]

Timing was an important factor in Fuller's radicalization, of course, and is another reason her response differed so much from Emerson's. While she was in France, Louis Philippe still sat on the throne, so whereas Emerson witnessed the chaos and turmoil the revolution brought in its wake, she beheld the misery and oppression suffered by the poor before the revolution and naturally advocated social and political change. In her accounts for the *Tribune*, she told of the starvation in France in the winter of 1846–47 and blamed the king. "While Louis Philippe lives," she wrote, "the gases, compressed by his strong grasp, may not burst up to light; but the need of some radical measures of reform is not less strongly felt in France than elsewhere, and the time will come before long when such will be imperatively demanded." In her eyes, the doctrines of Fourier, then gaining widespread attention, were making clear to all "the necessity of some practical application of the precepts of Christ, in lieu of the mummeries of a worn-out ritual." And her recognition of "the terrible ills which infest the body politic of Europe" increased her indignation "at the selfishness or stupidity of those in my own country who oppose an examination of these subjects,—such as is animated by the hope of prevention."[22] Emerson, arriving in Europe about six months before the French revolution, also noticed the progress the doctrines of Fourier were making, but as we have seen he belittled it at first. It was not until he had visited Paris after the revolution that he regarded French socialism sympathetically, and even then, when he reaffirmed his "true position of being priest & poet" of "the Movement party," he remained cool and aloof with regard to the struggling masses.[23]

As Emerson often and freely admitted, he lacked warmth in his feelings toward others ("a photometer cannot be a stove,"[24] he told Lidian). Fuller, on the other hand, possessed a warm and generous nature that made it natural for her to sympathize with the lowly and oppressed. And this difference in personalities is yet another explanation for the differences in their responses to the European scene. Whereas Emerson saw the revolutions motivated by greed, with one class wanting to acquire by force what another had acquired through talent and industry, she saw the revolutions motivated by a desire for freedom and justice. In her view, the commercial classes had heartlessly exploited the laboring poor, and ruling despots had denied them basic political rights. Writing of the painful degradation and misery suffered by the silk weavers in Lyons, she exclaimed to her American readers, "And there are those who dare to say that such a state of things is *well enough*, and what Providence intended for man,—who call those who have hearts to suffer at the sight, energy and zeal to seek its remedy, visionaries and fanatics! To themselves be woe, who have eyes and see not, ears and hear not, the convulsions and sobs of injured Humanity!"[25] Because Fuller had eyes that could see and ears that could hear, she found herself a radical when she arrived in Italy. "Art is not important to me now," she wrote her friend William Channing. "I take interest in the state of the people, their manners, the state of the race in them. I see the future dawning; it is in important aspects Fourier's future."[26] Fuller's new sociopolitical concerns, which supplanted her interest in art, resulted, paradoxically, in the best writing she ever did.

Fuller's *Tribune* Letters from Italy

Fuller's reputation as a writer, which has risen rapidly in the last decades, rests primarily upon her astute literary criticism published in the *Dial* and the *Tribune* and upon her well-known feminist work, *Woman in the Nineteenth Century*. As mentioned above, many Fuller scholars have expressed the belief that her "History of the Roman Republic" was probably her finest literary effort, but what has gone unnoticed is that her dispatches from Italy, when considered as a separate literary work, display more artistry and power than any of her other writings. Three features, especially, raise them far above mere journalism to the level of art: their shapely organic structure, their supple, powerful prose, and their use of a memorable persona.

Viewed in their totality, the *Tribune* letters from Italy divide into two balanced parts: twelve letters written between March 1847 and April 1848 and twelve letters written between December 1848 and January 1850. Here are their numbers and dates in her "Things and Thoughts in Europe" series (nos. 1–12 in the series were written before her arrival in Italy):

No. 13. No date (circa March 1847)	No. 25. 2 December 1848
No. 14. May 1847	No. 26. 2 December 1848
No. 15. 9 August 1847	No. 27. 20 February 1849
No. 16. October 1847	No. 28. 20 February 1849
No. 17. 18 October 1847	No. 29. 20 May 1849
No. 18. December 1847	No. 30. 27 May 1849
No. 19. 17 December 1847	No. 31. 21, 23 June 1849
No. 20. 30 December 1847	No. 32. 10 June 1849
No. 21. 10 January 1848	No. 33. 6, 8 July 1849
No. 22. 22, 27 January 1848	No. 34. 31 August 1849
No. 23. 29 March 1848	No. 35. 15 November 1849
No. 24. 19 April and 13 May 1848	No. 36. 6 January 1850

Informed by Fuller's recent radicalization, the entire twenty-four letters are shaped by the growth, flowering, and repression of the socialist-republican cause in Europe, especially as that cause was perceived, defined, and interpreted by Fuller herself. Her ideological commitment, her historical consciousness, and the exciting events she witnessed combined to yield a coherent historical narrative, one representing an insider's version of the rise and fall of the Roman Republic and the defeat of liberty in Europe.

Prior to writing her *Tribune* letters from Italy, Fuller seldom achieved coherence in her writings, a common problem for the Transcendentalists as a group. Emerson's inability to bind his sentences tightly together has long been recognized, ever since Carlyle characterized his paragraphs as canvas bags full of duckshot. And time spent in Thoreau's *Week on the Concord and Merrimack Rivers* or Fuller's *Summer on the Lakes* convinces one that whim and fancy played a great part in the shaping of these works. The organic principle, of course, has often been cited to defend the Transcendentalists' works from the charge of formlessness; however, only with the best, such as *Walden*, does the defense succeed. As Lawrence Buell has pointed out, although the Transcendentalists "relied heavily upon the analogy of nature" in their aesthetics, the analogy generally served "as a metaphor for the idea of inspiration rather than as a basis for hard thinking about structure."[27]

Fuller's first *Tribune* letters from abroad, written in England and France, display the same structural weaknesses as do her earlier writings; in these letters she discusses a multitude of topics related only by the fact that they happen to engage her interest at the time. Liverpool, peace and war, the Royal Institute, bathing, Wordsworth, and the bookselling trade are some of the topics found in these letters; and as Ernest Earnest has pointed out, what we have here is "a jumpy writer," one whose "headlong pace" and "insatiable curiosity" result in a "catch-all style."[28] Once she arrived in Italy, however, her subject matter became less and less a matter of whim and more one of necessity—dictated by her engagement in the Italian revolutionary movement—and her letters became truly organic, shaped not by disparate impulses and interests, but rather by the vital, developing ideology she had adopted as her own. Eventually, of course, she would subordinate all to the socialist-republican cause, including the safety of her husband, her child, and herself.

The political situation Fuller encountered upon her arrival in Italy in the spring of 1847 was chaotic, yet as she reported on it in her *Tribune* letters, it took on form and meaning. Italy, like contemporary Germany, was not a nation, but a group of small states, the product of the Congress of Vienna of 1815, which sought to repress nationalism and democracy by portioning out the spoils of the Napoleonic Empire. In the south of the peninsula, the Spanish Bourbon Ferdinand II ruled despotically over the degraded citizens of the Kingdom of Naples. In the north and northwest, hated

Austrian troops made certain that prosperous Lombardy and Venetia remained under the control of the Austrian Empire. In the northeast, Piedmont maintained a degree of independence from Austria, and Piedmont's king, Charles Albert, a vacillating monarch who desired to unite Italy under his rule, awaited his opportunity to wage a national war. In Tuscany, the grand duke Leopold, a Hapsburg, ruled as benevolently as he thought prudent. And further south, in the Papal States, which sliced across the middle of the peninsula, Pope Pius IX had begun to encourage European moderates and radicals by his recent reforms. A humble, unimaginative man, Pius appeared exceptionally liberal when compared to his regressive predecessor Pope Gregory XVI, who died in June 1846.

During her first summer in Italy, Fuller vacationed on the lakes of northern Italy and Switzerland, and as she reported on her sense of Italy she began to construct, perhaps unconsciously, a coherent account of the fate of liberty in Europe. Although at first, in Letters 13 and 14, she supplied her readers with discussions of a number of nonpolitical subjects, such as American artists, Italian paintings, and English travelers, with each new letter her focus on the socialist-republican cause became more sustained and sharp, until it alone held sway over all she wrote. Upon her first visit to Milan, in August 1847, she observed in Letter 15 the "great excitement in Italy" but chose not to write about it. "All things," she declared, "seem to announce that some important change is inevitable here, but what? Neither Radicals nor Moderates dare predict with confidence, and I am yet too much a stranger to speak with assurance of impressions I have received."[29] During her second visit to Milan one month later, however, she became good friends with a group of radicals intent upon the overthrow of Austrian rule, and in Letter 16 as she discussed their cause for her *Tribune* readers, she made it her own.

To Fuller, political change and social change were bound inextricably together, and in the role of prophetess she assumed in her dispatches, she referred to republicanism and socialism together as the "idea" or the "thought" or the "spirit," which she was convinced was animating the Old World and providing an example to the New. In Letter 16, she discusses the volatile political situation in Milan and declares, "In the middle class . . . *thought* ferments, and will yet produce a wine that shall set the Lombard veins on fire when the time for action shall arrive" (my italics). In the same letter, she declares that Americans "have no heart for *the idea*, for the destiny of our own great nation: how can they feel *the spirit* that is struggling now in this and others of Europe" (my italics).[30] Two months later, as revolution loomed nearer, she accurately predicted in Letter 18 a violent upheaval and declared that "still Europe toils and struggles with *her idea*, and, at this moment, all things bode and declare a new outbreak of the fire, to destroy old palaces of crime!" (my italics).[31]

By this sixth letter from Italy Fuller was writing almost exclusively about the "cause," and she would continue to do so throughout the remainder of her letters. Even when she was not describing specific revolutionary developments, she was interpreting them, explaining them, showing their relevance to her *Tribune* readers. In Letter 18, written to appear in the United States on New Year's Day, 1848, she uses the European scene as the basis for a severe indictment of American society, especially its capitalism and slavery. After confessing that she knows of no antidote to defend "that great, rich country" against "the evils that have grown out of the commercial system in the old world," she asserts that "voluntary association" will become "the grand means" for America "to grow and give a nobler harmony to the coming age." In her eyes Fourierism and Abolitionism have now much in common; admitting that before coming to Europe she had found the Abolitionists at home "tedious" and "narrow," she now admires them and finds "something eternal in their desire and life."[32]

When Fuller reported on the French revolution of February 1848, she treated it with unbounded enthusiasm, for to her it marked the dawn of a new era, a socialist-republican era. Having been in Paris, she understood, as many of her countrymen did not, the ideological background of that event. Whereas the American press interpreted the revolution, at first, as a triumph of democracy over despotism, Fuller knew that the Paris workers had been inspired by socialist doctrines, and she became convinced for a time that her prophecy of a "coming age" of harmony was at hand. In a private letter of 29 March 1849 to her friend William Channing, she confesses being "engrossed, stunned almost, by the public events that have succeeded one another with such rapidity and grandeur. It is a time such as I always dreamed of, and for long secretly hoped to see." In her *Tribune* Letter 23, written the same day, she lauds the French revolutionaries and tries to educate her readers about the true importance of what is happening. "To you, people of America," she writes, "it may perhaps be given to look on and learn in time for a preventive wisdom. You may learn the real meaning of the words FRATERNITY, EQUALITY: you may, despite the apes of the Past who strive to tutor you, learn the needs of a true Democracy. You may in time learn to reverence, learn to guard, the true aristocracy of a nation, the only really noble,—the LABORING CLASSES."[33]

Fuller's new ideological commitment, explicitly evident in the rhetoric of this passage, shaped even her public comments on her friend Mazzini, the father of the Italian *risorgimento*. Mazzini, who would head the Roman Republic, believed fervently in the people, but he, unlike the Parisian socialists and communists, viewed the people not merely as the laboring classes or the proletariat, but as everyone. Mazzini's beliefs were deeply religious, and his objections to French socialism were based upon not only its tendency to pit one class against another, but also its emphasis upon property as opposed to sacred ideals. Because of his opposition, Fuller chided her friend in the pages of the *Tribune*. "Mazzini sees not all," she writes in Letter 24, "he aims at political emancipation; but he sees not, perhaps would deny, the bearing of some events, which even now begin to work their way. Of this; more anon; but not to-day, nor in the small print of *The Tribune*. Suffice it to say, I allude to that of which the cry of Communism, the systems of Fourier, &c. are but forerunners." What Fuller meant by this remains uncertain, but in a letter to Mary Rotch she mentions "voluntary association in small communities,"[34] which coincides with the Fourieristic plans of Doherty, Considérant, Leroux, and others for establishing utopian socialist colonies in Europe and America.[35]

These plans, not coincidentally, resembled the experiments Fuller's friend the princess Belgiojoso conducted on her estate several years earlier. Beautiful, learned, of noble birth but republican sympathies, the princess represented, as Joseph Jay Deiss has pointed out, all that Fuller had dreamed of being since she was a child.[36] The princess, who enthralled Fuller when they met in the spring of 1848, had had her estate confiscated by the Austrians in the 1820s because of her subversive activities. She eventually won it back through the influence of friends, however, and, as Fuller points out in the *Tribune*, the princess then "made experiments in the Socialist direction with fine judgment and success," providing education, work, and care for her peasantry.[37] Fuller neglects to mention that the princess opened a glove factory and arranged for technical classes to be offered to the peasant children, both schemes showing the influence of Saint-Simonism, which Belgiojoso had studied in Paris in the 1830s.[38] Unlike the Fourierism Fuller apparently subscribed to, Saint-Simonism stressed large-scale organization and the use of technological knowledge. These distinctions, though, probably seemed inconsequential to Fuller, at least in her role as reporter to America. Her main point was that the princess has successfully put into practice socialist theory. (Marx, of course, expressed contempt for all such efforts, for unlike the utopian socialists, he called for revolution, not reform.)

Fuller's account of the princess served, like almost all of her other dispatches to the *Tribune* during 1848–49, to illustrate, explain, or support her belief in the socialist-republican cause. As insurrection in Sicily was followed by the revolution in France and the flight of Metternich from Vienna and the Five Glorious Days of Milan, Fuller kept her readers abreast of current events and the hope and enthusiasm they generated among the Italian people. After the Roman Republic was established in February 1849 and the Catholic powers of France, Austria, Naples, and Spain sent armies toward Rome to overthrow the new government and restore the pope, she was able to offer an eyewitness account of the initial successes of the Roman people as they routed the French, who were the first to arrive. As the siege of Rome progressed and the French began bombarding the city, and no other power in Europe could, or rather would, come to the aid of the Romans, Fuller saw that the cause was doomed, yet she elevated all to an epic level in her letters by focusing on the bravery and heroism of the people and their leaders, especially Mazzini and Garibaldi.

Even after the fall of Rome, Fuller, or rather her persona in the *Tribune*, refused to abandon hope for her cause (privately Fuller wrote despairing letters to friends). In exile, she fashioned stirring jeremiads of the American kind, that is, prophecies of doom coupled with celebrations of the glorious future that would follow the destruction of the present corrupt order. (As chapter 6 will show, these letters were probably the immediate inspiration for Whitman's poem "Resurgemus," the beginning of *Leaves of Grass*.) In Florence, as she studied Blanc's powerful socialist indictment of Louis Philippe's reign, *History of the Ten Years, 1830–1840*, and Lamartine's dramatic narrative of the great French Revolution, *History of the Girondists*, Fuller worked on her own history and wrote her final letters to the *Tribune*. In her penultimate dispatch, no. 35, she prophesies an imminent "peaceful though radical revolution." Claiming to have viewed socialism before she came to Europe "as the inevitable sequence to the tendencies and wants of the era," she declares, "but I did not think these vast changes in modes of government, education and daily life would be effected as rapidly as I now think they will, because they must. The world can no longer stand without them." In her last letter for the *Tribune*, written two months later when it had become more and more apparent that the revolutions of 1848–49 had left reaction, reprisals, and repression in their wake, she became more fiercely radical, calling not merely for the creation of a new social order, but also for the complete destruction of the old. By the time she concluded her dispatches for the *Tribune*, Fuller could not help but see that the chances for her cause's success had been reduced to nothing; nevertheless, she hid her despair. Throughout the *Tribune* letters her thesis had been that the cause, because it was morally right, would prevail; thus, although the Roman Republic had suffered defeat, she insisted to the last that a new day was dawning, or, in Thoreau's terms, that the sun was a morning star. "O Lucifer," she exclaimed, "son of the morning, fall not this time from thy chariot, but herald in at last the long looked for, wept for, bled and starved for day of Peace and Good Will to men."[39]

The *Tribune* letters are distinguished not only by their overall thematic and structural unity, achieved through Fuller's new ideological commitment, but also by the power and grace they display at the level of individual sentences and passages. As Bell Gale Chevigny has said, "In these dispatches, all her values are intact and so focused and actualized that they make her accounts of hopefulness, restlessness, political suspense, and battle, riveting even now."[40] Fuller writes poetically at times, polemically at others, and prophetically at still others; she creates colorful and romantic scenes; yet she also pens stark and restrained descriptions of the fighting and dying around her. And in almost all cases, her style is organic in the sense that its selection arises from the history she chooses to tell. Rarely calling attention to itself, the style enhances, clarifies, and dramatizes the various subjects it treats.

Fuller, of course, had not always demonstrated such skill, and many have commented upon the extravagant, preening, labored prose that debilitates much of her earlier writing. Ann Douglas has put it most pointedly by observing that "much of her prose before 1843 reminds one of the heroic ridiculous spectacle of Isidore [*sic*] Duncan trying to dance out with her small rather ill-trained self the whole meaning of Beethoven's Fifth Symphony played deafeningly by a full attendant orchestra."[41] The egoism and pretension of Fuller's writing became, in time, one of Lowell's targets in his *Fable for Critics*, in which he parodies Fuller as Miranda, who with an "I-turn-the-crank-of-the-Universe air" unfolds a "tale (of herself, I surmise, / For 't is dotted as thick as a peacock's with I's)."[42] In her *Summer on the Lakes* (1844), Fuller's style became clearer and less self-referential as she offered observations on social and economic conditions,[43] and her journalism for Greeley's *Tribune*, which began in 1844, led to even better writing, which did not go unnoticed at the time. Her friend James Freeman Clarke, for one, informed her in the summer of 1845 that he read her *Tribune* pieces regularly, adding, "They seem to me to be better written than anything of yours I have read. There is more ease, grace, freedom and point to them."[44] It was some three years later, however, in her *Tribune* dispatches from Italy, that Fuller's style reached its peak of excellence by displaying more diversity and control than it ever had before.

Fuller's first letters from Italy show traces of her earlier style, but while they reflect wide mood swings resulting from changes in her private life, they draw upon the personal rather than exhibit it. Letter 19, for example, written during her romantic interlude with Ossoli, contains a paean to Rome as a city of love and beauty, a city where "the seven hills tower, the innumerable temples glitter, and the Via Sacra swarms with triumphal life once more."[45] Similarly, Letter 20, which soon followed, apparently after she learned she was pregnant, reflects her depression as she describes the rain, the discomfort, the drabness of the Roman scene. By the spring of 1848, her prose began to move even farther away from the personal and to become eloquently polemical, as we have seen, under the stimulus of the French revolution of February. Soon after the revolution, however, a six-month hiatus occurred in her reporting when she retired to the countryside to bear her child.

Her retreat from Rome, a fearful and lonely experience, affected her dispatches in several ways. First of all, it kept her from recognizing and being sensitive to the reactionary turn that occurred in the thinking of many Americans with regard to the socialist movement in 1848. Although she shared her reader's euphoric response to the early days of the French revolution, she was out of touch with their reaction to the Bloody June Days in Paris. Certainly she learned about the events of June, but they must have seemed dim and inconsequential to her at the time, because of her isolation and her concern about Ossoli's safety and her own. For months she was convinced she would die in childbirth, and although she did not, this ordeal, too, affected her work, for she was a different woman by the time she returned to Rome—more militant, more Italian, more certain than ever that her hopes were bound up with the fate of the socialist-republican cause in Europe. The letters written after her return to Rome in December 1848 are obviously influenced by the psychological and physical pain she had suffered. For the most part they are hard-hitting and unsentimental; often they are spare, understated, tightly controlled. Exclamation gives way to careful, precise argumentation, and her purpose seems no longer to dwell upon her impressions (although she sometimes does), but to educate and persuade. In the early letters when she wrote of "my Italy," the phrase rang hollow, because it obviously referred to what she had learned through her readings in history and poetry; now "my Italy" refers to the living present as perceived not by a tourist, but by a resident struggling with poverty, loneliness, and the fear of death. During the battle of Rome, as Fuller nursed the wounded in the hospital on Tiber Island and her husband (a captain in the civic guard) manned his post on the Pincian Hill, she provided descriptions of the battle such as the following:

> The attack began before sunrise, and lasted all day. I saw it from my window, which, though distant, commands the gate of St. Pancrazio. Why the whole force was bent on that part, I do not know. If they could take it, the town would be cannonaded, and the barricades useless; but it is the same with the Pincian Gate. Small parties made feints in two other directions, but they were at once repelled. The French fought with great bravery, and this time it is said with beautiful skill and order, sheltering themselves in their advance by movable barricades. The Italians fought like lions, and no inch of ground was gained by the assailant. The loss of the French is said to be very great: it could not be otherwise. Six or seven hundred Italians are dead or wounded.[46]

The short sentences, the focus upon facts, the freedom from bias (even the hated French are given their due) endow the material with a dignity of Fuller's making; only the intrusive "like lions" mars the crystalline quality of the passage.

Although once she saw that republican Rome would fall, Fuller expressed anger toward the French, the pope, the London *Times*, and even her own country (which she mistakenly thought was unsupportive of the Roman republicans); she linked this anger to the sufferings of the Italian

Battle at the Porta San Pancrazio. (From *Illustrated London News* 14 (23 June 1849), 432.)

people rather than to herself. And whenever she indulged in self-pity, she provided the concrete details necessary to justify her feelings and evoke sympathy from her readers. During the bombardment, for example, after relating that "men are daily slain, and this state of suspense is agonizing," she adds,

> In the evening 't is pretty, though terrible, to see the bombs, fiery meteors, springing from the horizon line upon their bright path, to do their wicked message. 'T would not be so bad, methinks, to die by one of these, as wait to have every drop of pure blood, every childlike radiant hope, drained and driven from the heart by the betrayals of nations and of individuals, till at last the sickened eyes refuse more to open to that light which shines daily on such pits of iniquity.[47]

Here the literal reality of the first sentence justifies the metaphoric abstractions of the second. Fuller convinces us of the reality of the bombs by the visual precision of their "springing from the horizon line"; we consequently accept and share the sense of outrage and despair she then expresses. Moreover, by linking the imagery of the "fiery" bombs to the dimmed "radiant hope" and both to the "light which shines" on the "pits of iniquity," she gives her meditation on death figurative unity that enhances its rhetorical force.

Once republican Rome fell, Fuller's anger and bitterness toward its enemies became intense, yet in passages in her dispatches she successfully channeled these feelings into powerful understated descriptions of the scenes before her. After the fighting ended, for example, she described her visit to the battlefield: "I then entered the French ground, all mapped and hollowed like a honey-comb. A pair of skeleton legs protruded from a bank of one barricade; lower a dog had scratched away its light covering of earth from the body of a man, and discovered it lying face upward all dressed; the dog stood gazing on it with an air of stupid amazement."[48] Strikingly similar to passages in the works of Stephen Crane and Ernest Hemingway, such writing, before photojournalism desensitized readers, represented a fresh and powerful treatment of war. And this style apparently grew out of Fuller's confrontation with the subject matter itself. "What shall I write of Rome in these sad but glorious days?" she had asked on 10 June 1849. "Plain facts are the best; for my feelings I could not find fit words."[49] Her plain facts, however, conveyed her feelings superbly.

When she learned that the French general Oudinot had claimed that the Battle of Rome had been fought to "put an end to the reign of terror," Fuller, outraged, again used plain facts to enlighten her *Tribune* readers and refute the "impudent falsehood": "I, a woman, walked alone at all hours, in all quarters of Rome; I stood alone amid the throng of soldiers and of citizens; I took with me little girls to help me at the hospitals, and their parents thought my protection sufficient; I was at the gates, at the post-office, in the nearer quarters of Trastevere, in the Vatican gardens—I never saw an act of violence, was never even jostled in the excitement of the crowd; I do not believe ever people or soldiery showed a finer spirit."[50] The details here of the "little girls" and the "hospitals"—ubiquitous contrivances in the sentimental fiction of the day—seem natural because of the factual, eyewitness context in which Fuller places them; so placed they evoke pathos and contribute to the effectiveness of the passage. The parallelism of the clauses ("I walked"; "I stood"; "I took"; "I was at"; "I never saw") also gives, as Fuller knew it would, an emotional impact to her factual refutation.

The felicity and diversity of Fuller's style can be seen not only in her restrained, realistic passages, but also in her colorful, romantic ones, which she uses to endow her material with epic grandeur. The best of these focuses upon Garibaldi and his lancers as they prepare to flee Rome:

> We followed them to the piazza of St. John Lateran. . . . The sun was setting, the crescent moon rising, the flower of the Italian youth were marshalling in

that solemn place. . . . They must now go or remain prisoners and slaves. *Where* go, they knew not, for except distant Hungary there is not now a spot which would receive them, or where they can act as honor commands. They had all put on the beautiful dress of the Garibaldi legion, the tunic of bright red cloth, the Greek cap, or else round hat with Puritan plume, their long hair was blown back from resolute faces; all looked full of courage. . . . I saw the wounded, all that could go, laden upon their baggage cars, some were already pale and fainting, still they wished to go. I saw many youths, born to rich inheritance, carrying in a handkerchief all their worldly goods; the women were ready, their eyes too were resolved, if sad. The wife of Garibaldi followed him on horseback. He himself was distinguished by the white bournouse [tunic]; his look was entirely that of a hero of the middle ages, his face still young, for the excitements of his life, though so many, have all been youthful, and there is no fatigue upon his brow or cheek. Fall or stand, one sees in him a man engaged in the career for which he is adapted by nature. He went upon the parapet and looked upon the road with a spy-glass, and, no obstruction being in sight, he turned his face for a moment back upon Rome, then led the way through the gate.[51]

Drawing upon the techniques of the historical novelist ("I longed for Sir Walter Scott to be on earth again," she says as she assays her description), Fuller provides a dramatic setting, filled with adversity and tension, and focuses upon the hero's features as he prepares to meet his fate. Although in several sentences of the passage (omitted here), the writing becomes overwrought, Fuller nevertheless demonstrates throughout a keen sense of history in the making. It is almost as if she could sense that Garibaldi, who would barely escape the country alive, would return ten years later as a conquering hero and help unite Italy at last. In Letter 34, she asserts that "the voice of this age shall yet proclaim the names of some of these Patriots whose inspiring soul was JOSEPH MAZZINI—men as nobly true to their convictions as any that have ever yet redeemed poor, strained Humanity";[52] and the course of history has validated her assertion. Both Garibaldi and Mazzini have acquired and maintained, in the eyes of most Italians, the heroic stature Fuller in her dispatches early credited them with.

After Fuller left Rome for Rieti (to get her son) and then Florence (to live and finish her "History"), she wrote several more letters to the *Tribune* (which to date no biographer or critic has ever discussed), and in them her style grew like fire in the wind, becoming biblically prophetic. Her brother Arthur did not include her last three letters in his edition *At Home and Abroad*, probably because he felt the apocalyptic socialism they expressed reflected poorly upon his sister. Whereas most Americans saw the June Days of Paris as confirming the perniciousness of socialist and communist doctrines, for Fuller, who had been distracted during the June Days and had just witnessed the brutality of reactionary forces, these doctrines had become sacred truths, and she advocated them with skill. In her last *Tribune*

Garibaldi and His Men. (From *Illustrated London News*, 15 (21 July 1849), 37.)

letter, she produced a fierce visionary beauty unmatched elsewhere in her works:

> The seeds for a vast harvest of hatreds and contempts are sown over every inch of Roman ground, nor can that malignant growth be extirpated, till the wishes of Heaven shall waft a fire that will burn down all, root and branch, and prepare the earth for an entirely new culture. The next revolution, here and elsewhere, will be radical. Not only Jesuitism must go, but the Roman Catholic religion must go. The Pope cannot retain even his spiritual power. . . . Not only the Austrian, and every potentate of foreign blood, must be deposed, but every man who assumes an arbitrary lordship over fellow man, must be driven out. It will be an uncompromising revolution. . . . The New Era is no longer an embryo; it is born; it begins to walk—. . . . That advent called EMMANUEL begins to be understood, and shall no more so foully be blasphemed. Men shall now be represented as souls, not hands and feet, and governed accordingly. A congress of great, pure, loving minds, and not a congress of selfish ambitions, shall preside. Do you laugh, Editor of the *"Times*?" (Times of the Iron Age.) Do you laugh, Roman Cardinal, as you shut the prison-door on woman weeping for her son martyred in the cause of his country? Do you laugh, Austrian officer, as you drill the Hungarian and Lombard youth to tremble at your baton? Soon you, all of you, shall *"believe* and tremble."[53]

Fuller's use here of epistrophe (repetitions at the end of successive clauses), of anaphora (repetitions at the beginning of successive clauses), of metaphor, antithesis, and climax reveals a gifted prose stylist, one who is employing rhetoric as the last means of defense against a brutal adversary. The revelation she creates, moreover, although historically inaccurate, provides a dramatic conclusion to the coherent narrative she has given in her letters as a whole.

Fuller's last letter appeared, as did her earlier ones, not over her name or initials, but over an asterisk, and this device indicates perhaps the most artful dimension of the *Tribune* letters, namely, the public persona she created for herself within them, one that differed considerably from the self she presented to family and friends. Fuller, as is well known, had an affinity for the histrionic, and the European revolutionary scene inspired her to assume the role of Liberty in her dispatches, even though she found herself constrained in her private life by her pregnancy, her baby, her poverty, and her husband's social and intellectual limitations (that is, his outcast state and childlike mind). In the spring of 1848, as news of the revolutions in Paris, Vienna, Milan, Venice, and elsewhere reached her at Rome, she wrote to Emerson, "I am deeply interested in this public drama, and wish to see it *played out.* Methinks I have *my part* therein, either as actor or historian."[54] At the time she wrote this, Fuller was indulging in wishful thinking, for she was some five months pregnant and making plans to leave Rome to conceal this fact. It was her new friend, the princess Belgiojoso, who acted the part Fuller wished for herself. Hearing of the revolution in Milan, the Five Glorious Days, the princess, who was in Naples at the time, took two hundred Neapolitan volunteers by steamer to Milan to fight in the revolutionary cause. Although her followers never saw the enemy, and in fact ended up being a nuisance to the new government, the princess became a goddess of Liberty in the eyes of many Italians.[55]

Only through her writings could Fuller emulate her friend. Before the French revolution, Fuller often referred to Christ in her appeals for the liberation of the lowly and oppressed of Europe. When she lauded Fourier and Fourierism, for example, it was the Christian nature of both that she emphasized. Once the revolutions occurred, however, her persona became more fierce, resembling Liberty in her martial pose. As I noted earlier, Lowell in his "Ode to France" had described the two Liberties familiar to the public, one "a maiden mild and undefiled / Like her who bore the world's redeeming child," the other "Vengeance, axe in hand, that stood / Holding a tyrant's head up by the clotted hair."[56] Although Fuller never became openly bloodthirsty in the *Tribune,* she came close. The first glimpse of her martial spirit and willingness to shed blood can be seen in her dispatch of 27 May 1849, in which she declares, "The struggle is now fairly, thoroughly commenced between the principle of Democracy and the old powers, no longer legitimate. That struggle may last fifty years, and the

The Princess Belgiojoso. (From H. Remsen Whitehouse, *A Revolutionary Princess*. London, 1906.)

earth be watered with the blood and tears of more than one generation, but the result is sure. All Europe, including Great Britain, . . . is to be under Republican Government in the next century." After King Charles Albert's betrayal of Milan to the Austrians, she became even more violently republican as she asserted in December 1848; "Had the people slain him in their rage, he well deserved it at their hands; and all his conduct since had confirmed that sudden verdict of passion." In an even more revolutionary spirit, after Count Rossi was assassinated, Fuller applauded the murder, declaring in the *Tribune* that "certainly, the manner *was* grandiose."[57] (He had been stabbed in the back as he was entering the Roman Assembly, and in Fuller's mind he thus suffered a fate similar to that of the tyrant Caesar.)

By adopting this public persona that was fiercely committed to republicanism, Fuller became in the eyes of sympathetic readers a romantic revolutionary heroine. Some twenty years after her death, her friend Christopher Cranch paid tribute to this heroine in the following lines:

> Nor honor less, nor praise
> To her whose later days
> Were pledged to lift wronged Justice to her seat.
> And though Rome's new-lit torch
> Blew backward, but to scorch
> The hand that held it, dropping at her feet,
> Quenched in the patriots' blood, not incomplete
> Her task, though all the heroic strains she sang
> To chronicle a struggling nation's pang—. . .
> Were strewn upon the wind like withered flowers,
> And gulfed in roaring floods,—Italia's loss, and ours![58]

The "torch" Cranch refers to is of course that of Liberty, while the "heroic strains" certainly refers to Fuller's lost "History of the Roman Republic." Even though Cranch's poetry is wretched, his lines express the admiration for Fuller, or rather for her *Tribune* persona, felt by many of her contemporaries.

A few of her readers, however, regarded her not as a bearer of Liberty's torch, but as a misguided subversive. Hawthorne viewed her in this way, and even her friends the Springs, both Quakers, expressed their disapproval of her militance in a letter to her. Conservative Catholics probably formed the most hostile group of readers, and their spokesman, Bishop John Hughes of New York City, castigated the *Tribune* and sneered at Fuller. Claiming that the republicans had established "a reign of terror over the Roman people," Hughes asserted, "They wield the stiletto and sacrifice by assassination the human victims who are to propitiate the young goddess of Liberty in Italy." Turning to the evils of socialism and Margaret Fuller, Hughes added, "And this is the phalanx recognized by Mr Greeley as the Roman republic! Yet no ambassador from foreign countries has recognised such a republic, except it be the female plenipotentiary who furnishes the Tribune with diplomatic correspondence."[59]

Although Fuller's private sentiments about Rossi's assassination corresponded to her public ones ("this act affected me as one of terrible justice," she wrote her mother),[60] her private letters confirm that the woman who spoke on behalf of Italian liberty in the *Tribune* was an artful creation. Whereas the *Tribune* persona is bold, resolute, optimistic, the persona of the private letters is frightened, uncertain, and pessimistic. Whereas the *Tribune* persona is dedicated to the Italian people and the republican cause, the private Fuller calls the people "coarse," "selfish," and "ignorant,"[61] worries about her husband and child, and wonders what will become of them all. In the *Tribune*, Fuller tells of seeing the blood stains on the Vatican walls, but she does not tell about spending the night with Ossoli at his post on the Pincian Hill, expecting a terrible bombardment, convinced they both would die. In the *Tribune*, she tells of tending the wounded in the hospitals, but she does not reveal that her service undermined her courage. In a revealing letter written to her brother Richard in July 1849, Fuller confessed that if she could have influenced Mazzini, she "should have prayed him to capitulate." She adds, "I feel that no honorable terms can be made with such a foe, and that the only way is *never* to yield; but the sound of the musketry, the sense that men were perishing in a hopeless contest, had become too terrible for my nerves." Similarly, in response to Channing's praise for her, Fuller wrote him a month later, "You say, you are glad I have had this great opportunity for carrying out my principles. Would it were so! I found myself inferior in courage and fortitude to the occasion. I knew not how to bear the havoc and anguish incident to the struggle for these principles. . . . I forget the great ideas, to sympathize with the poor mothers, who had nursed their precious forms, only to see them all lopped and gashed."[62] In many ways, the private Fuller, the woman concerned with human beings as opposed to abstract ideas, is more heroic, because of her vulnerability, than the persona of the *Tribune* letters, and perhaps Fuller knew this. Because loving relatives and friends formed the audience for the private correspondence, she knew they would discount her self-criticism and admire her even more for expressing it. She could not assume, however, that the readers of the *Tribune* would be similarly prejudiced in her favor. For them a more ideal and stoic revolutionary was in order.

The relationship between Fuller's public and private selves ultimately brings one to the issue that has been at the center of Fuller criticism for years: her writing versus her conversation. Fuller, of course, was known as a minor writer and a premier conversationalist, an estimate that has enjoyed a long life, even though Fuller herself sought to overturn it. Barbara Welter, in her book *Dimity Convictions*, has credited Fuller with pointing out that "woman's preoccupation with the personal frequently leads her to trivial conversation, which degenerates into gossip, all for want of a genuine goal, a 'high object' to her life."[63] In many respects, Fuller's private letters to her mother, to Emerson, to Channing, to Ossoli can be seen as forms of conversation, or at least as her attempts to approximate the spoken word in her written correspondence. It is easy to recognize that the private letters have an immediacy, an intimacy, an earnestness that made her a valued and engaging friend; furthermore, they tell us more about her hopes and fears than any of the *Tribune* letters. However, because of their personal, conversational nature, they at times treat what can be considered trivial by a stranger (for example, the baby's cough, the servant's quarelling, the landlord's lechery). Her *Tribune* letters, on the other hand, are polished, objective, and elevated. And because they focus upon the fate of the socialist-republican cause in Europe, they are of interest to the world and not just to a small circle of family and friends. They tell of events that will affect the lives of thousands of people for years to come and thus move in the direction of the permanent as opposed to the ephemeral.

Thoreau, in the journal he kept at Walden, entered an observation that explains the important distinction between Fuller's public and private correspondence. "There is a memorable intervale," he wrote, "between the written and the spoken language—the language read and the language heard. The one is transient—a sound—a tongue—a dialect—and all men learn it of their mothers— It is loquacious, fragmentary—raw material— The other is a reserved select matured expression—a deliberate word addressed to the ear of nations & generations."[64] Fuller, I think, was aware of this distinction, and although she believed that "newspaper writing is next door to conversation, and should be conducted on the same principles,"[65] she realized how to elevate it. When we write for the newspaper, she declared, "we address not our neighbor, who forces us to remember his limitations and prejudices, but the ideal presence of human nature as we feel it ought to be and trust it will be. We address America rather than Americans."[66] In Italy, Fuller assumed such an ideal presence not only for her audience, but for herself as well, and it was this artful public achievement that established her image in the American mind as a nineteenth-century revolutionary heroine. The history she told to America as she witnessed it imposed form and meaning upon a failed revolution and upon her life as well.

5

The Scarlet Letter and Revolutions Abroad

Dearest, thou didst not come into my dreams, last night; but, on the con-
trary, I was engaged in assisting the escape of Louis XVI and Marie Antoinette from Paris, during the French revolution. And sometimes, by an
unaccountable metamorphosis, it seemed as if my mother and sister were
in the place of the King and Queen.

— HAWTHORNE, Letter to Sophia Peabody (26 March 1840)

Near the end of *The Scarlet Letter*, Hawthorne in a summary tells us about
Hester's eventual change of heart, about how she at last forsook radicalism
and recognized that the woman who would lead the reform movements of
the future and establish women's rights must be less "stained with sin," less
"bowed down with shame" than she. This woman must be "lofty, pure, and
beautiful, and wise, moreover, not through dusky grief, but the ethereal
medium of joy."[1] More than one reader has correctly surmised that this ending to the novel constitutes a veiled compliment to Hawthorne's little Dove,
Sophia, and a veiled criticism of Margaret Fuller—radical, advocate of
women's rights, and subject of gossip because of her child and questionable
marriage.[2] Hawthorne's ambivalent feelings toward Fuller indeed informed
this and other parts of the novel, and although a number of women have
been discussed as models for Hester, including Anne Hutchinson, Ebe
Hawthorne, and Elizabeth Peabody, Fuller seems to have served in this
capacity most provokingly. As Francis E. Kearns has pointed out, a number
of parallels exist between Fuller and Hester: both had the problem of facing
a Puritan society encumbered by a child of questionable legitimacy; both
were concerned with social reform and the role of woman in society; both
functioned as counselor and comforter to women; and both had children
entitled to use the armorial seals of a non-English noble family.[3] A more
important parallel, which Kearns does not mention, is that for Hawthorne
both women were linked to the figures of Liberty and Eve, that is, to the
ideas of revolution and temptation, which lie at the heart of the novel.

   Fuller was the most intelligent, articulate, and passionate woman Hawthorne ever knew. She lacked beauty, of course, and in fact, as both Emerson and Greeley admitted, her plainness, her nasal voice, her blinking
eyelids, and her haughty demeanor at first repelled; however, once an individual came to know her, her vitality, wit, and generosity of spirit exerted

a strong attraction. "The eyes," wrote Emerson, "which were so plain at first, soon swam with fun and drolleries, and the very tides of joy and superabundant life."[4] "I found myself," confessed Greeley, "drawn, almost irresistibly, into the general current. I found that her faults and weaknesses were all superficial and obvious to the most casual . . . observer. They rather dwindled than expanded upon a full knowledge; or rather, took on new and brighter aspects in the light of her radiant and lofty soul."[5]

In the summer of 1844, while the Hawthornes were still at the Old Manse, Fuller, who was friends with them both, came to visit, and it was then that Hawthorne became most intimate with her. Throughout the month of July, they went boating at dusk on the Concord, took moonlit walks through the woods, and conversed at length on a variety of subjects. (Sophia was occupied with the new baby, Una.) And surprisingly, given his reserve and shyness, it was Hawthorne who initiated many of their hours alone together.[6] After Fuller moved to New York City that fall and thence to Europe and Rome, she and Hawthorne never saw one another again; however, ten years after her death, Hawthorne in a long and famous passage in his Italian notebook ridiculed her husband and called her "a great humbug" with a "defective and evil nature."[7] This outburst seems inexplicable, given Hawthorne's previous friendliness, but it does make sense if one sees it as motivated by guilt and anger about his attraction to her. As Paula Blanchard has pointed out, "There is no possible way that anyone can accuse Margaret of being evil—if he is thinking of Margaret herself. But Hawthorne was not; he was thinking of what she represented to him."[8] During the summer of 1849, when Fuller and her fellow republicans fought their losing battle against the invading French, capturing the attention and admiration of the American public, Hawthorne certainly noticed, and when he wrote *The Scarlet Letter* several months later, he then too had in mind what Fuller represented: a female revolutionary trying to overthrow the world's most prominent political-religious leader, a freethinking temptress who had almost subverted his right-minded thoughts and feelings.

Fuller's activities in Italy enhanced the influence that revolution exerted upon Hawthorne as he composed his masterpiece. That this influence was compelling is revealed in "The Custom-House" sketch, when he forewarns the reader of the darkness in the story to follow and explains that "this uncaptivating effect is perhaps due to the period of hardly accomplished revolution and still seething turmoil, in which the story shaped itself" (43). His explicit reference is to his recent ouster from the Salem custom house, his "beheading" as he calls it, but we know that the death of his mother and anxiety about where and how he would support his family added to his sense of upheaval. Lying behind all these referents, however, are the actual revolutions, past and present, which he had been pondering and reading about for almost twenty consecutive months.

Although the European revolutions all failed, from the spring of 1848 to the fall of 1849, the American public, as we have seen, displayed its interest and sympathy by mass gatherings, parades, fireworks, proclamations, speeches, and constant newspaper coverage. As Hawthorne was defending himself from the attacks of the Salem Whigs and battling to be reinstated as surveyor, the developments in Italy received a predominant amount of American attention. On 20 June, the Boston *Daily Advertiser* reported that the French, in order to restore the power of the pope, were marching on Rome with eighty thousand men, and it quoted Mazzini's declaration "We shall fight to the last against all projects of a restoration." The following day, alongside Hawthorne's public letter to Hillard, this same newspaper reported Garibaldi's arrival upon Neapolitan territory and printed Louis Napoleon's lengthy speech explaining his government's support of the pope. During the next two months, as Hawthorne ceased careening through the public prints in his decapitated state, accounts by Fuller and others of the defeat of the Roman revolutionaries made their way to the United States, where they were greeted by most with sadness or outrage. Although Fuller's former devotee Sophia (in her dutifully childlike manner) expressed approval of the republican successes in Europe as they were occurring in 1848,[9] her husband shared neither her optimism nor the enthusiasm of their literary friends, particularly Fuller. The book that he wrote in the wake of the revolutions indicates that they reaffirmed his skepticism about revolution and reform and inspired a strong reactionary spirit, which underlies the work.

Revolution had been a fearful thing in Hawthorne's mind for some time, even though he found the ends it wrought at times admirable.[10] Violent reform and the behavior of mobs particularly disturbed him,[11] as the final scene of "My Kinsman, Major Molineux" makes clear. This story may celebrate the beginnings of a new democratic era, as some have suggested, but it cannot be denied that Molineux is presented as a noble victim of a hellish mob. "On they went," Hawthorne wrote, "like fiends that throng in mockery round some dead potentate, mighty no more, but majestic still in his agony."[12] Similarly, in "The Custom-House" sketch, Hawthorne presents himself as the victim of another "bloodthirsty" mob, the Whigs, who, acting out of a "fierce and bitter spirit of malice and revenge," have struck off his head with the political guillotine and ignominiously kicked it about. This presentation, humorous in tone but serious in intent, gives *The Scarlet Letter* its alternate title, "THE POSTHUMOUS PAPERS OF A DECAPITATED SURVEYOR," and foreshadows the use and treatment of revolutionary imagery in the novel proper.

This imagery, of course, is drawn from the French Revolution of 1789, which was at the forefront of Hawthorne's mind for several reasons. First of all, the spectacular excesses of that revolution provided the language and metaphors used by conservatives to describe events in 1848–49. Bishop Hughes, who claimed the Italian revolutionaries had established "a reign of terror" in Rome, was but one of many who saw a replay of history in events abroad. Evert Duyckinck, keeping his brother George (who was in Paris) abreast of American attitudes in the spring of 1848, reported that "people look at this Revolution [the February French revolution] with recollections of the Era of Robespierre and suspect every revival of the old political phraseology of that period. An article attributed to Alison is going the rounds from Blackwoods in which he sets Satan grinning over the shoulders of Lamartine."[13] The *Blackwood's* article referred to had echoed the theme of "Earth's Holocaust" as it declared, "Experience will prove whether, by discarding all former institutions, we have cast off at the same time the slough of corruption which has descended to all from our first parents. We shall see whether the effects of the fall can be shaken off by changing the institutions of society; whether the devil cannot find as many agents among the Socialists as the Jacobins; whether he cannot mount on the shoulders of Lamartine and Arago as well as he did on those of Robespierre and Marat."[14]

The Bloody June Days of 1848 seemed to confirm such skepticism, and even George Duyckinck, an ardent supporter of the French people, was reminded of the Reign of Terror and the role women played in it as he reflected upon recent events. "Human nature," he wrote his brother, "seems to be the same it was sixty years ago. Heads were stuck on pikes or swords and women danced about them as they did then and who can doubt but that if the insurgents had succeeded the guillotine would have been as busily at work today as it was then."[15] Although use of the guillotine had been discontinued (General Cavaignac used the firing squad during the June Days), the shadow of that instrument loomed over all, and after Louis Napoleon reinstituted it in March of 1849, it became a potent political symbol. For publishing an article entitled "The Restoration of the Guillotine," which called Louis Napoleon an assassin, the owner of the Paris newspaper *Le Peuple* was fined and sentenced to five years' imprisonment; similarly the proprietor of *La Révolution Démocratique et Sociale* was fined and sentenced to three years' imprisonment for issuing a radical article entitled "The Political Scaffold."[16] In America, the guillotine and the scaffold carried not quite so much import, except, of course, in the mind of one "decapitated" surveyor.

Predictably, the American press drew careless comparisons between the European revolutions and the American political scene. When Zachary Taylor began his series of political appointments in the spring and summer of 1849, they were reported in the Democratic papers as terrorist acts, as symbolic beheadings of Democratic party members. Some seven times in May and June, for example, the Boston *Post* printed, in conjunction with the announcement of a political appointment and removal, a small drawing presumably of General Taylor standing beside a guillotine, puffing a cigar,

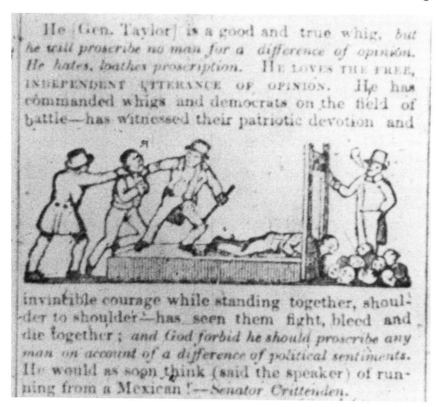

He [Gen. Taylor] is a good and true whig, but he will proscribe no man for a difference of opinion. He hates, loathes proscription. HE LOVES THE FREE, INDEPENDENT UTTERANCE OF OPINION. He has commanded whigs and democrats on the field of battle—has witnessed their patriotic devotion and invincible courage while standing together, shoulder to shoulder—has seen them fight, bleed and die together; and God forbid he should proscribe any man on account of a difference of political sentiments. He would as soon think (said the speaker) of running from a Mexican!—*Senator Crittenden.*

Woodcut in the Boston *Post*, 14 June 1849.

surrounded by heads (presumably of Democrats) at his feet. One of these drawings appeared on 11 June, and on the following day, a letter to the editor appeared objecting to Hawthorne's removal from the Salem custom house. "This is one of the most heartless acts of this heartless administration," the anonymous writer declared. "The head of the poet and the scholar is stricken off to gratify and reward some greedy partizan! . . . There stands, at the guillotine, besides the headless trunk of a pure minded, faithful and well deserving officer, sacrificed to the worst of party proscription, Gen. Zachary Taylor, now President." As Arlin Turner has pointed out, this letter was probably a source of Hawthorne's beheading metaphor;[17] however, behind the reference were two years of revolutionary events in Europe, two years of revolutionary rhetoric and imagery.

Hawthorne's Readings

Such rhetoric and imagery appeared not only in the newspapers, of course, but also in contemporary books, some of which dealt with revolution in a serious historical manner. Although *The Scarlet Letter* has often been praised for its fidelity to New England history, the central setting of the novel, the scaffold, is, I believe, a historical inaccuracy intentionally used by Hawthorne to develop the theme of revolution. The Puritans occasionally sentenced a malefactor to stand upon a shoulder-high block or upon the ladder of the gallows (at times with a halter about the neck),[18] but in none of the New England histories Hawthorne used as sources (namely, Felt, Snow, Mather, Hutchinson, and Winthrop) are these structures called scaffolds. In fact, I have been unable to find the word *scaffold* in them. The common instruments of punishment in the Massachusetts Bay Colony were, as Hawthorne shows in "Endicott and the Red Cross," the whipping post, the stocks, and the pillory. (The gallows, located in Boston at the end of town,[19] was used for hangings and serious public humiliation.) Although Hawthorne in his romance identifies the scaffold as part of the pillory, his narrator and his characters refer to it by the former term alone some twenty-six times, calling it the scaffold of the pillory only four times and the pillory only once.[20]

As early as 1557 and then later with increasing frequency during the first French Revolution, the word *scaffold* served as a synecdoche for a public beheading—by the executioner's axe or the guillotine. And, because of its role in the regicides of overthrown kings, the word acquired powerful political associations, which it still retains.[21] When King Charles I was beheaded with an axe following the successful rebellion led by Cromwell, Andrew Marvell in his "An Horatian Ode" used the word in the following tribute to his king:

> thence the royal actor born
> The tragic scaffold might adorn:
> While round the armed bands
> Did clap their bloody hands.
> *He* nothing common did or mean
> Upon that memorable scene:
> But bowed his comely head
> Down, as upon a bed.[22]

One hundred and forty-four years later, when Louis XVI became a liability to the new French republic, he too mounted what was termed the scaffold and there became one of the victims of the new device being advocated by Dr. Guillotin. The association of a scaffold with revolution and beheading, particularly the beheading of Charles I and Louis XVI, explains, I think,

The Execution of Charles I. (Courtesy of National Portrait Gallery, London.)

why Hawthorne uses it as his central and dominant setting. It links the narrator of "The Custom-House" sketch with the two main characters in the romance proper, and it raises their common predicaments above the plane of the personal into the helix of history.

Hawthorne's desire to connect his narrative with historic revolutions abroad is further shown by the time frame he uses. The opening scenes of the novel take place in May 1642 and the closing ones in May 1649.[23] These dates coincide almost exactly with those of the English Civil War fought between King Charles I and his Puritan Parliament. Hawthorne was familiar with histories of this subject and had recently (June 1848) checked out of the Salem Atheneum François Guizot's *History of the English Revolution of 1640, Commonly Called the Great Rebellion*.[24] Guizot, professor of modern history at the Sorbonne when he wrote this work, became Louis Philippe's prime minister, and the policies he proclaimed while occupying this position provoked the French revolution of 1848. During the spring of 1848 Guizot's name became familiar to Americans, and probably the man's recent notoriety led Hawthorne to a reading of his work in the summer of 1848.

Examination of the simultaneity between fictional events in *The Scarlet Letter* and historical events in America and England verifies that the 1642–49 time frame for events in the romance was carefully chosen to enhance the treatment of revolutionary themes. When the beadle, crying "Make way, good people, make way, in the King's name," leads Hester Prynne from the prison, less than a month has passed since Charles's Puritan Parliament had sent him what amounted to a declaration of war. Five months later, in October 1642, the first battle between Roundheads and Cavaliers was fought at Edgehill, and word of the open hostilities reached America in December.[25] Then and in the years that followed, the Bay Colony fasted and prayed for victory by Parliament, but these became times of political anxiety and stress in America as well as England. According to one of Hawthorne's sources, Felt's *Annals of Salem,* in November 1646 the General Court (presided over by Messrs. Bartholomew and Hathorne) ordered "a fast on Dec. 24th, for the hazardous state of England . . . and difficulties of Church and State among themselves, both of which, say they, some strive to undermine."[26] By the final scenes of the novel, when Arthur is deciding to die as a martyr, Charles I has just been beheaded (on 30 January 1649); thus, when Chillingworth sarcastically thanks Arthur for his prayers, calling them "golden recompense" and "the current gold coin of the New Jerusalem, with the King's own mint-mark on them" (224), Hawthorne adds to Chillingworth's irony his own. Furthermore, given the novel's time frame, the tableau of Arthur bowing "his head forward on the cushions of the pulpit, at the close of his Election Sermon" (250), while Hester stands waiting beside the scaffold, radiates with ominous import, particularly when one recalls that Arthur is not a graduate of Cambridge, as most of the Puritan ministers of New England were,[27] but rather of Oxford, the center of Laudian and Royalist sympathies and the place of refuge for King Charles during the revolution.

By thus setting events in an age when "men of the sword had overthrown nobles and kings" (164), Hawthorne provides a potent historical backdrop for the revolutionary and counterrevolutionary battles fought, with shifting allegiances, among the four main characters and the Puritan leadership. Furthermore, his battle imagery, such as Governor Bellingham's armor and Pearl's simulated slaying of the Puritan children, draws upon and reflects the actual warfare abroad and thus illuminates the struggles being fought on social, moral, and metaphysical grounds in Boston.

Bearing upon the novel perhaps even more than its connections with the English "Rebellion" and its attendant regicide are its connections with the first French Revolution and the execution of Louis XVI. In the romance itself, Hawthorne first alludes to one tie when he describes the scaffold in the opening scenes: "it constituted," he writes, "a portion of a penal machine, which . . . was held, in the old time, to be as effectual an agent in the promotion of good citizenship, as ever was the guillotine among the terrorists of France" (55). This allusion may be derived from the imagery appearing, as discussed above, in the contemporary press; but it is also shaped, in a more profound way, by an overlooked source of *The Scarlet Letter*, Alphonse de Lamartine's *History of the Girondists*.[28]

As I have already discussed, Lamartine became a heroic figure to the American public following the February 1848 revolution in France. And after he fell from power due to his unwillingness to align himself with the radical republicans or the right-wing Bonapartists, he was treated as a noble martyr in the American press. The New York *Evening Post* on 23 June 1849, the day after Bryant's editorial on Hawthorne's behalf appeared there, devoted two and a half front-page columns to a glowing summary of Lamartine's literary and political career. "[His] brief administration," the article concluded, "born of the barricades of February, expired amidst the roar of the cannon of June," proved "that Lamartine is too righteous a man to be a politician." "He was no demagogue; he appreciated the crisis, approved the revolution, but dreaded its excess. To save his country from terrorism and communism, he cheerfully laid down his popularity, as he would have laid down his life."

Before this political martyrdom, which would have engaged Hawthorne's sympathy, Lamartine's career had been advanced by his writings; his *History of the Girondists*, as we have seen, became almost as popular as its author during the revolutions of 1848–49. Unlike Guizot, Lamartine was not a scholarly historian, and his account of the first French Revolution is an imaginative and dramatic construct that gains much of its power from its sympathetic treatment of Louis XVI and its suspenseful narrative structure, which includes a tableau at the scaffold as its climactic scene. Throughout the first volume and a half of his history, Lamartine, while detailing the political infighting of the National Assembly and their struggle with the king for power, generates sympathy for Louis. He and his family are seldom free from danger, and the two high points of volume 1 are their unsuccessful attempt to flee the country and their confrontation with a mob of thousands at the Château of the Tuileries. In volume 2, Lamartine shows the situation of the royal family becoming more desperate and the king acquiring strength and character as his fate unfolds. In terms a decapitated surveyor could appreciate, Lamartine observes that "all the faults of preceding administrations, all the vices of kings, all the shame of courts, all the griefs of the people, were accumulated on his head and marked his innocent brow for the expiation of many ages" (1:27). "He was the scape-goat of olden time, that bore the sins of all" (2:323).

Lamartine shifts from third-person omniscient narration to third-person limited after the National Assembly renders its verdict of guilty and its judgment of death. Thus, unlike Carlyle's clipped, brusque, and almost sarcastic account of the regicide, Lamartine's treatment generates sympathy; the reader is beside the king for some thirty intensely moving pages—as he parts with his family, as he rides in the carriage with his priest, who hears his confession, and as he sees and enters the Place de la Révolution to be beheaded. "There," Lamartine writes, "a ray of the winter's sun . . . showed the place filled by 100,000 heads, the regiments of the garrison of Paris drawn up round all sides of the scaffold, the executioners, awaiting the victim, and the instrument of death prominent above the mob, with its beams and posts painted blood-color. It was the guillotine!" (2:370). Stationed around the scaffold are "unscrupulous and pitiless ruffians," who desire "the punishment should be consummated and applauded" (2:371). In contrast, the king steps forward composed and aloof. Humiliated by being bound, he regains his composure, mounts the scaffold, faces the multitude, casts a farewell glance on his priest, and meets his death. "The plank sunk, the blade glided, the head fell" (2:373), Lamartine writes, as this chilling and memorable scene comes to an end. Appearing in almost the exact center of the narrative, on the 867th page of 1,578, the scene dominates the history; all that goes before anticipates it; all that follows refers back to it. The rest of volume 2 and all of 3 detail the excesses of the Revolution: the assassination of Marat, the Reign of Terror, the wave upon wave of bloodletting, and so on, all of which become horrifyingly repetitive.

Lamartine's stirring treatment of revolutionary events and political martyrdom and especially his unprecedented use of the scaffold as both a dramatic setting and a unifying structural device lead one to speculate that Hawthorne may have read this work before he wrote *The Scarlet Letter;* however, speculation is unnecessary. He did. The records of the Salem Atheneum reveal that on 13 September 1849, he checked out the first two volumes of Lamartine's *History.*[29] Moreover, Sophia Hawthorne's letters to her sister and mother, combined with Hawthorne's notebook entries, reveal, as no biographer has yet pointed out, that it was about ten days later, most likely between September 21 and September 25, that Hawthorne began work in earnest on *The Scarlet Letter.*[30] On 27 September, he checked out the third volume of Lamartine's *History,* and on that date Sophia, in an often-quoted letter, informed her mother, "Mr. Hawthorne is writing morning & afternoon. . . . He writes immensely—I am almost frightened about it—But he is well now & looks very shining."[31] (He returned the first two volumes of the *History* on 6 November and the third volume 12 November.) This correlation in dates plus Hawthorne's allusions to the terrorists of France suggest that what has become one of the most celebrated settings in American literature, the scaffold of *The Scarlet Letter,* was taken from the

MORT DE LOUIS CAPET 16.ᵉ DU NOM LE 21 JANVIER 1793

The Death of Louis XVI. (Courtesy of Bibliothèque Nationale, Paris.)

Place de la Révolution of eighteenth-century Paris, as described by Lamartine, and transported to the Marketplace of seventeenth-century Boston, where it became the focal point of Hawthorne's narrative. Along with it came, most likely, a reinforced skepticism about violent reform.

A Reading of *The Scarlet Letter*

Recognition that revolutionary struggle stirred at the front of Hawthorne's consciousness as he wrote *The Scarlet Letter* not only accounts for many structural and thematic details in the novel, but also explains some of the apparent inconsistencies in his treatment of his characters, especially Hester and Arthur. The issue of the degree and nature of Hawthorne's sympathies in the novel has been debated for years, at times heatedly, and I have no hope of resolving the debate here; however, I think the revolutionary context of events provides a key for sorting out Hawthorne's sympathies, or more accurately those of his narrator (whose biases closely resemble Hawthorne's). The narrator, as a member of a toppled established order, an ancien régime so to speak, possesses instincts that are conservative and antirevolutionary, consistently so, but the individuals he regards undergo

Hester Standing on the Scaffold. (Illustration by Eric Pape in *The Scarlet Letter*. Large-Paper Edition. Boston, 1900.)

considerable change, thus evoking inconsistent attitudes on his part. Specifically, when Hester and Arthur battle to maintain or regain their rightful place in the social or spiritual order, the narrator sympathizes with them; when they become revolutionary instead and attempt to overthrow an established order, he becomes unsympathetic.[32] The scaffold serves to clarify the political and spiritual issues raised by events in the novel, and the decapitated surveyor of the custom house, not surprisingly, identifies with whoever becomes a martyr upon it.

Hawthorne's use of the scaffold as a structural device has long been recognized; in 1944 Leland Schubert pointed out that the novel "is built around the scaffold. At the beginning, in the middle and at the end of the story the scaffold is the dominating point."[33] The way in which the scaffold serves as a touchstone for the narrator's sympathies, however, has not been fully explored, particularly with reference to the matter of revolution.

As every reader notices, at the beginning of the story, Hester is accorded much sympathy. Her beauty, her courage, her pride, all receive emphasis; and the scaffold, meant to degrade her, elevates her, figuratively as well as literally. The narrator presents her as an image of Divine Maternity, and more important, as a member of the old order of nobility suffering at the hands of a vulgar mob. Her recollection of her paternal home, "poverty-stricken," but "retaining a half-obliterated shield of arms over the portal" (53, 58) establishes her link to aristocracy. Furthermore, although she has been sentenced by the Puritan magistrates, her worst enemies are the coarse, beefy, pitiless "gossips" who surround the scaffold and argue that she should be hanged or at least branded on the forehead. The magistrates, whom Hawthorne characterizes as "good men, just, and sage," have shown clemency in their sentence, and that clemency is unpopular with the chorus of matrons who apparently speak for the people.

As the dream that appears in the epigraph to this chapter shows, the vision of a mother with child assuming the role of a king facing a revolutionary mob had been part of Hawthorne's imagination for some time, as had his personal involvement in such a scene. It is not surprising then that through the first twelve chapters, half of the book, Hester is dealt with sympathetically as she represents, like Charles I, Louis XVI, and Surveyor Hawthorne, a fallen aristocratic order struggling in defense of her rights against an antagonistic populace. The poor, the well-to-do, adults, children, laymen, clergy, all torment her in various ways; but she, the narrator tells us, "was patient,—a martyr, indeed" (85). It is Pearl, of course, who anticipates what Hester will become—a revolutionary—and reveals the combative streak her mother possesses. "The warfare of Hester's spirit," Hawthorne writes, "was perpetuated in Pearl" (91), and this is shown by Pearl's throwing stones at the Puritan children ("the most intolerant brood that ever lived" [94]), her smiting and uprooting the weeds that represent these children, and her splashing the governor himself with water. "She never created a friend, but seemed always to be sowing broadcast the dragon's teeth, whence sprung a harvest of armed enemies, against whom she rushed to battle" (95). ("The struggle is now fairly, thoroughly commenced between the principle of democracy and the old powers," Fuller had written in the spring of 1849. "Every struggle made by the old tyrannies . . . only sow more dragon's teeth; the crop shoots up daily more and more plenteous.")[34]

Hester's own martial spirit comes to the fore in the confrontation with Bellingham, but here she fights only to maintain the status quo and thus keeps the narrator's sympathies. She visits the governor not to attack him in any way, but to defend her right to raise Pearl. Undaunted by Bellingham's shining armor, which "was not meant for mere idle show," Hester triumphs, because she has the natural order upon her side and because Arthur comes to her aid. Drawing Pearl forcibly into her arms, she confronts "the old Puritan magistrate with almost a fierce expression"; and Arthur, prompted into action by Hester's veiled threats, responds like a valiant Cavalier. His voice, as he speaks on her behalf, is "sweet, tremulous, but powerful, insomuch that the hall reechoed, and the hollow armour rang with it" (114).

In the central chapters of the novel, when the narrator turns his attention toward Arthur and evidences antipathy toward him, it is not only because of the minister's obvious hypocrisy, but also because of the intellectual change that he has undergone at Chillingworth's hands. Subtly, Arthur becomes radicalized and anticipates Hester's ventures into the realm of speculative and revolutionary thought. "There was a fascination for the minister," Hawthorne writes, "in the company of the man of science, in whom he recognized an intellectual cultivation of no moderate depth or scope; together with a range and freedom of ideas, that he would have vainly looked for among the members of his own profession" (123). And if Arthur is the victim of the leech's herbs and poisons, he is a victim of more deadly intellectual brews as well. The central scene of the novel, Arthur's "vigil" on the scaffold, is inspired, apparently, by the "liberal views" he has begun to entertain. "On one of those ugly nights," we are told, "the minister started from his chair. A new thought had struck him" (146). This thought is to stand on the scaffold in the middle of the night, but by so doing he joins the ranks of Lucifer's rebellious legions. As he indulges in "the mockery of penitence" upon the scaffold, his guilt becomes "heaven-defying" and reprehensible, in the narrator's eyes. Rather than seeking to reestablish his moral force, which has been "abased into more than childish weakness," Arthur, in his imagination, mocks the Reverend Wilson, the people of Boston, and God himself. Furthermore, as Henry Nash Smith as pointed out, the "lurid playfulness" Arthur indulges in upon the scaffold, calls into question "the very idea of a solid, orderly universe existing independently of consciousness."[35] The questioning remains Arthur's, however, not the narrator's, and the scene itself, with the scaffold as its setting, serves to reveal the cowardice and licentiousness Arthur has been reduced to. The blazing A in the sky, which Arthur sees "addressed to himself alone," marks Governor Winthrop's death, according to the townspeople, and thus further emphasizes (by its reference to Winthrop's famous leadership and integrity) the nadir Arthur has reached by his indulgence in defiant thought and behavior.

The transformation Hester undergoes in the middle of the novel (which only appears to be from sinner to saint) is a stronger version of that which Arthur has undergone at her husband's hands; she too becomes, like the French revolutionaries of 1789 and the Italian revolutionaries of 1849, a radical thinker engaged in a revolutionary struggle against an established political-religious order. And as such, she loses the narrator's sympathies (while gaining those of most readers). The transformation begins with her regaining, over the course of seven years, the goodwill of the public, which "was inclined to show its former victim a more benign countenance than she cared to be favored with, or, perchance, than she deserved" (162). The rulers of the community, who "were longer in acknowledging the influence of Hester's good qualities than the people," become, as time passes, not her antagonists but rather the objects of her antagonism. We first see her impulse to challenge their authority when Chillingworth tells her that the mag-

istrates have discussed allowing her to remove the scarlet letter from her
bosom. "It lies not in the pleasure of the magistrates to take off this badge"
(p. 169), she tells him. Similarly, when she meets Arthur in the forest several days later, she subversively asks, "What hast thou to do with all these
iron men and their opinions? They have kept thy better part in bondage too
long already!" (197).

The new direction Hester's combativeness has taken is political in nature and flows from her isolation and indulgence in speculation. In a passage
often quoted but seldom viewed as consistent with the rest of the novel
because of its unsympathetic tone, the narrator explains that Hester Prynne
"had wandered, without rule or guidance, in a moral wilderness. . . .
Shame, Despair, Solitude! These had been her teachers,—stern and wild
ones,—and they had made her strong, but taught her much amiss" (199–
200). Hester's ventures into new areas of thought link her, significantly, with
the overthrow of governments and the overthrow of "ancient prejudice,
wherewith was linked much of ancient principle." "She assumed," the narrator points out, "a freedom of speculation, then common enough on the
other side of the Atlantic, but which our forefathers, had they known of it,
would have held to be a deadlier crime than that stigmatized by the scarlet
letter" (164). Referring for the second time to the antinomian Anne Hutchinson, whom Hawthorne in another work had treated with little sympathy,
the narrator speculates that if Pearl had not become the object of her mother's devotion, Hester "might, and not improbably would, have suffered
death from the stern tribunals of the period, for attempting to undermine
the foundations of the Puritan establishment" (165).[36]

Although Hester does not lead a political-religious revolt against the
Puritan leadership, these speculations are quite relevant to the action which
follows, for Hawthorne shows her radicalism finding an outlet in her renewed relationship with Arthur, which assumes revolutionary form. When
they hold their colloquy in the forest, during which she reenacts her role as
Eve the subversive temptress, we learn that "the whole seven years of outlaw and ignominy had been little other than a preparation for this very hour"
(200). What Hester accomplishes during this hour (other than raising the
reader's hopes) is once again to overthrow Arthur's system and undermine
his loyalty to the Puritan community and the Puritan God. She establishes
a temporary provisional government within him, so to speak, which fails to
sustain itself. Although Hester obviously loves Arthur and seeks only their
happiness together, her plan, which most readers heartily endorse, challenges, in the narrator's eyes, the social order of the community and the
spiritual order of the universe, and thus earns his explicit disapproval.

When Hester tells Arthur that the magistrates have kept his better part
in bondage, the narrator makes it clear it is Arthur's better part that has
actually kept his worse and lawless self imprisoned, For some time the

prison has proved sound, but "the breach which guilt has once made into the human soul is never, in this mortal state, repaired," the narrator declares. "It may be watched and guarded; so that the enemy shall not force his way again into the citadel. . . . But there is still the ruined wall" (200–01). Thus, as Hawthorne draws upon the popular revolutionary imagery of 1848–49 to present Hester as a goddess of Liberty leading a military assault, she prevails; however, her victory, like that of the first Bastille day, sets loose forces of anarchy and wickedness. Arthur experiences "a glow of strange enjoyment" after he agrees to flee with her, but to clarify the moral dimensions of this freedom, Hawthorne adds, "It was the exhilarating effect— upon a prisoner just escaped from the dungeon of his own heart—of breathing the wild, free atmosphere of an unredeemed, unchristianized, lawless region" (201).

Unlike the earlier struggle that Hester and Arthur had fought together to maintain the status quo—the traditional relationship between mother and child—this struggle accomplishes something far more pernicious: "a revolution in the sphere of thought and feeling." And because it does, it receives unsympathetic treatment. "In truth," Hawthorne writes, "nothing short of a total change of dynasty and moral code, in that interior kingdom, was adequate to account for the impulses now communicated to the unfortunate and startled minister. At every step he was incited to do some strange, wild, wicked thing or other, with a sense that it would be at once involuntary and intentional" (217).

Donald A. Ringe among others has suggested that this abrupt change in Arthur's system is beneficent, a fortunate fall, in other words, that gives him insight and powers of expression;[37] however, the narrative emphasizes that it is unfortunate and unholy. Arthur's impulses to blaspheme, curse, and lead innocence astray are a stronger version of those seen during his vigil, and they confirm the narrator's assertion that the minister has acquired "sympathy and fellowship with wicked mortals and the world of perverted spirits" (222). The success of Arthur's sermon, which is so eloquent, so filled with compassion and wisdom, depends ultimately not upon his new revolutionary impulses, but upon older counterrevolutionary sources that are spiritually conservative. He draws upon the "energy—or say, rather, the inspiration which had held him up, until he should have delivered the sacred message that brought its own strength along with it from heaven" (251).

The final change of heart and spirit that Arthur undergoes and that leads him to his death on the scaffold is foreshadowed by events in the marketplace prior to his sermon. There the exhibition of broadswords upon the scaffold suggests that while the minister's better self has been overthrown, a struggle is still being waged. The procession in which Arthur appears dramatizes the alternative to the lawless freedom Hester has offered. Here, as Michael Davitt Bell has observed, we have "the greatest tribute in all of Hawthorne's writing to the nobility of the founders."[38] The people, we are told, had bestowed their reverence "on the white hair and venerable brow of age; on long-tried integrity; on solid wisdom and sad-colored experience; on endowments of that grave and weighty order, which gives the idea of permanence, and comes under the general definition of respectability" (237–38). These are the qualities that distinguish Bradstreet, Endicott, Dudley, Bellingham, and their compeers. And, although we are not told who the new governor is (it was Endicott), we know that his election represents orderly change, in contrast to the rebellion and regicide that has recently occurred in England. "Today," Hester tells Pearl, "a new man is beginning to rule over them," and, in harmony with this event, Arthur acts to reestablish his place within the order of the community and within the order of the kingdom of God.

During the sermon Arthur seems to regain some of his spiritual stature and is described as an angel, who, "in his passage to the skies, had shaken his bright wings over the people for an instant,—at once a shadow and a splendor." Because Arthur is still a hypocrite, considerable irony exists within this description; however, when the minister walks to and mounts the scaffold, the narrator's irony seems to disappear. Arthur attempts, before he dies, to regain God's favor, and as he nears the scaffold, where Hester and Chillingworth will both oppose his effort to confess, we are told that "it was hardly a man with life in him, that tottered on his path so nervelessly, yet tottered, and did not fall!" The exclamation mark indicates the double sense of "fall" Hawthorne wishes to suggest, and at the end Arthur seems to escape from the provisional control over him that both Chillingworth and Hester have had.

"Is not this better than what we dreamed of in the forest?" he asks Hester, and although she replies, "I know not! I know not!" the revolutionary context of the novel, the bias toward restoration and order, indicate we are supposed to agree that it is.[39] Arthur's final scene upon the scaffold mirrors Hester's first scene there, even though he proceeds from the church whereas she had proceeded from the prison. But, unlike Hester, Arthur through humility and faith seems to achieve peace, whereas she, through "the combative energy of her character," had achieved only "a kind of lurid triumph" (78). In the final scaffold scene, Pearl acts as an ethical agent once again and emphasizes Hawthorne's themes about peace and battle, order and revolt. At the moment of his death, Arthur kisses Pearl, and the tears she then sheds are "the pledge that she would grow up amid human joy and sorrow, nor for ever do battle with the world, but be a woman in it." In what seems to be a reward for her docility, she marries into European nobility (thereby accomplishing a restoration of the ties with aristocracy her maternal relatives once enjoyed); similarly, Hester at last learns to forsake her radicalism, to be neither Eve nor Liberty.

Certainly Hawthorne's knowledge of and interest in the New England past were considerable, as Michael J. Colacurcio has so painstakingly shown; however, as Thomas Woodson has pointed out, his interest in his contemporary world was far greater than the critical emphases of recent decades would indicate.[40] In writing *The Scarlet Letter* he drew upon the issues and rhetoric he was encountering in the present, especially those relating to himself as a public figure. Moreover, he responded strongly and creatively to accounts of foreign revolutions and revolutionaries that he found in the newspapers, the magazines, and books new to the libraries. Although to most of his countrymen the overthrow of kings and the triumph of republicanism were exhilarating events, to a man of Hawthorne's temperament, the violence, the bloodshed, the extended chaos that accompanied the revolutions of 1848–49 were deeply disturbing. Associated in his own mind with his personal plight, they, along with his reading in Guizot and Lamartine, shaped *The Scarlet Letter* in Burkean ways the reader of today finds difficult to accept. We value too highly Thomas Paine and the rights of woman.

6

Moby-Dick and the Matter of France

It was the summer of 1797. . . . the bluejackets, to be numbered by thousands, ran up with huzzas the British colors with the union and cross wiped out; by the cancellation transmuting the flag of founded law and freedom defined, into the enemy's red meteor of unbridled and unbounded revolt.

—MELVILLE, *Billy Budd*

While Hawthorne was writing *The Scarlet Letter* in his third-floor study in Salem with Lamartine's history of the French Revolution near at hand, Melville was sailing to England and Europe aboard the packetship *Southhampton*, where on the night of 27 October 1849 he listened to a conversation about Lamartine that he would recall and draw upon some twenty years later when he wrote *Clarel* (1870). After the Bloody June Days of 1848, Lamartine became more and more an outcast in his own country, and his disillusionment with the public and their rejection of him led Melville to view him as an alter ego of sorts. In *Clarel* the spirit of Lamartine reaches out like a dead hand from the past to reveal the futility of revolutionary action on behalf of the common man.

Melville and Lamartine

Lamartine died in his Paris house on the evening of 28 February 1869 (a year before Melville began *Clarel*), and at his death, he was suffering from poverty, illness, and despair.[1] The irony of his plight would have interested Melville, of course, for it resembled that of his own. As we have seen, during the spring of 1848, Lamartine's popularity soared; his writings and leadership inspired his nation and the world. As the *Democratic Review* put it, Lamartine arose "like the spirit of the storm-king riding triumphantly on the tempestuous deep, bidding the winds and waves of popular tumult to hush, and cease their murmuring;—then by his impassioned eloquence . . . did he breast and stay that onward march of death."[2] The horrible workers' revolt, however, pulled him down and drowned his hopes for a distinguished political career. To many Americans, though, Lamartine seemed, especially after the Red Revolution, a heroic man of peace, a living part of heaven (like the sky-hawk of *Moby-Dick*), too divine for the world of men. In his ode "To Lamartine, 1848," James Russell Lowell paid him high tribute:

> The highest duty to mere man vouchsafed
>   Was laid on thee,—out of wild chaos,
> When the roused popular ocean foamed and chafed
>   And vulture War from his Imaus
>   Snuffed blood, to summon homely Peace,
> And show that only order is release.
>   .   .   .   .
> If France reject thee, 't is not thine,
>   But her own, exile that she utters;
> Ideal France, the deathless, the divine,
>   Will be where thy white pennon flutters,
>   As Once the nobler Athens went
> With Aristides into banishment.
>   .   .   .   .
> France is too poor to pay alone
>   The service of that ample spirit;
> Paltry seem low dictatorship and throne,
>   Weighed with thy self-renouncing merit;
>   They had to thee been rust and loss;
> Thy aim was higher,—thou hast climbed a Cross![3]

As Lowell's imagery suggests, Lamartine seemed a Christlike martyr in American eyes. Among the French, however, he fared poorly. Blamed by leftists and rightists alike for failing to maintain law and order in Paris, this formerly elegant and eloquent spokesman for moderate republicanism was reduced to accepting charity from friends to survive. As the years passed, his appearance became shabbier; he remained silent in conversation; and he evidenced increasing bitterness. He felt betrayed by the various classes of his countrymen and especially by the bankers of Paris, whom he identified as "a band of cutthroats for poor men of letters." Toward the end of his life, Lamartine felt he had nothing to live for and kept repeating to his friend Jean-Marie Dargaud, "I want to die."[4]

Although we cannot be certain Melville knew about the circumstances of Lamartine's final years, it seems likely he did, for American newspapers took notice of his plight. Walt Whitman, in his role as editor of the Brooklyn *Daily Times*, for example, reported in 1858 that "the embarrassments of authors . . . are just now the topic of conversation. In France we have Lamartine in the attitude of a pauper invoking pecuniary aid by private or national subscriptions to discharge his liabilities."[5] In *Clarel*, Melville has Rolfe sympathize with "poor Lamartine" whose "fine social dream" was destroyed by "Fate,"[6] and he presents a character named Mortmain whose life seems modeled on Lamartine's. Mortmain is of noble birth and Swedish

nationality (it was a Frenchman and a Swede whose conversation about Lamartine Melville listened to on board the *Southhampton* in 1849). At the
present he is a bitter monomaniac who has come to the Holy Land to cleanse
his soul and to die; however, in his past he was an idealist and a leader in
the French revolution of 1848:

> Europe was in a decade dim:
> Upon the future's trembling rim
> The comet hovered. His a league
> Of frank debate and close intrigue:
> Plot, proselyte, appeal, denounce—
> Conspirator, pamphleteer, at once,
> And prophet. Wear and tear and jar
> He met with coffee and cigar:
> These kept awake the man and mood
> And dream. That uncreated Good
> He sought, whose absence is the cause
> Of creeds and Atheists, mobs and laws.
>
> [155]

"That uncreated Good" Mortmain sought, however, he never found; he was
betrayed by his friends and witnessed the failure of his dream.

As Rolfe tells about Mortmain's bitter experiences, he draws from them
two conclusions, which appear in *Mardi* and *Moby-Dick* and are consistent
features of Melville's conservative response to the French revolution. The
first has to do with mankind. "The world is portioned out, believe:" Rolfe
says, "The good have but a patch at best, / The wise their corner; for the
rest—/ Malice divides with ignorance"(156–57). The second rings like the
fine hammered steel of woe, Ecclesiastes:

> The flood weaves out—the ebb
> Weaves back; the incessant shuttle shifts
> And flies, and wears and tears the web.
> Turn, turn thee to the proof that sifts:
>
> What if the kings in Forty-Eight
> Fled like the gods? even as the gods
> Shall do, return they made; and sate
> And fortified their strong abodes.
>
> [157]

Mortmain offers a far different and more blasphemous explanation of
those events in 1848–49 which eventually led to his loss of faith. Like Ahab,
he has come to believe that a demonic deity is responsible for the bloodshed, hate, and terror he has seen:

> Recall the red year Forty-Eight:
> He storms in Paris; thence divides;

> The menace scarce outspeeds the fate:
> He's over the Rhine—He's at Berlin—
> At Munich—Dresden—fires Vien;
> He's over the Alps—the whirlwind rides
> In Rome; London's alert—the Czar:
> The portent and the fact of war,
> And terror that into hate subsides.
> There, through His instruments made known,
> Including Atheist and his tribes,
> Behold the prophet's marching One,
> He at whose coming Midian shook—
> The God, the striding God of Habakkuk.

[281]

Although Melville presents Mortmain as a man driven insane by his bitter loss of faith in man and God, he nevertheless treats him compassionately. As Walter E. Bezanson has pointed out, Melville's own psychic involvement with Mortmain is considerable. And, while Mortmain appears on the surface to have much in common with Ahab, even to the extent of having his hat stolen by a great bird shortly before his death, he differs from him by being at heart not a revolutionary, but a peacemaker: "*Peace and good will* was his acclaim— / If not in words, yet in the aim: / *Peace, peace on earth:* that note he thrilled" (155).[7] Mortmain's disillusionment with human nature—"Man's vicious: snaffle him with kings" (154)—has not, the narrator explains, made him evil even though it has embittered him: "Innocent be the heart and true— / Howe'er it feed on bitter bread—"(265), says a hovering spirit about him. Mortmain's distrust of men, like Lamartine's and Melville's, is a result of life's experiences, not of a naturally misanthropic cast of mind, and as a tribute to the lofty spirit of this character, Melville has him die peacefully and nobly, with an eagle feather on his lips, "wafted from the skies" (399).

Melville and France

Although there is no evidence Melville saw Lamartine while he was in Paris in 1849, he did see, as Hawthorne had yet to do, the renamed Place de la Révolution (Concorde), which he termed "magnificent," and he noted in his journal the "great numbers of troops marching all about," which made Paris seem "like a garrisoned town."[8] In December 1848 Louis Napoleon had been swept into the presidency by nostalgia for the power and glory associated with the name of his uncle, and in the spring of 1849, the *Illustrated London News* reported that the lower classes, who had suffered "the delusion of utopian socialism and tyrannical red-republicanism," were turning to Louis Napoleon "as a plank to which to cling in the ocean of misery into which the storm of revolution has plunged them."[9] In the summer of 1849 Napoleon, who had been both socialist and republican before rising to power, destroyed the Roman Republic, and by the time Melville arrived in Paris, he had instituted a reactionary government that, like those in Austria and Germany, relied upon military force to maintain its control. "Whoever should visit the principal countries of Europe at the present moment," Bryant had written from Paris several months before Melville arrived, "might take them for conquered provinces, held in subjection by their victorious masters, at the point of the sword. . . . Those who maintain that France is not fit for liberty, need not afflict themselves with the idea that there is at present more liberty in France than her people know how to enjoy."[10] (Louis Napoleon would stage his outrageous coup d'état in December 1851 and make himself Emperor Napoleon III in December 1852.)

Although Melville's cryptic journal entries made during this trip to Europe reveal little about his response to the revolutions, we know from *Mardi* and the works which followed that he was keenly interested in their fate and attached much significance to the course they ran. Like Hawthorne, he maintained a lifelong skepticism toward violent popular uprisings, and the developments in Europe, especially the French revolution, affected him deeply and endowed his work, in a lasting manner, with the dark hues of the conservative side of his thought. Although intimations of his conservatism can be found in his first two books, it was not until *Mardi* and the events of 1848 that he gave open and explicit political expression to his doubts about the masses and radical reform. After the Bloody June Days, distrust and dislike for the "people" permeated his writings, where they are consistently linked with the idea of revolution, particularly revolution in France.

The French revolution of 1848 had a deep and lasting effect upon Melville because of the importance of France to his imagination. In fact, prior to 1848 and *Mardi* he had already acquired a full reservoir of strong feelings toward that nation. Perhaps no stronger evidence exists of Melville's near obsession with the matter of France than its presence throughout his writings, from the very beginning of the first book that he wrote to the very end of his last. In the opening pages of *Typee* (1846), as the narrator describes his entrance into the lovely bay of Nukuheva, we learn that it is not the beauty of this Eden he recalls; "that beauty was lost to me then," he declares, "and I saw nothing but the tri-colored flag of France trailing over the stern of six vessels, whose black hulls and bristling broadsides proclaimed their warlike character."[11] Similarly, in the posthumously published *Billy Budd* (1924), when Captain Vere's fate is reported in the epilogue, we learn that his death was caused by a musket ball fired from the main cabin of a French man-of-war, once named the *St. Louis* but renamed the *Athée* (the *Atheist*)[12] in the revolutionary fleet.

Although in *Typee* and *Billy Budd*, the French men-of-war are instru-

French Men-of-War in Typee Bay. (Courtesy of Old Dartmouth Historical Society Whaling Museum, New Bedford, Massachusetts.)

ments of warfare and death, in *Redburn* (1849) this same image is associated with magnetic beauty and refinement. Here the ship is a small glass one, and Melville, speaking as the older Redburn, declares, "That which perhaps more than any thing else, converted by vague dreamings and longings into a definite purpose of seeking my fortune on the sea, was an old-fashioned glass ship, about eighteen inches long, and of French manufacture, which my father, some thirty years before, had brought home from Hamburgh as a present to a great-uncle of mine." [13] While this ship inspires wonder and delight, it has the same darker associations as the full-size ships in *Typee* and *Billy Budd* because of the two tiers of black guns along its two decks. "Often I used to try to peep in at the portholes to see what else was inside," the narrator says, "but . . . it looked so very dark indoors, that I could discover little or nothing." Although this dark mysteriousness attracted him, he confesses, "Often I used to feel a sort of insane desire to be the death of the glass ship, case, and all, in order to come at the plunder" (8).

Readers familiar with Melville's life and psyche will perceive the subconscious connection between this recurring image of the French man-of-war (with its associations of beauty, refinement, and grandeur on the one hand and of loss, death, and violent upheaval on the other) and Melville's memory of his father, an importer of French goods who died when Herman was only twelve, after having become bankrupt and then insane. (Vere, in the scene referred to above, plays the same paternal role as does Redburn's father in the reminiscence.) Another French warship, that in *Moby-Dick*, seems consonant with the three above, related as it is to loss and martial display. Near the end of *Moby-Dick*, as Ahab goes on deck, leaving the insane and pathetic Pip behind, he says to the boy, "God for ever bless thee; and if it come to that,—God for ever save thee, let what will befall." After Ahab leaves, Pip steps forward and says, "Here he this instant stood; I stand in his air,—but I'm alone"; sitting down, he then declares, "Here, our old sailors say, in their black seventy-fours great admirals sometimes sit at table, and lord it over rows of captains and lieutenants. Ha! what's this? epaulets! epaulets! the epaulets all come crowding! Pass round the decanters; glad to see ye; fill up, monsieurs!"[14]

The web of Melville's feelings toward France, when spun into rational thought, eventually formed two strands of political ideas, both of them conservative. On the one hand, he developed a strong admiration for the aristocratic tradition of France, with its emphasis on elegance, refinement, and grandeur; on the other, he learned to identify France with revolution, violence, and warfare and to interpret these as confirmation of man's primeval savageness. The dual associations France held for Melville found their most explicit expression in *Israel Potter* in a description of John Paul Jones. Finely dressed, complete with ruffled shirt and Parisian rings, Jones rolls up his sleeve to admire the cabalistic tattoo on his arm, acquired from some pagan artist. He then resumes pacing his Paris hotel room awaiting orders that will quench his thirst for battle.

> So at midnight, [Melville writes,] the heart of the metropolis of modern civilization was secretly trod by this jaunty barbarian in broad-cloth; a sort of prophetical ghost, glimmering in anticipation upon the advent of those tragic scenes of the French Revolution which levelled the exquisite refinement of Paris with the blood-thirsty ferocity of Borneo; showing that broaches and finger-rings, not less than nose-rings and tattooing, are tokens of the primeval savageness which ever slumbers in human kind, civilised or uncivilised.[15]

The two concepts of "exquisite refinement" and "primeval savageness," each supporting one side of Melville's political thought, acquired their French affiliation during his childhood.

Melville's father, Allan (whose death struck his son Herman as a cruel betrayal), took great pride in his French manners, friends, and possessions. While a youth, Allan visited France a number of times, and during the years 1801–02, he spent some twenty months with his brother Thomas in Paris, where he mastered the language.[16] In 1803 he saw at first hand Napoleon's regime nearing its height, and in 1818, the year before Herman was born, returned once again, this time to invest in the silks, shawls, hose, gloves, and "fancy articles" for the ill-fated business he would establish in New York

City. While in Paris, he visited a number of distinguished American friends and dined with notable Frenchmen, including the Count de Legun and the Marquis de Lafayette.[17] After his return home, Allan cultivated his French connections through the Société Française de Bienfésance, employed a French servant to whom he spoke French, and maintained a library in which French works were prominent.[18]

In *Redburn* (1849), Melville as narrator describes the French ambience of his youth created by his father. He recalls that in his home there were oil paintings and rare engravings his father had bought in Paris; large green French portfolios of colored prints, containing "pictures of Versailles, its masquerades, its drawing-rooms, its fountains, and courts, and gardens" (6); and a library case with long rows of old books printed in Paris and elsewhere. "There was a copy of D'Alembert in French," the narrator recalls, "and I wondered what a great man I would be, if by foreign travel I should ever be able to read straight along without stopping, out of that book, which now was a riddle to every one in the house but my father, whom I so much liked to hear talk French, as he sometimes did to a servant we had" (7). In context, the above passage serves a thematic purpose, of course, related as it is to Redburn's quest to become a man like his father, but it also documents how France (and Versailles) acquired positive associations for the youthful Melville.

Allan Melvill's brother Thomas has similarly strong ties to France, and Herman, after his father died, felt drawn to this uncle and later identified with him. Thomas had spent some sixteen years in France as a banker and financial entrepreneur during the period 1795–1811.[19] As Melville related in the affectionate memoir he wrote of him, Thomas "was familiar with the stirring events which took place in that country from the closing years of the Republic through the Consulate, and down to a period towards the collapse of the first Empire."[20] In Paris, Thomas circulated among the best society and entertained Frenchmen of note, including Lafayette. Melville does not mention in his memoir that Thomas may also have participated in some of the shady financial dealings of the Directory and apparently acted, for a price, as a secret agent for the corrupt Viscount de Barras in peace negotiations with the British prime minister, William Pitt.[21]

In 1802 Thomas married the young daughter of M. Lamé Fleury, a Frenchman from Nantes who during the Revolution was sent to Paris for trial by the infamous *Tribunal révolutionnaire* but who was liberated from prison after the guillotining of Robespierre in July 1794.[22] Fleury's daughter Françoise Raymonde Eulogie Marie des Douleurs Lamé Fleury was a beautiful woman who would die in 1814 at the age of thirty-three. "A miniature I have seen of her," her nephew Herman later wrote, "presents a countenance of much beauty of that kind which forcibly arrests the attention."[23]

Although Melville never knew Françoise, he did know her daughter Anne
Marie Priscilla, and this cousin, who was born in France, would serve as
one model for the beautiful, mysterious, and destructive Isabel of *Pierre*,
whose mother emigrated from France during the Reign of Terror.[24]

Melville first came under the influence of his uncle Thomas after the
man and his family had relocated in Pittsfield. Melville's first recollection of
him dated from 1831, and three years later, when he himself was fifteen,
Priscilla twenty-four, and his uncle fifty-eight, he spent "the greater portion
of a year an inmate of [his] uncle's family," later writing about the impression
his uncle made upon him then. "His manners were mild and kindly," Melville recalled, "with a faded brocade of old French breeding which—contrasted with the surroundings at the time—impressed me as not a little
interesting, nor wholly without a touch of pathos. He . . . would at times
pause . . . and taking out his smooth-worn box of satin-wood, gracefully help
himself to a pinch of snuff, . . . making some little remark, quite naturally;
and yet with a look, which—as I now recall it—presents him in the shadowy
aspect of a courtier of Louis XVI, reduced as a refugee, to humble employment, in a region far from the gilded Versailles."[25]

Although a Democrat while in Pittsfield, the impoverished Thomas became a Whig after moving to Galena, Illinois, to escape his creditors. There
on the frontier he found his conservative sensibilities strongly provoked by
the immigrants who controlled local politics. "The good people call us the
aristocracy of the place,"[26] Cousin Julia reported in a letter to Melville's
sister Augusta, but the term was an aspersion, and Uncle Thomas faced
increasing frustration at the failure of the Irish and German "rabble" to recognize his superiority. Writing to his friend Lemuel Shaw in Boston, he
explained why he knew in advance he would lose for the second time in an
election for justice of the peace. "There was but little chance of success," he
wrote, "against the overwhelming force, of the whole *Catholic alien vote*,
which can be brought to bear *in a mass* in all our elections on the side of the
selfstyled democratic party—or more properly Jacobins, thro' the influence
of the *Priests*."[27]

Thomas Melvill's aristocratic manners and conservative social outlook,
at least as the latter developed on the frontier, seem to have influenced
those of his nephew Herman, who visited him in Galena in 1840 before
returning to the East and putting out to sea on a whaler. As Merton M.
Sealts, Jr., has pointed out, Melville came to see his uncle as "another 'iso
lato,' another Ishmael driven into the wilderness, sometimes presenting
himself in the altered guise of a John Marr, a Jimmy Rose, or a Jack Gentian.
All of these roles, moreover, are semi-autobiographical characterizations as
well."[28] Verification of Sealts's view is given by one of Melville's best friends
during his Berkshire years, J. E. A. Smith, who reported that in Pittsfield

Melville "seemed to have modelled himself as a 'gentleman of the old school' upon the pattern of his Boston-born and Parisian bred uncle, the democratic aristocrat Major Thomas Melville."[29]

Before moving to the Berkshires in the summer of 1850, Melville visited there regularly, staying at his uncle's farm mansion called Broadhall, to which Thomas's family returned following his death in Galena in 1845. Along with a French ambience, which apparently suggested the Parisian furnishings and wallpaper of "Jimmy Rose,"[30] Broadhall possessed features that reminded Melville, interestingly, of a man-of-war. In his memoir of his uncle (who acquired a modicum of military experience and the title of major during the War of 1812), he describes the "ample hall and staircase, carved wood-work and solid oaken timbers," adding that "these timbers as viewed from the cellar, remind one of the massive gun deck beams of a line-of-battle-ship." According to his cousin Priscilla, Melville had strong attachments to the place, which would, of course, be one model for the Saddle Meadows of *Pierre*. In April of 1848, as he was about to plunge forward with the final stage of *Mardi*, Melville paid a visit to Broadhall, and at this time Priscilla wrote to his sisters and new wife expressing her pleasure that Herman had "manifested so much constancy toward the object of his *first love, our Berkshire* farm—as to *tear* himself from the idol of his heart to indulge again in the unfetter'd freedom of Batchelor days."[31]

Priscilla, as her letters show, was a playful, dramatic, intelligent young woman, and Melville was apparently fascinated by her.[32] As the recently discovered Melville family papers reveal, she, like her father, was a kindred spirit who shared Melville's frustrations at having fallen from high social station. Like him, and like Ishmael, she learned that being ordered about "touches one's sense of honor, particularly if you come of an old established family in the land" (*Moby-Dick*, 14), and in a letter of 1849 written from the Ontario Female Seminary, where she had gone to teach, Priscilla tells her cousins in New York City that it is not the "galling sense of the yoke" that disturbs her most. "It is *more this* circumstance of *birth* & *taste* that causes my spirit to chafe under the burden, than aught else—& doubtless I should consider my lot a most enviable one—did not my *native* aristocracy rebel."[33]

Priscilla's birth and taste, of course, were French (although her only valid claims to aristocracy were based upon her father's Scottish lineage).[34] And just as Thomas Melvill was associated in Melville's imagination with the elegance and manners of the ancien régime, his daughter probably was as well, thus reenforcing the conservative political tone of Melville's familial sympathies. That Melville was disposed to adopt this tone even before the stimulus of the revolutions of 1848–49 and the bitter failures of *Moby-Dick* and *Pierre* can be seen in a letter of 1846 he wrote to his brother Gansevoort telling about preparations for the war against Mexico. "Nothing is talked of but the 'Halls of the Montezumas,'" he wrote. "And to hear folks prate about

those purely figurative apartments one would suppose that they were another Versailles where our democratic rabble meant to 'make a night of it'
ere long."[35] Melville's disdain for the "democratic rabble" and his corre-
sponding admiration for the refinement represented by Versailles formed
only one pole of his political thought, of course, but with the French revolution of 1848, which stimulated the strong feelings associated with his father, his uncle Thomas, and his cousin Priscilla, this pole immediately became charged and potent.

As discussed in chapter 1, the events in the spring of 1848 surrounding
the French revolution engaged Melville so thoroughly and strongly that he
felt compelled to treat them in the book he was struggling to complete, even
though this meant borrowing money to live on and plunging into debt. "The
book is done now, . . . and the copy for the press is in progress," Melville's
wife reported to her stepmother on 5 May 1848;[36] however, because of his
additions, some twenty-five chapters in length, Melville did not finish with
the last proof sheets until almost nine months later, on 27 January 1849.[37]

Mardi (1849) marked, as is well known, the turning point in Melville's
career, for while writing it he discovered not only the depth and breadth
of his own mind, but the limitless possibilities for the courageous writer of
fiction. Having begun the book as another travel adventure on the order of
Typee (1846) and *Omoo* (1847), he transformed it into a fanciful romantic
quest that served as the foundation for weighty disquisitions on religion,
politics, philosophy, science, and art, offered by the Mardian travelers. Although the first two-thirds of the book are farfetched and tedious, the later
chapters, which treat contemporary world events, compose a solid political
allegory both original and interesting.

Melville's account of the French revolution of 1848 teems with conservative and unsympathetic reflections,[38] although at first he allows for the possibility that it may bring good results over the course of time. He has the
travelers leave Dominora (England), where they witnessed the riotous mob
(of Chartists), and, after they lament the plight of Verdanna (Ireland), they
near Franko (France), where they see a violent eruption accompanied by
the din of warfare, showers of embers, and whirling blasts. "The fiery storm
from Franko, kindled new flames in the distant valleys of Porpheero [Eu-
rope]," Melville writes, "while driven over from Verdanna came frantic
shouts, and direful jubilees. Upon Dominora a baleful glare was resting"
(499). In an exchange that anticipates the imagery of *Billy Budd*, in which
"live cinders [are] blown across the Channel from France in flames" (54),
one of Melville's characters, Media, the king, cries, "See! how the flames
blow over upon Dominora!" while the philosopher Babbalanja is made to
answer, "Yet the fires they kindle there are soon extinguished. No, no; Dominora ne'er can burn with Franko's fires; only those of her own kindling may
consume her" (499). The travelers debate the value of the burning red vol-

canoes in Franko and question whether a desert of ashes or fruitful vineyards
will eventually result. No conclusion is reached in the chapter, however,
leading one to suspect that Melville wrote it sometime before the Bloody
June Days, when the rioting of the mobs of Parisian workers and their
slaughter at the hands of General Cavaignac's troops presaged the end of
republican government in France.

Eight chapters later, after the travelers arrive in Vivenza (the United
States), Melville again addresses the subject of the revolutions, but here, as
we have seen, they receive harsher treatment, indicating he has decided
where his sympathies lie. The mysterious scroll, which appears in chapter
161, reveals an author who has become impatient with the chauvinistic bombast of sympathy meeting speakers, even though their rhetoric differed only
in degree from the chauvinistic bombast of Young America to which he paid
pen service. Within the scroll, Melville challenges the democratic beliefs
and assumptions of the American people, even though he shared these beliefs and assumptions when he regarded his fellow man idealistically, that is,
as "a grand and glowing creature" (*Moby-Dick*, 104). The scroll's interpretation of the past contains nothing antidemocratic. However, when it comments upon recent revolutionary events, it offers a pessimistic view of human nature and radical reform that would remain thereafter a salient feature
of Melville's thought and art. Although in the works which followed, he
would maintain and express, quite fervently, his "unconditional democracy
in all things" (*Letters*, 127) he would also reveal, albeit symbolically and
dramatically, his "dislike to all mankind—in the mass" (*Letters*, 127), which
was the other, less popular side of his thought. His use of the scroll, with its
unknown authorship, shows his uneasiness about publicly acknowledging
his lack of confidence in the American civil religion; however, by calling the
scroll "a Voice from the Gods" (523), he takes it beyond the static points of
view represented by his five travelers and shows his regard for its contents.

Moby-Dick, Napoleon, and Workers of the World

Once one recognizes the strong conservative reflections elicited from Melville by the French revolution of 1848, it becomes possible to trace both the
short- and long-term effect it had upon his thought and his art. Although he
responded to America's renewed spirit of chauvinism (caused by events
abroad) with passages freighted with messianic nationalism,[39] he also expressed new hostility toward the mass of mankind and admiration for superior individuals who stood above the mass. This elitism can be discerned in
White-Jacket (1850),[40] and it is prevalent in *Redburn* (1849) as well. The
novel he wrote between the spring of 1850 and the summer of 1851, however, is of far more importance than these "two *jobs*" (*Letters*, 91), as he
called them: *Moby-Dick* (1851), his masterpiece, viewed in the new light of

the French revolution of 1848 and in the rekindled light of the first French Revolution, reveals its political features with new clarity.

Although *Moby-Dick* has often been read as a political allegory, it has invariably been linked to political figures and events in America.[41] In their major studies of the politics of Melville's fiction, James Duban and Paul Michael Rogin, for example, use and extend earlier interpretations that identify Ahab and Ishmael with American political figures and issues. Duban agrees with earlier critics that Ahab is modeled on spokesmen for expansionism and slavery such as Lewis Cass and John Calhoun, and he identifies Ishmael as "an unwitting post facto accomplice to his captain's worst nationalistic transgressions." Rogin, whose interpretation of the novel is Marxist, sees Ahab not only as a representative of American expansionism and slavery, but also of American industrial capitalism. For him, the crew of the *Pequod* is a "multiracial proletariat" enslaved by Ahab, who reunites all fragments of Jacksonian Democracy—"Free-Soilers, secessionists, Young America expansionists, and conservative proslavery Unionists"—into "a new, communal body, which also contained within it the industrial core of patriarchal New England Whiggery—Webster and Shaw—and then led that ship of state to its doom."[42]

Studies such as these offer useful observations, for Melville indeed paid close attention to the American political scene; nevertheless, they use a closeup lens where a wide-angle is needed. Melville's political interests, like those of the magazines and newspapers of his day, were international as well as national (and historical as well as current). Thus, to focus upon American political developments in an attempt to capture the political meanings of the novel can result in an incomplete reading. To his credit, Rogin, in his chapter "*Moby-Dick* and the American 1848," offers a number of suggestive observations (to which this study is indebted) on political developments in Europe in 1848 that preceded Melville's writing of the novel in 1850 ("the American 1848"); he views these developments, though, as but illustrative parallels, not as formative influences in their own right, which they were.

Before turning to the international dimensions of *Moby-Dick*, I wish to acknowledge how much greater the work is than any examination of its parts can show. Lewis Mumford once identified *Moby-Dick* as "a symphony," and Henry A. Murray, in a classic essay, echoed him by calling it "Beethoven's *Eroica* in words," citing the "masterly orchestration of harmonic and melodic language, of resonating images and thoughts in varied meters. . . . the spacious sea-setting of the story; the cast of characters and their prodigious common target; the sorrow, the fury, and the terror, . . . and finally the fated closure, the crown and tragic consummation of the immense yet firmly welded whole."[43] Melville's inspiration for his symphony came, of course, from almost countless sources. Dante, Milton, Shakespeare, Goethe, Carlyle, Hawthorne, Byron, the Bible have all been identified as major influences upon him, while the characters convincingly identified as Ahab's prototypes include Prometheus, Satan, Lear, Macbeth, Hamlet, Faust, Teufelsdröckh, Ethan Brand, Manfred, Cain, Adam, Job, King Ahab, and even Christ. But though the richness of the novel and the extent of its sources have long been recognized, the influence of revolution in France upon the novel as a whole and of the figure of Napoleon upon the characterization of Ahab has yet to be demonstrated. Such a demonstration will show that Murray's comparison of the novel with the *Eroica* is far more apt than even he realized, given the circumstances of that symphony's composition and the fate of its dedication.[44]

In *Heroes and Hero-Worship*, Carlyle explains how a new king naturally emerges from revolutions, because of their natural movement from chaos toward order. "There is not a *man* in them, raging in the thickest of the madness," he writes, "but is impelled withal, at all moments, towards Order. . . . While man is man, some Cromwell or Napoleon is the necessary finish of a Sansculottism."[45] Although the revolution Ahab rages at the center of during the voyage of the *Pequod* is primarily metaphysical rather than political, and although his cause, like Lucifer's, appears anarchical and destructive, he is at heart a man impelled toward order. This can easily be seen in his military bearing and in his touching insistence that life should be governed like a boxing match, by rules of fair play. Ahab's quarrel, in its most heroic form, is not with the clarity, harmony, and integrity of creation, but rather with "all that most maddens and torments; all that stirs up the lees of things; all truth with malice in it; all that cracks the sinews and cakes the brain; all the subtle demonisms of life and thought" (160). And these, of course, are what Moby Dick personifies for him, and why this imperial, godlike creature is the object of his hatred.

While Ahab's military bearing and affinity for order link him to the king who emerged from the last phase of the first French Revolution, these are only two of many subterranean linkages. In profound ways, Napoleon served as a prototype for Ahab, and Napoleon's political development served as a paradigm for Ahab's own. Melville, like Beethoven and others, viewed Napoleon as the heroic representative of the French Revolution who ultimately betrayed the democratic ideals that revolution embodied, and this, in part, is the role assigned to Ahab in *Moby-Dick*.[46] Moreover, because Melville, like many of his contemporaries, saw history repeating itself in France during and after the revolution of 1848, especially with another Napoleon rising to the head of state, he also incorporated a damning commentary on current French political radicalism into the novel.

Allusions to the first French Revolution appear throughout *Moby-Dick*, at times to bind apparently unrelated material to the main narrative. "The Town-Ho's Story," for example, is a polished set piece which seems only loosely connected to Ahab's quest; however, in it Melville introduces and develops the theme of revolution integral to the book as a whole. As Ishmael tells this story of injustice and violence, images of upheaval in Paris provide key elements of the setting. Steelkilt's origins, of course, are thoroughly American; he is an Erie Canaller, a "man of violence," "abundantly and picturesquely wicked" (215). In his rebellion against Radney and his Captain, however, Steelkilt acquires the attributes of a French revolutionary. After he staves in Radney's jaw, he and his men become "sea-Parisians," slewing large casks in front of them and entrenching "themselves behind the barricade." Steelkilt also exhibits the theatrical behavior found in revolutionary iconography as he leaps "on the barricade, and striding up and down there, defied the worst the pistols could do" (216). Betrayed by his own comrades and flogged by his cowardly adversary, Steelkilt nevertheless has his revenge, with help from Moby Dick, and he and his men, after "seizing a large double war-canoe of the savages" reach Tahiti, where they embark, appropriately, on two ships "about to sail for France" (223). Melville thus allows his readers to speculate that Steelkilt's violent, rebellious character fulfills its destiny abroad, perhaps in the "red year Forty-Eight."

Although "The Town-Ho's Story" seems curiously out of place in the novel, by treating a violent rebel whose adversary seems intent upon demeaning him, it encapsulates Ahab's situation, a situation likewise tied to revolution in France through a series of linked allusions and images. To begin with, Ishmael, in a famous phrase, calls the crew of the *Pequod* "an Anacharsis Clootz deputation from all the isles of the sea, and all the ends of the earth" (108). Because Baron Cloots led his ragtag group of Parisians before the French National Assembly in June 1790 to symbolize the support of the human species for the French Revolution, the allusion places the voyage of the *Pequod* within the context of historic revolutionary action. Ahab strengthens the association between his quest and the course of the French Revolution when he uses the red banner of revolt as the flag of his ship; and when Ishmael notices that the *Pequod* has a complexion "darkened like a French grenadier's, who has alike fought in Egypt and Siberia" (67), the Napoleonic nature of the voyage and Ahab's resemblance to that future king are strongly suggested. Ahab himself reenforces the identification when he imagines upon his head the Iron Crown of Lombardy, which Napoleon placed upon his own head when he declared himself king of Italy in 1805. And consonant with Ahab's role as a military commander, the three mates, Starbuck, Stubb, and Flask, are introduced as "captains of companies" due to "that grand order of battle in which Captain Ahab would probably marshal his force to descend on the whales" (106).[47]

Whaling is linked with the great battles of Napoleon through indirect allusions as well as such direct ones. Commenting on Garneray's engravings of whaling scenes, Ishmael declares, "Go and gaze upon all the paintings of Europe, and where will you find such a gallery of living and breathing com-

"Pêche de la Baleine" (detail) by Ambroise Louis Garneray. Engraved by Martens and Published by Goupil & Vibert, Paris. (Courtesy of Nantuckett Historical Association.)

"Battle of Marengo, 1800" (detail) by L. F. Lejeune. (Courtesy of Musées Nationaux, Paris.)

motion on canvas, as in that triumphal hall at Versailles; where the beholder
fights his way, pell-mell, through the consecutive great battles of France;
where every sword seems a flash of the Northern Lights, and the successive
armed kings and Emperors dash by, like a charge of crowned centaurs? Not
wholly unworthy of a place in that gallery, are these sea battle-pieces of
Garneray" (230).

Melville had visited Versailles in the fall of 1849 and there found hundreds of paintings of Napoleon dominating the gallery, as he knew they
would. Dr. Augustus Kinsley Gardner, "perhaps the most stimulating of all
of [Melville's] acquaintances" in the Duyckinck circle,[48] had written about
Napoleon and the gallery in his book *Old Wine in New Bottles: or, Spare
Hours of a Student in Paris* (1848), which he gave to Melville in the spring
of 1848 before the latter went to France.[49] "Here are vivid pictures of the
principal battles where he triumphed," Gardner declared. "Wagram, Aus-
terlitz, Marengo, and Moscow, are exhibited with a power and faithfulness,
which, while they chill the blood at the sight of so much suffering and carnage, exalt the consummate general who achieved them, and stands out the
most conspicuous object in the groups. The effect of these paintings is wonderful." Telling how the paintings affect an observer, Gardner related, "I
defy the greatest advocate of peace that lives, to look upon these paintings
calmly; to view with cool composure the brown coat, the cocked hat, the
white horse, the calm features of the man of destiny, who subdued all—
even himself and his own feelings,—for ambition—for glory—for France.
Had I lived in those tempestuous times, my heart tells me, how easily I
could have shouldered the musket, and drawn the trigger, under the aus-
pices of that glorious commander."[50]

Melville, even before he went to Paris (where he stayed in lodgings
recommended by Dr. Gardner)[51] and visited Versailles, had heard much
about Napoleon and had probably developed strong feelings toward him.
His father, Allan, we know, had followed the emperor's career with great
interest. In 1818, Allan informed his wife in a letter from Paris that his
arrival on the French coast had reminded him of what he had seen there
some fifteen years before. "Here were those veteran Legions," he wrote,
"who had spread dismay throughout Europe, assembled for the invasion of
England in 1803 most of whom I had seen reviewed in Paris by the projector
of this mighty enterprise, who is now in hopeless exile, while on the same
spot where his soldiers were encamped, I saw in 1818 [the present] British
Troops who were quartered in the vicinity."[52] From his uncle Thomas, another eyewitness to Napoleon's career, Melville sought and received impressions of the emperor's glory. In the memoir of his uncle, he recalled
how Thomas "often at my request described some of those martial displays
and spectacles of state which he had witnessed in Paris in the time of the
first Napoleon. But I was too young and ignorant then, to derive the full

benefit from his pictorial recollections."[53] Thomas admired the emperor so ardently that he even named his second son Napoleon, and members of the Melville family apparently shared Thomas's enthusiasm for the man. Among the recently discovered Melville family papers, there is a letter from Melville's beloved younger brother Tom who, as he was about to go to sea in 1846 at the age of sixteen, wrote home (in care of his sister Helen), "Before I come back I will proberably visit the France of Napoleon, that beacon of Modern history and you may tell Miss Lizzy Shaw that I will fetch her a peace of one of the willows (that droope their heads over the spot honnoured by being chouse as the rasting place of one of the greatest men that ever lived) to put in her collection of ods and ends."[54] (One of the two curios Melville himself purchased while in Paris three years later was a medallion of Napoleon and Josephine, which may have been, like Tom's prospective willow leaf, for Lizzy, who had become Herman's wife. He also acquired, perhaps on the same trip, a striking engraved bust of Napoleon.)

Napoleon—admired by the Melvilles, brought to mind by the revolution of 1848 and the rise of his nephew, viewed in all his glory in the paintings of Versailles—surely strode naturally to the front of Melville's imagination as he created the "mighty pageant creature"(71) of *Moby-Dick*. Nevertheless, for many of the details of Ahab's character, especially those that distinguish him from traditional tragic heroes and make him a modern (that is, nineteenth-century) protagonist, Melville I think drew upon a particular account of Napoleon, that of Emerson in *Representative Men*, a book Melville probably read in the Hawthornes' small sitting room during a September morning in 1850.[55]

Emerson, fascinated in spite of himself by Napoleon, describes him as a representative of the "class of industry and skill," someone able to "carry with him the power and affections of vast numbers," because "the people whom he sways are little Napoleons."[56] Unlike the effete kings he defeated, Napoleon was, according to Emerson, "a worker in brass, in iron, in wood. . . . He knew the properties of gold and iron, of wheels and ships, of troops and diplomatists, and required that each should do after its kind" (228–29). He "would not hear of materialism" (250), however, and fondly indulged in abstract speculation, especially concerning religion and justice. Although Emerson attributes to Napoleon a deadly "absorbing egotism" (257) and admits he had no scruples, he nevertheless defends him from the charge of cruelty, claiming he must not "be set down as cruel, but only as one who knew no impediment to his will; not bloodthirsty, not cruel,—but woe to what thing or person stood in his way! . . . He saw only the object: the obstacle must give way" (234).

Once one considers Ahab in the light of Emerson's Napoleon, the similarities become striking. And in fact, if one listens closely, echoes of Emerson's observations on Napoleon can be heard throughout the novel, in Ish-

Engraved Bust of Napoleon Owned by Herman Melville. (Courtesy of Osborne Collection of Melville Materials at Southwestern University, Georgetown, Texas.)

mael's comment on "Ahab's iron soul" (438), in Ahab's boast that "naught's an obstacle, naught's an angle to the iron way!"(147), in Starbuck's lament that "flat obedience to thy flat commands, this is all thou breathest. Aye, and say'st . . . all of us are Ahabs."[57] The unique link between Ahab and Emerson's Napoleon, however (one not found between Ahab and his other prototypes), is a technical knowledge of the workaday world. As Ahab pores over his charts and calculates, from his knowledge of tides and currents, where to find Moby Dick, as he stands at the forge welding the shank of his own harpoon, as he smites the iron rod and uses it to magnetize the compass needle, he becomes, indeed, a representative of "the class of industry and skill," and thus, like Napoleon, and unlike figures such as King Lear, Manfred, and Job (or Daniel Webster, John Calhoun, and Lewis Cass, if you will), a laboring participant in the modern democratic, and pragmatic, age.

Ultimately though, Ahab is a much more complex and heroic figure than Emerson's representative man of the world. Most of this is due to the many sources, unrelated to Napoleon, that enriched Melville's characterization of his shaggy old whale hunter. Some of it though resulted from another book Melville turned to in the summer of 1850, Carlyle's *Heroes and Hero-Worship*,[58] which contained a treatment of Napoleon and the French Revolution that supplemented Emerson's chapter and showed Melville an intriguing way of perceiving and presenting political revolt as ontological heroics.[59]

In a key passage, Carlyle rebuts the notion that "the French Revolution was a general act of insanity" (200–01), defining it and all revolution as part of "the struggle of men intent on the real essence of things, against men intent on the semblances and forms of things" (204). "We will hail the [next] French Revolution," Carlyle writes in 1840, "as shipwrecked mariners might the sternest rock, in a world otherwise all of baseless sea and waves. A true Apocalypse, though a terrible one, to this false withered artificial time; testifying once more that Nature is *preter*natural; if not divine, then diabolic; that Semblance is not Reality; that it has to become Reality, or the world will take fire under it, —burn *it* into what it is, namely Nothing!" (201–02). When Ahab tells Starbuck, "All visible objects, man, are but as pasteboard masks. . . . If man will strike, strike through the mask!" (144), he is formulating the purpose of his quest in Carlyle's transcendental terms. Similarly, when Ishmael offers his meditation on the whiteness of the whale and ends with the question "Wonder ye then at the fiery hunt?"(170), he has explained Ahab's motives in the same terms that Carlyle's passage explains the French Revolution, that is, as a response to the maddening notion that what we see around us "are but subtile deceits, not actually inherent in substances, but only laid on from without."[60]

"The Hero as King" is the chapter in which Carlyle's passage appears, and the hero and king he discusses in the context of the French Revolution is Napoleon. Like Emerson, Carlyle sees Napoleon in his first period as "a true Democrat" (240). "There was an eye to see in this man, a soul to dare and do. He rose naturally to be the King" (240). By the end of his career, however, Napoleon, according to Carlyle, had become unjust and tyrannous. Not only did he begin to rely heavily upon his conviction of the useful "*Dupeability* of men" (241), but he began to mistake semblances, such as coronations and consecrations, for realities. By the end, Napoleon "had gone that way of his," writes Carlyle with pity, "and Nature also had gone her way. Having once parted with Reality, he tumbles helpless in Vacuity; no rescue for him. He had to sink there, mournfully as man seldom did; and break his great heart, and die" (243). This last sentence, of course, could serve as a description of Ahab's death as well as Napoleon's.

Although Ahab never develops Napoleon's appreciation of grandeur, never sees the material world as of ultimate importance, he does, during the course of the voyage, become more and more contemptuous of his men, more and more willing to sacrifice human life to attain his own "topmost greatness." While he begins as an archdemocrat, a Promethean figure willing to defy all "the omniscient gods" who are "oblivious of suffering man" (428), by the end he too has become oblivious because of his fatal egotism. Perhaps his most despicable act is his refusal to help Captain Gardiner search for his son; but earlier, of course, his characterization of his men as tools makes this behavior unsurprising. "May I forgive myself," he says to Captain Gardiner, thus revealing how great his sense of godlike power has become. But, of course, in his last battle he rediscovers his fatal human limitations, as the hemp grips his neck and he's pulled beneath the waves.

In two discernible ways, Melville merges his treatment of Ahab as a Napoleonic figure with a treatment of contemporary international politics. First, he intimates, as he did in *Mardi,* that there is nothing new under the sun and that the lesson time teaches is that all is vanity, including political struggle, for the cycle of republics and monarchies is endless. When Ishmael facetiously identifies Napoleon as a modern masthead stander (as a statue atop the column of Vendôme), he says, "There is Napoleon; who . . . stands with arms folded, some one hundred and fifty feet in the air; careless, now, who rules the decks below; whether Louis Philippe, Louis Blanc, or Louis the Devil" (136). Louis Philippe, of course, was the French king ousted by the French revolution of 1848; Louis Blanc was the radical French journalist and member of the provisional government who devised the ill-fated scheme of national workshops for the unemployed Parisian workers in the spring of 1848; and Louis the Devil is Melville's reference to Louis Napoleon, the emperor's nephew, whose movement toward absolutism Melville had glimpsed in Paris. Melville's idea here is that kings and revolutionaries alike are most notably part of the "wilful world" that "hath not got hold of unchristian Solomon's wisdom yet" (355).[61] And this is also the key idea he develops in his use of the Hotel de Cluny in Paris to hint at "Ahab's larger, darker, deeper part." Like a tour guide addressing political exiles such as Louis Philippe, Metternich, and Charles Albert, Ishmael says,

> Winding far down from within the very heart of this spiked Hotel de Cluny where we here stand—however grand and wonderful, now quit it;—and take your way, ye nobler, sadder souls, to those vast Roman halls of Thermes; where far beneath the fantastic towers of man's upper earth, his root of grandeur, his whole awful essence sits in bearded state; an antique buried beneath antiquities, and throned on torsoes! So with a broken throne, the great gods mock that captive king. . . . Wind ye down there, ye prouder, sadder souls! question that proud, sad king! A family likeness! aye, he did beget ye, ye young exiled royalties; and from your grim sire only will the old State-secret come. [161]

This secret, assuming the dead king could speak, would be on the order of "All is Vanity, ALL" (355), and like Shelley in "Ozymandias," Melville relies upon irony to convey it.

A second way Melville uses his narrative to develop a theme about contemporary French politics is his association of the crew of the *Pequod* with workers engaged in a fated revolt. Admittedly, as many critics have pointed out, Melville throughout the novel emphasizes the importance of the liberty, equality, and brotherhood of man, especially in his treatment of the Ishmael–Queequeg relationship, in the impassioned paean to the great democratic God in the first "Knights and Squires" chapter, and in the closing paragraphs of the "Fast-Fish and Loose-Fish" chapter; nevertheless, the Ishmael that tells the tale of the *Pequod*'s voyage only appears to share the pure democratic sensibilities of his younger self.[62] In many ways, he, like Ahab, perceives that the "people" measure up to no ideal, and his narrative continually dramatizes the primeval savageness that lies beneath the surface character of the crew, a savageness that appears when Ahab in his role as revolutionary incites them to "make war on the horrors of the deep!" (443). "We are all killers, on land and on sea," Ishmael admits at one point, "Bonapartes and Sharks included" (125).

The murderous action of "Forecastle—Midnight," the unholy tableaux of "The Quarter-deck," "The Try-works," and "The Candles" all serve to verify Starbuck's estimate of the men as "a heathen crew that have small touch of human mothers in them!" And even when viewed apart from their wild participation in Ahab's hellish rites, they are, as Ishmael says, no more than "mongrel renegades, and castaways, and cannibals—morally enfeebled" by Starbuck's "mere unaided virtue," Stubb's "invulnerable jollity of indifference," and Flask's "pervading mediocrity" (162).

Singling out two representatives of the people, the carpenter and the blacksmith, for chapter-length study, Melville provides a damning appraisal of the workingman, at least as he exists on the *Pequod*. "A stript abstract; an unfractioned integral" (388), the carpenter is a pure manipulator of wood, nothing more. He is skilled at "repairing stove boats, spring spars, reforming the shape of clumsy-bladed oars" (387), but he nevertheless cannot think. "His brain," Ishmael relates, "if he had ever had one, must have early oozed along into the muscles of his fingers" (388). The old blacksmith Perth, who has ruined his life by drinking, is a similarly sad representative of the working class. "Silent, slow, and solemn; bowing over still further his chronically broken back, he toiled away, as if toil were life itself, and the heavy beating of his hammer the heavy beating of his heart. And so it was.—Most miserable!" (400).

Both the carpenter and the blacksmith wield hammers, and this tool is a key image in the novel; it identifies the crew of the *Pequod* as workingmen, and it supports Melville's theme that mankind in the mass often become mere thoughtless tools during a revolt. When Ahab nails the doubloon to the mast, he assumes the role of a manipulative leader of the workers of the ship: "Receiving the top-maul from Starbuck, he advanced towards the main-mast with the hammer uplifted in one hand, exhibiting the gold with the other" (142). (As the props suggest, we also see here Ahab's belief that the forces which move the men are fear on the one hand and greed on the other.) Ishmael, excited and incited by Ahab like all the others, explains himself by saying, "My oath had been welded with theirs; and stronger I shouted, and more did I hammer and clinch my oath, because of the dread in my soul" (155). And when the chase for Moby Dick is under way, Melville again uses the image of the hammer in his description of the crew. During the night that follows the second-day chase, "the sound of hammers, and the hum of the grindstone was heard till nearly daylight, as the men toiled by lanterns in the complete and careful rigging of the spare boats" (460). And finally, on the third day, as Moby Dick bears down upon the *Pequod*, the crew form a workingman's tableau, as they await in static, emblematic poses their destruction. "From the ship's bows," Melville writes, "nearly all the seamen now hung inactive; hammers, bits of plank, lances, and harpoons, mechanically retained in their hands, just as they had darted from their various employments; all their enchanted eyes intent upon the whale" (468).

In the United States, the icon of an arm holding a hammer symbolized the workingman or a workingman's association during the eighteenth century and the first half of the nineteenth century. It appeared on membership certificates of mechanic societies, on campaign posters, and on allegorical representations of American progress and western expansion, and its associations were primarily social and fraternal.[63] During the mid and late 1840s, however, with the rise of labor unionism and labor radicalism, the symbol became politicized, appearing in newspapers such as *Working Man's Advocate* and *Champion of American Labor*.[64] The European revolutions, moreover, with their attendant spotlighting of workers revolting at the instigation of communist and socialist intellectuals, tied the image to the "Red Revolution." With the Bloody June Days, the symbol of the arm and hammer, along with those of the sickle, the red flag, and the liberty cap, became exceptionally potent and to conservative thinkers connoted popular violence. In *Mardi*, when Melville refers to the hammers and sickles of the mob, when he mentions the red banner they carry, his imagery is familiar to us because we have seen its proliferation in the twentieth century. We all recognize its link to communism, and when Melville wrote *Moby-Dick*, many of his readers did as well.

"A specter is haunting Europe—the specter of Communism. All the Powers of old Europe have entered into a holy alliance to exorcise this specter: Pope and Tsar, Metternich and Guizot, French Radicals and German police spies."[65] Thus began the *Communist Manifesto*, which appeared in early February 1848. As I have discussed, Marx and Engels had anticipated the European revolutions but found themselves rushing to keep abreast of events on the Continent once the upheavals began. Communists and social-

Illustration from the *Working Man's Advocate*, 15 March 1845.

ists, however, were at the center of revolutionary events, and the press in England and America portrayed their influence as pernicious and dangerous. Lamartine's courageous rejection of the red flag when it was raised by the mob on the steps of the Hôtel de Ville on 25 and 26 February earned him special praise, as we have seen, for it was interpreted as a rejection of political radicalism and popular violence. When conservatives reacted to the Bloody June Days, they invariably alluded to the red flag of the communists, which Lamartine had rejected. Ik Marvel's dispatches, we know, sensationalized the violence of the frightening "Reds," and other reports did the same. On 1 July 1848, the *Illustrated London News* explained the recent events in Paris by observing, "The 'Red Republicans' have justified their name. They have filled the streets of Paris with blood. . . . The working classes or 'Red Republicans,' were imbued with the doctrines of Communism. The middle classes, however, did not share these ideas. They wanted no red flag, which was to them an emblem of terror alone." Similarly, the New York *Herald* concluded, "In the main, this terrible catastrophe springs from the evil effects of incendiary doctrines, instilled into the minds of the resident populace by the Communists and Fourierites, and others of that ilk, who have made Paris their headquarters. This is placed almost beyond the shadow of a doubt, by the banner of red, the banner *Republique Democratique et Sociale,* which was hoisted during the insurrection by the insurgents."[66]

What becomes clear, once one appreciates the historical context of

The People of Paris during the February Revolution. (From Stern, *Histoire de la Révolution de 1848.*)

Moby-Dick and Melville's conservative response to the French revolution, is that within the novel is imbedded the allegory of a group of workingmen incited to violence and revolt by a political radical who plays upon their fear and greed and inspires them to destroy themselves. If this allegory sounds familiar, it is because of its resemblance to that beneath Melville's treatment of the Chartists in *Mardi*. It also parallels, of course, the tale of Lucifer's rebellion against God and the casting of that revolutionary and his minions into Hell. Although each member of the *Pequod*'s crew, whom Ishmael so flatteringly calls the "kingly commons," has an inherent nobility apparent when Melville touches "that workman's arm with some ethereal light" or spreads "a rainbow over his disastrous set of sun" (104–05), each also has an inherent savageness that surfaces when he acts as part of a revolutionary mob.

Perhaps the strongest evidence for the point I am making (which, of course, calls into question the multitude of Marxist and New Left interpre-

Lamartine and the Red Flag. (From Stern, *Histoire de la Révolution de 1848.*)

tations that dwell upon Melville's sympathies for the proletariat)[67] occurs in the final chapter of the novel. Here, in an odd tableau that makes sense only when interpreted allegorically, the *Pequod* has sunk from sight, with only a few inches of the mainmast still visible and Ahab's red flag streaming from it: "At that instant," Melville writes, "a red arm and a hammer hovered backwardly uplifted in the open air, in the act of nailing the flag faster and yet faster to the subsiding spar." With the vivid conjunction of the red flag, the red arm, the hammer, and the sinking ship, we have I think a pictorial commentary on European political radicalism, namely, communism and "Red Republicanism." Thus, although Ishmael has celebrated that "abounding dignity" that shines "in the arm that wields a pick or drives a spike" (104), Melville here expresses, implicitly, his distrust of the "people" and his revulsion at their capacity for self-destructive violence. The moral implications of the final tableau are, of course, made quite clear as Melville introduces a sky-hawk to convey them. This bird, it will be recalled, "chanced to inter-

The End

The End of *Moby-Dick*. Illustration by Rockwell Kent. (Courtesy of The Rockwell Kent Legacies.)

cept its broad fluttering wing between the hammer and the wood" and Tashtego, with uncharacteristic savagery, will not let it go. "The submerged savage beneath, in his depth-grasp, kept his hammer frozen there; and so the bird of heaven, with archangelic shrieks . . . went down with his ship, which, like Satan, would not sink to hell till she had dragged a living part of heaven along with her, and helmeted herself with it" (469).

In the years following *Moby-Dick*, Melville remained a student of mob action and a conservative in his response to it, never forgetting the lesson he saw demonstrated by the revolutions of 1848–49: the terror, the hate, the bloodshed, the futility, and, most important, the evil of popular uprisings. A number of his works reveal these sentiments—his poem "The House-Top" (1863) most forcefully—but it is in *Clarel* (1871) that we can see most clearly how his response remained inextricably linked to the matter of revolution in France:

The Revolution, whose first mode,
Ere yet the maniacs overrode,
Despite the passion of the dream
Evinced no disrespect for God; . . .
But yesterday—how did they then,
In new uprising of the Red,
The offspring of those Tuileries men?
They made a clothes-stand of the Cross
Before the church; . . .
Transcended rebel angels!

[478–79]

Thus declares Ungar, the disillusioned monomaniac of *Clarel*, as he gives voice to Melville's distrust of political radicalism and his perception of it as comparable to Lucifer's revolt against God. As Walter E. Bezanson has aptly pointed out, "A major political theme of *Clarel*" is "intense distrust of French revolutionary politics in the 19th century, and of radicalism generally." Throughout the poem, Rolfe, the Dominican, Mortmain, and Ungar speak critically of the "Vitriolists," "Red Caps," "Communists," and "Atheists" aligned with the "Red Republic." While the revolution of 1871 and the Paris Commune surely evoked the reactionary sentiments of *Clarel*, Melville's references are general, not specific. As Bezanson has observed, "In some passages it is not entirely clear which of 3 major revolutions is being referred to, the sense often being collective—1789, 1848, or 1871."[68] The Revolution of 1789, linked in Melville's memory with the reversals of his father, his uncle Thomas, and especially himself, formed the basis for his latent antipathy toward radicalism; the revolution of 1848, as we have seen, inspired him to express this antipathy in his works; and the revolution of 1871 intensified what he already felt and believed. That the three revolutions merge in *Clarel* is thus not surprising. To the very end of his life, as *Billy Budd* reveals, Melville regarded revolution in France as symbolic, fraught with meaning about the dark side of man.[69]

7

Revolution, Martyrdom, and *Leaves of Grass*

O to struggle against great odds, to meet enemies undaunted!
To be entirely alone with them, to find how much one can stand!
To look strife, torture, prison, popular odium, face to face!
To mount the scaffold, to advance to the muzzles of guns with perfect nonchalance!
To be indeed a God!

—WHITMAN, "A Song of Joys" (1860)

Like Melville, Walt Whitman regarded the matter of France with deep interest and emotion. The French language, French manners, French books and paintings, and especially French political revolt engaged his attention throughout his life.[1] Like Fuller and Melville, Whitman was profoundly stirred by the French revolution of 1848; moreover, the events it precipitated, especially the heroism and martyrdom of the European revolutionaries, shaped his poetic persona and inspired the major themes of *Leaves of Grass* (1855).

For years a central challenge to Whitman scholars has been to account for the miraculous appearance of the first edition of *Leaves,* to explain what it was that transformed the conventional journalist of 1848 into the revolutionary poet of 1855. Although no one has traced this transformation to the revolutions of 1848–49, many other explanations have been given. A New Orleans love affair, a mystical experience, unsatisfied homosexual desires, all have been advanced as psychological causes behind the writing of the 1855 *Leaves.*[2] As for literary sources, Emerson's essays, George Sand's *The Countess of Rudolstadt,* Jules Michelet's *The People,* and Thomas Carlyle's *Heroes and Hero-Worship* have each been identified as a key inspiration for Whitman's new poetry.[3] Looking at Whitman's politics from a Soviet point of view, Maurice Mendelson has argued that *Leaves of Grass* grew out of Whitman's involvement in the antislavery movement in the late 1840s and early 1850s. "It was not political passion alone, of course, that made Whitman a poet," Mendelson writes. "But when the mighty emancipatory movement opened Whitman's eyes to the magnificence of the people's cause, penetrating the depths of his soul, the poet's dormant poetic powers were awakened."[4]

Mendelson explains, more fully than any other commentator has to date, the importance of "political passion" to Whitman's mature poetry; however, he does not notice that the European revolutionary movement, rather than abolitionism, precipitated this passion.[5] Whitman in his old age implied he had been an abolitionist as a young man, but this was simply not the case. In his editorials for the Brooklyn *Daily Eagle* during the late 1840s, he attacked the abolitionists and blamed them for retarding the end of slavery by their fanaticism.[6] He did disapprove of slavery, of course, but mainly because of its inconsistency with American ideals. He held a low opinion of Negroes, as his Civil War correspondence with his mother reveals, and his sympathy for them was limited.[7] It was the revolutions in Europe, not abolitionism, that inspired him to become a poet of liberty, one whose attitude, as he described it in the 1855 preface, was "to cheer up slaves and horrify despots."

The road by which Whitman's interest in revolutions abroad led to the 1855 *Leaves* has several distinct stages. First, in his childhood, Whitman acquired from his family a reverence for political radicalism and for the heroes of the American and French revolutions. Next, as editor of the Brooklyn *Daily Eagle* in 1846–48, he watched intently the European scene and with bloodthirsty rhetoric prophesied the violent upheavals soon to occur there. During his stay in New Orleans in the spring of 1848, he was deeply stirred by the accounts of the 1848 revolutions, which he came to know thoroughly. He then returned to New York City with a new set of revolutionary heroes, and during the years that followed he identified with them in their martyrdom. "Resurgemus," his June 1850 tribute to the defeated revolutionaries, became the first poem Whitman selected for inclusion in *Leaves of Grass* (1855), and in its imagery, themes, and experimental prosody it represents the beginning of Whitman's great career. Both the preface to the 1855 *Leaves* and many of the poems of later editions reflect Whitman's conception of himself as "the sworn poet of every dauntless rebel the world over."[8] And although the last editions of *Leaves of Grass* became more religious and less political, more serene and less angry, Whitman nevertheless remained loyal to his early sentiments, and he retained "Resurgemus," retitled "Europe, in the 72nd and 73d Years of These States," as a part of his book from the first edition to the last.

Whitman's Interest in Revolution in France

As a young boy, Whitman learned to place a high value on political revolt. From his grandmother he heard stories about the Revolutionary War, told from a patriot's point of view, and these formed a valued part of his education. Washington, naturally, became one of his heroes, and from his father, as is well known, he acquired a love of radical democrats. Whitman's father knew personally and admired Thomas Paine and Frances Wright (an ardent Scottish-born democrat and freethinker), and these two gained young Walt's reverence. Whitman became familiar with the writings of both, and *Leaves of Grass*, as Justin Kaplan has pointed out, "borrowed the insurgent and questioning spirit of these mentors along with literal quotations from their writings."[9]

The American and French revolutions assumed great importance in Whitman's imagination, perhaps because of his father's interests, perhaps because of Whitman's own youthful encounter with a central figure in both. General Lafayette came to Brooklyn to lay the cornerstone for the Brooklyn free public library on 4 July 1825, when Whitman was six. Some of the children in attendance were lifted into spots where they could see; young Walt was among them, and General Lafayette was the adult who lifted him. "It is one of the dearest of the boyish memories of the writer," Whitman recalled some thirty-six years later, "that he not only saw, but was touched by the hands, and taken a moment to the breast of the immortal old Frenchman."[10] Whitman eventually wrote three versions of what transpired that day; in two he was held by Lafayette, in the third he was kissed by him as well.[11]

The connections Whitman saw between the American and French revolutions included their common intellectual ancestry, which he claimed as his own. Extending a toast on Bastille Day in 1888, he declared, "What America did for the Fourth France did for the Fourteenth: both acts were of the same stock."[12] Being well aware that the writings of Paine, Jefferson, and Wright, which he so admired, were informed by the philosophy of the French Enlightenment, he studied for himself the works of the French philosophes Volney, Rousseau, and Voltaire. As a boy, he read his father's copy of Count Volney's *Ruins*, and before the 1855 publication of *Leaves*, he read Rousseau's *Confessions* and probably Voltaire's *Philosophical Dictionary*.[13] Later, he responded enthusiastically to the republican writings of his French contemporaries George Sand, Jules Michelet, and Victor Hugo, whose indebtedness to French revolutionary thought and whose love for the common people resembled his own.

Whenever Whitman wrote about the French Revolution in his prose or poetry, he sympathized passionately with the people and their behavior, even justifying the Reign of Terror. In his editorial for 21 January 1847 in the *Eagle*, he noted that it was on this day that Louis XVI was guillotined in Paris, a central event of "that era of bloodshed—when a nation's accumulated wrongs and wrath burst over the tyrants of France in one wild whirlwind whose fury, even wild as it was, did not half equal the horror of the long train of *quiet* outrage and wretchedness which millions had previously endured."[14] Whitman wrote this while reading Hazlitt's biography of Napoleon, and when he published his review of that work two months later, he expressed the same thought in physiological terms: "We hear of the 'horrors' of the French Revolution: as if mere blotches on the skin, an unsightly eruption athwart the face of a man, were more horrible than the long, dreary deadness, the lethargy and decay, of the vital organs within. . . . For thus it was with France—the Revolution being the blotch—the ages before it, tallying that dreary deadness." The conservative response to revolutionary violence, he adds, alluding to Burke, "simply appeals to our sympathies for passing physical pain, not one tithe as intense and suffered by not one tithe as many, as in the years before—merely because the latter was borne passively and beneath the surface." [15] When Whitman read Lamartine's book on the 1789 French Revolution in the summer of 1847, he found himself, as Hawthorne would two years later, moved by the drama surrounding the guillotining of Louis XVI and Marie Antoinette, and he sympathized with them. Near the end of his review, however, he retracted his sympathy and angrily declared, "In the overthrow of that despotism of that period we hail a glorious work, for which whole hecatombs of royal carcasses were a cheap price indeed!" [16]

Whitman's comments contain a primitive sense of justice, yet they are also uncharacteristically bloodthirsty and savage. This strong emotional response to revolution, especially the great French Revolution, is linked, I suspect, to his personal feelings toward his father. While Walter Whitman, Sr., directly taught his son to love political radicals, he may have indirectly taught him to hate despots. A savage fury pervades Whitman's responses to and descriptions of political revolution, and what we may be seeing in these is the sublimation of his feelings toward his father. Whitman's early short fiction deals a number of times with a young boy suffering from an unjust father. This is the case in "Wild Frank's Return"; it is also the case in "Bervance." As Gay Wilson Allen has said, "The young author seemed to have almost a compulsion to write about cruel fathers." [17] In the transparently autobiographical poem "There Was a Child Went Forth" we see: "The father, strong, self-sufficient, manly, mean, anger'd, unjust, / The blow, the quick loud word, the tight bargain, the crafty lure" (365). The image of an unjust father, as Ronald Paulson has shown, has often been used to represent the king in paintings and descriptions of revolution, while images of sons, such as America's "Sons of Liberty," have been used to represent revolutionaries. [18] Such traditional imagery may have established a natural connection in Whitman's mind between his father and the French Revolution.

Whatever the psychology behind Whitman's fury at despotism and his empathy for French revolutionaries, the fact remains that these emotions, evoked and brought to full force by the 1848 French revolution, pulsed at the heart of his poetry. Whitman himself recognized their vital importance to his art, as can be seen in his comments on the paintings of Millet. "The Leaves are really only Millet in another form," he told Horace Traubel: "—they are the Millet that Walt Whitman has succeeded in putting into words." [19] Whitman first viewed Millet's paintings in Boston in 1881, and in

The Sower (1850) by Jean-François Millet. (Courtesy of Museum of Fine Arts, Boston.)

Specimen Days, he relates, "Never before have I been so penetrated by this kind of expression. I stood long and long before 'The Sower' . . . . There is something in this that could hardly be caught again—a sublime murkiness and original pent fury." (Millet painted *The Sower* in the wake of the 1848 French revolution, and the socialist and revolutionary implications of its subject, the dark figure of a peasant striding powerfully down a slope throwing seeds from his fist as he goes, was commented upon by contemporary French critics.)[20]

In Millet's paintings of peasant life, Whitman saw not only sympathy for oppressed workers but also justification of revolutionary violence and revenge. Commenting on the paintings as a whole, he wrote,

> To me all of them told the full story of what went before and necessitated the great French revolution—the long precedent crushing of the masses of a heroic people into the earth, in abject poverty, hunger—every right denied, humanity

attempted to be put back for generations—yet Nature's force, titanic here, the stronger and hardier for that repression—waiting terribly to break forth, revengeful—the pressure on the dykes, and the bursting at last—the storming of the Bastile [*sic*]—the execution of the king and queen—the tempest of massacres and blood. Yet who can wonder?

> Could we wish humanity different?
> Could we wish the people made of wood or stone?
> Or that there be no justice in destiny or time?[21]

The three lines Whitman quotes, or rather misquotes, here are his own, found in his poem "France, the 18th Year of these States," where he celebrates 1794, the last year of the Reign of Terror. The poem presents not only Whitman's acceptance of the violence of the French Revolution but also the familial, and perhaps Oedipal, associations it holds for him:

A great year and place,
A harsh discordant natal scream out-sounding, to touch the mother's heart closer than any yet.

I walk'd the shores of my Eastern sea,
Heard over the waves the little voice,
Saw the divine infant where she woke mournfully wailing, amid the roar of cannon, curses, shouts, crash of falling buildings,
Was not so sick from the blood in the gutters running, nor from the single corpses, nor those in heaps, nor those borne away in the tumbrils,
Was not so desperate at the battues of death—was not so shock'd at the repeated fusillades of the guns.

Pale, silent, stern, what could I say to that long-accrued retribution?
Could I wish humanity different?
Could I wish the people made of wood and stone?
Or that there be no justice in destiny or time?

[235–36]

Although the slaying of a father-king is not described in the poem, new hope for mother and child does emerge from "that long-accrued retribution." Invariably, thoughts of revolution abroad evoked almost a visceral reaction from Whitman, and the 1789 French Revolution, with its terror, violence, and revenge, struck him as especially gratifying and just. When a new French revolution loomed on the horizon in the late 1840s, he looked forward to it eagerly.

The *Eagle* and Whitman's Interest in Europe

During 1846 and 1847, when Whitman served as editor of the Brooklyn *Daily Eagle*, his interest in the international political scene permeated his book reviews and editorials. Although he is often thought of as the quintes-

sential national poet, this is probably because he expressed his internationalism at relatively low volume; nevertheless, like his "gong of revolt" (52), it
sounds throughout his writings, early and late. Of the twenty-two historical
books he reviewed for the *Eagle*, fourteen dealt with the Old World, the
remainder with America.[22] His selections and comments indicate that histories dealing with the revolutionary movements in England and France
especially interested him.[23] Among the books he reviewed were Guizot's
History of the English Revolution, Michelet's *History of France*, and Lamartine's *History of the Girondists*. His review of *The Girondists*, the longest he would write, reveals that he was deeply moved by Lamartine's treatment of the great French Revolution. For him the book provided "glimpses
into some of the nooks of that revolution, which the more uniform, disci-
plined track of other works on the same subject, has precluded them from
touching upon. Indeed the 'History of the Girondists,' compared with other
histories is much as a play compared with an ordinary prose volume: it is,
we think we can say, the most dramatic work we ever read—too dramatic,
perhaps, for the higher purposes of history—though its intensity of interest
is increased by the same cause."[24] Other works Whitman read during his
Eagle years, such as Carlyle's *French Revolution*, Hazlitt's *Napoleon*, and
George Sand's *Journeyman Joiner*, likewise turned his thoughts to Europe
and its revolutionary tradition. These reviews as a whole highlight the international features of Whitman's "long foreground." As Gay Wilson Allen
has said, "Whitman was far less the great, unique, untutored American bar-
barian than the child of French pre- and post-revolutionary thought."[25]

Like Fuller and Engels, Whitman as journalist anticipated the 1848–49
upheavals on the Continent and stood ready to applaud and justify them.
His editorials throughout 1846 and 1847 boil with anger, and he relates
various topics—the hanging issue, marriage of royalty, slave owners in the
South—to the great French Revolution, time and again prophesying a new
revolution, one that will bring apocalyptic destruction and vengeance. Although anger at kings and priests is the strongest of Whitman's emotions in
his editorials on Europe, it is almost balanced by his sympathy for oppressed
peoples. Like Melville when he wrote *Redburn*, Whitman used what he saw
at home—masses of poor immigrants crowding the streets of New York—to
make accurate inferences about the situation abroad. In June of 1846 he
commented on the "panting multitudes" on the shores of Europe: "Partly
through the excess of population, and partly through the grossly partial na
ture of the laws and the distribution of property, half the aggregate number
of the natives of the Old World live in squalor, want and misery." Addressing
the platform of the American Republican party, which sought to deny immigrants political rights in the United States, he asked, "Ah, who can look
on the condition of the Old World, and assent to the views of this proscrip-
tive party?"[26] Repeatedly, Whitman rejected narrow nationalism by refer-

ring to "the lover of his race—he whose good-will is not bounded by a shore or a division line—" and arguing for opening up America's "immense territory" to all seekers of freedom. "The degrading, starving and ignorant ones of the Old World, whatever and whosoever they are, should be transplanted thither, where their cramped natures may expand, and they do honor to the great humanity they so long have been a blot upon."[27] Like other romantic writers, Whitman thought nature could shape character. America's great landscape could make for a great people.

As a supporter of the Young America movement through his contributions to the *Democratic Review* and his *Eagle* editorials, Whitman subscribed to its messianic nationalism, and he believed that America's example of freedom would precipitate changes in Europe. As early as the summer of 1846, he looked upon American expansion "with the faith which the Christian has in God's mystery" and anticipated the impulse of freedom nourishing itself "in a few short years" to full development abroad. "Who shall say what spectacles will be witnessed on the breast of Old Earth, our mother, then?" he asked. As the months passed and the crop failures and financial crises proceeded apace in Europe, Whitman became more concerned about the European scene and the plight of its people. In November of 1846, he wrote about two royal marriages arranged by the French minister Guizot, commenting, "It sickens one quite, to think that thousands and millions of people . . . are governed by a complicated tangle of which selfishness, treachery, sensuality, and depravity, make up so large a portion, and of which such doings as we have mentioned are the fruits." Reflecting upon how Americans would respond to such doings, he thought in revolutionary terms, saying it would be "with one unanimous, prompt, shrieking yell of scorn, hate, and horror, so wild and high that the old fabric of royalty itself might come tumbling in ruins to the ground!"[28]

Because Whitman believed in the Jeffersonian doctrine that "the best government is that which governs least," he had difficulty supporting the idea of legislated reforms; radical change, however, such as the overthrow of a corrupt government, was another matter, and this seemed to be what he looked for abroad. On 11 February 1847, he observed that "the signs bode the heaving up in Europe of the downtrodden people—and their efforts at throwing off those oppressive burdens of government, that, after all, are so closely connected with their evils. . . . For though we are not of the school which believes that government can confer happiness, the signs are plain that they have sovereign potency in the prevalence of misery." The signs of impending upheaval Whitman saw he described in metaphors similar to Fuller's: "In France, the smothered fires only wait the decay of the false one, the deceiver Louis Philippe, to burst forth in one great flame . . ."; in Austria, the empire "is filled with the seeds of rebellion—with thousands of free hearts," while "the numerous petty German states, too, have caught the sacred ardor," and in Switzerland, "an insurrectionary movement is mentioned by the last accounts."[29]

By March 1847, Whitman was ready not just to report on the horrible conditions abroad or to welcome immigrants to America's shores or to predict change, but ready also to advocate revolution. Professing to "dread the horrors of the sword and of violence," Whitman declared, "but we would rather at this moment over every kingdom on the continent of Europe, that *the people* should rise and enact the same prodigious destructions as those of the French Revolution, could they thus root out the kingcraft and priest-craft which are annually dwindling down humanity there to a lower and lower average." As for the magnitude of the "destructions" he called for, Whitman extended his metaphor of human health to declare that because the "fangs" of kingcraft have sunk deeply and the "virus" of priestcraft has spread widely, "only some great retching of the social and political structure can achieve the blessed consummation."[30] He was right of course. And because of his sustained and keen interest in the fate of Europe, as demonstrated by this and his other *Eagle* pieces, he responded with passion to the revolutions of 1848–49, eventually creating a new poetry to convey his strong feelings.

From New Orleans to "Resurgemus"

Whitman was one of those rare individuals who cling to principle regardless of personal cost, which made him often a martyr. He lost his editorship of the *Eagle* because he supported the Wilmot Proviso while his publisher, Isaac Van Anden, an Old Hunker, opposed it. After his firing, Whitman was offered a job on the New Orleans *Crescent*, and he arrived in New Orleans on 25 February 1848 to begin his new editorial duties. In New Orleans, he continued to observe the European scene steadily and intently. As one of the *Crescent* editors, he "made up" the foreign news by reading incoming newspapers, clipping out sections for reprinting, and writing his own commentary to accompany them, a "pen and scissors" job[31] that he was well suited for, given his background and interests. Fortuitously, Whitman began this work at a time when the foreign news could not have been more exciting. The first issue of the *Crescent* appeared on 5 March, and within three weeks, news of the French revolution began arriving in the city. As Paul Zweig has said, "It was one of the few times in Whitman's life when he was in the right place to share the excitement of a great event. New Orleans swarmed with European refugees who were delirious with joy at the news from across the ocean."[32] One suspects, moreover, that to Whitman it must have seemed as if his readings, his anger, his hopes and prophecies had somehow led to these climactic events. In any case, all evidence indicates he became totally absorbed by them.

His first columns on the upheaval in France, before he knew exactly what had transpired, were tentative and cautious; once it became clear that few had died in the revolution and that France had gone republican, however, he let out the stops, castigating the deposed Louis Philippe, applauding the acts of the provisional government, and anticipating with passionate joy the overthrow of other European despots. In the *Crescent* on 31 March, he told of feeling the blood rush through his veins and grow hot within him when he thought "of this news from the continent of Europe!" "Is it not glorious?"[33] he asked his readers.

Particularly stimulating to Whitman was the fact, reported in the *Crescent* on 8 April, that "literary men seem to have been not only the prime starters of this French revolution—but to be recognized as the ones from whom liberalism is to take body and form in a new Government there." The socialist Louis Blanc was one of these "literary men," but the poet and historian Lamartine interested Whitman most. Before he learned about the February revolution, Whitman had written for the *Crescent* another review of Lamartine's *Girondists*, claiming that as a history of "that wonderful era, the French Revolution," it was "beyond comparison, the best book yet written." When Lamartine as political leader soon moved to the center of events in France in the spring of 1848, Whitman agreed that "'The Girondists' had a great effect in producing the late revolution," and he found it "fitting that Lamartine, himself, should be a principal agent in developing the great drama, whose introduction he has caused."[34]

As Whitman reported on this "great drama" for his readers, he made Lamartine his hero, emphasizing the man's defiance, his courage, his eloquence, his serenity—traits that he would later attribute to his ideal poet–prophet as described in his 1855 preface. On 7 April, Whitman quoted from Lamartine's address on France's preparedness to wage war and to increase France's strength and glory, and he commented, "This may be construed only as the language of firmness, and a consciousness of power, but it is more. It is the language of defiance." Rather than objecting to Lamartine's sabre rattling, Whitman praised it. Asking, "What will be—what has already been the natural effects of such language?" he answered, "The people will rise in every quarter against domestic wrong and foreign oppression—certain of the sympathy of the French people—hopeful of the aid of French arms." This prophecy, which resembles those in his *Eagle* editorials, proved accurate, and ten days later, he could exult: "The example of France has acted upon the rest of Europe as a spark applied to gunpowder. The whole civilized world is in commotion—. . . . Everywhere the people have arisen against the tyrannies which oppress them, and the success which has so far attended their efforts is marvellous indeed."[35] The euphoric sense of savage, justified vengeance Whitman felt during these days, he would recall in his poem "Resurgemus," which begins:

> Suddenly, out of its sta[l]e and drowsy [l]air, the [l]air of slaves,
> Like lightning Europe le'pt forth,
> Sombre, superb and terrible,
> As Ahimoth, brother of Death.
>
> God, 'twas delicious!
> That brief, tight, glorious grip
> Upon the throats of kings.[36]

For those revolutionaries outside of France, the grip could not hold, for Lamartine never came through with French arms. He had his hands full establishing and protecting the new French Republic from enemies within.

Lamartine's abilities as a leader, which Dana and others later questioned, seemed to Whitman worthy of praise, not the least because the man was a poet. Whitman described at length in the *Crescent* Lamartine's address to the crowds at the Hôtel de Ville, where he rejected the red flag of the socialists. After dramatizing the scene for his readers, Whitman concluded, "Lamartine carried his point, and succeeded so far in subduing the people as to induce them to become themselves the safeguard of the Provisional Government. And yet this man is sneered at . . . as a poet and philosopher. Could your 'practical men' have done better in the crisis?" In other columns, Whitman accorded Lamartine hyperbolic praise and elevated him to the level of his old childhood heroes. On 21 April 1848, he characterized Lamartine's speech of 17 March as "a model of dignity, firmness, and wisdom" and asserted that had Lamartine's "whole public life been confined to the delivery of that speech alone, it would, under the circumstances, have entitled him to immortality." On 3 May, in a column on Lamartine's denial of French military aid to Irish liberals, Whitman praised him as the "embodiment" of moderation and added, "God seems to have raised up this man as Washington was raised for us in our great struggle. . . . What a destiny! Even if he were to die this moment, his life would be of more worth to history—to patriots too—than the lives of all the kings and warriors that ever governed France, or led her children to slaughter!" Finally, on 18 May in an article entitled simply "Lamartine," Whitman summarized:

> More and more noble grows the character of Lamartine, the more he is surrounded with trials, and the greater the dangers that menace him. It is beautiful to see such a man! It works out a stronger argument against Kings than all the philosophy of the most scholastic radicals. For where is there—where has there ever been—such a King! Lamartine has a wondrous union of physical and moral courage, to begin with; the first of which the masses must always admire, and the other clinches the respect of every intellectual person. Then his godlike serenity—the balance on which he always seems to be calmly poised! Does he not indeed, as we said a fortnight ago, resemble our own Washington?[37]

Whitman left New Orleans for New York on 26 May, having gained during his stay much that would contribute to the volume of poetry he would publish in 1855. As Justin Kaplan has pointed out, he had seen "democratic vistas of city and wilderness, river and lake, mountain and plain,"[38] and these would become important features of his poetry. Also, as Betsy Erkkila has observed, in New Orleans he acquired new words, French words, that he would use as "a means of flaunting pro-French sympathies and defying the more conservative political and moral attitudes of his countrymen."[39] More important than the new landscape and the new language, however, was Whitman's new understanding of the great events that had transpired in Europe and the examples of heroism they provided. Most noticeable of these examples was Lamartine's, whose idealism and eloquence were reshaping Europe and showing the importance of a great poet to history. Soon other writers, Mazzini in Italy and Kossuth in Hungary, would provide similar examples through their eloquent radicalism.

After Whitman arrived back in Brooklyn on 15 June, the *Advertiser* reported seeing him, "large as life, but quite as vain, and more radical than ever."[40] At first Whitman channeled his heightened radicalism into wholehearted participation in Barnburner politics. On 5 August, he spoke at a Barnburner meeting in Brooklyn and was elected, along with thirteen others, as a delegate to the Buffalo convention. One of his fellow delegates was Marcus Spring, the socialist Quaker with whom Margaret Fuller had traveled throughout Europe in 1846–47 and with whom she still corresponded. "I never met Margaret Fuller, but I knew much about her those years," Whitman later said; and Spring, whom Fuller regarded as a dear friend, could have been a source of this knowledge.[41] Whitman's political passion, like Fuller's, had been inflamed by the French revolution, and after the Buffalo convention, he directed it into his new paper, *The Freeman,* whose revolutionary motto, "Liberty, equality, fraternity," showed the influence of French radicalism, according to the *Advertiser,* which also called Whitman one of the "hot-headed ultras."[42] Only the first issue of the *Freeman* survives, so we know little about Whitman's handling of the paper. By the time he resigned as editor in September 1849, republicanism was on the defensive in Europe; Lamartine had fallen from public favor, France was under the control of Louis Napoleon, the Roman Republic had fallen to French troops, Mazzini had been driven into exile, the Hungarians had been defeated by the combined forces of Austria and Russia, Kossuth had escaped to Turkey, and revolutionaries everywhere were being subjected to brutal reprisals, including flogging, hanging, and shooting. Oddly enough, however, Whitman, like Fuller, found in these events a source of inspiration, and his radicalism soon flowed into a poetry of political protest.

Always harboring a sense of defeat himself, a sense of isolation and despair, Whitman identified with the failed revolutionaries and insisted upon their dauntlessness. For all his celebration of life and his songs of joy, Whitman, as Roger Asselineau has shown, is "the poet of anguish."[43] His

family, of course, was filled with life's outcasts and failures. His improvident
father and self-sacrificing mother certainly led difficult lives, and their children led worse ones: Eddie, crippled and feebleminded; Jesse, violent, hys-
terical, and finally insane; Andrew, tubercular and alcoholic; Hannah, hy-
pochondriacal, battered, eventually psychopathic. And as for Whitman
himself, his problems were substantial. Even if we set aside as unknowable
the nature of his feelings toward his father and mother and of his homo-
eroticism or homosexuality, there remains the unhappiness he felt being
a spiritual, idealistic, compassionate individual in a society that was pre-
dominantly materialistic, pragmatic, and grasping. The sense of alienation
Whitman experienced, however, resulted not in angry self-pity, such as we
see in Melville's middle period, nor in arrogant disdain, such as lay beneath
Hawthorne's gentle Custom-House persona; rather, he tended, in his notebooks and poetry, to conceive of himself as a great undaunted martyr—half
religious, half political. And it was this tendency, of course, that reenforced
his identification with the failed revolutionaries of Europe. "Did we think
victory great?" he asks in "To a Foil'd European Revolutionaire":

> So it is—but now it seems to me, when it cannot be help'd, that defeat is great,
> And that death and dismay are great.
>
> [371]

These sentiments, of course, echo those in "Song of Myself" and later
poems. The celebration of defeat and death which was his way of dealing
with the disheartening news from abroad at midcentury evolved into the
powerful lyricism of his greatest poems.

The most engaged and engaging accounts in the American press of the
foiled European revolutionaries were those of Margaret Fuller published in
the *Tribune*, a paper Whitman read regularly. That her dispatches influenced him seems likely. We know that her earlier essay "American Literature" (1846), in which she called for spiritual American poems, made a lasting impression upon him, for he referred to it several times, quoting a
portion of it from memory; we also know that after Fuller left for Europe he
read closely at least one of her dispatches to the *Tribune*, an account of her
night on Ben Lomond, for a clipping from it was found among his papers at
his death.[44] Fuller, it seems, was one of the women who, along with his
mother, Frances Wright, George Sand, and the soprano Marietta Alboni,
shared his highest regard. Her writings and heroic persona, moreover,
probably inspired his insistence upon the equality of the female with the
male in his poetry.

Fuller's last dispatches from Italy, those apocalyptic rhetorical jeremiads that her brother omitted from *At Home and Abroad*, appeared in the
Tribune in January and February of 1850. Their subject matter, the suffering
revolutionaries of Europe and the eventual triumph of democracy and free-

dom, had been, as we have seen, of intense interest to Whitman for years, and Fuller's treatment was affecting. Writing from Florence, Fuller tells how the Austrian general Radetzky has "applied the bastinado" to more than four hundred men and women in Parma, how in the kingdom of Naples, "there are thirty thousand in the prisons, and new arrests constantly made," and how in Rome the priests, now back in power, are "tracking out their prey," even "those who had received the amnesty from Pio IX." She also, as we have seen, singles out particular villains, asking, "Do you laugh, Roman Cardinal, as you shut the prison-door on woman weeping for her son martyred in the cause of his country? Do you laugh, Austrian officer, as you drill the Hungarian and Lombard youth to tremble at your baton?" For these she has a revelation: "Soon you, all of you, shall '*believe* and tremble.'" And she expresses hope: "I gaze on the beauty of nature, and seek thus to strengthen myself in the faith that the Power who delighted in these creations will not suffer his highest, ardent, aspiring, loving men, to live and die in vain, that immortal flowers bloom on the grave of all martyrs, and phenix [*sic*] births rise from each noble sacrifice."[45]

Within four months of the appearance of Fuller's last letter, Whitman completed and sent to Greeley his poem "Resurgemus," which Greeley published in the *Tribune* on 21 June 1850. Its title, which translates "We will rise again," recalls the Italian *risorgimento* and is unique among Whitman's poetry by being in Latin, which was perhaps Whitman's way of acknowledging the Italian inspiration of the poem. Its subject matter, sentiments, and imagery match those in Fuller's last letters, and its purpose seems the same: to cheer up the oppressed and to horrify their oppressors. When Whitman quoted eighteen lines from the poem at the end of an 1851 lecture, they were placed in the context of the struggle for liberty in Naples, Rome, and Venice, a placement further indicating the Italian, and Fullerean, inspiration of the work.

"Resurgemus" begins by recalling the joy of the uprisings of 1848 and then laments the return of "frightened rulers" with their "bitter destruction":

> Each comes in state, with his train,
> Hangman, priest, and tax-gatherer,
> Soldier, lawyer, and sycophant.

For these Whitman has an apocalypse:

> behind all, lo, a Shape
> Vague as the night, draped interminably,
> Head, front and form, in scarlet folds;
> Whose face and eyes none may see,
> Out of its robes only this,
> The red robes, lifted by the arm,

> One finger pointed high over the top,
> Like the head of a snake appears.

With less fantastic imagery, he indicates the fates of those who fought in the revolutions:

> Meanwhile, corpses lie in new-made graves,
> Bloody corpses of young men;
> The rope of the gibbet hangs heavily,
> The bullets of tyrants are flying,
> The creatures of power laugh aloud.

(The laughter here seems a clear echo of that Fuller described.) The young men who have been hanged and shot, Whitman goes on to insist, have not died in vain: "all these things bear fruits, and they are good." As he elaborates upon this hope, he introduces an image that would become identified with his poetry, an image that resides at the center of *Leaves of Grass* and has been admired by countless readers:

> Not a grave of those slaughtered ones,
> But is growing its seed of freedom,
> In its turn to bear seed,
> Which the winds shall carry afar and resow,
> And the rain nourish.

As Justin Kaplan has observed, the poem moves "beyond its topic toward his matured style and concerns. Invoking some of his shaping metaphors, the benign and ever-renewing cycle of sour corpses and sweet grass, it links insurgency with eternal life."[46] In its final stanza, the poem also develops what would become a central theme in Whitman's poetry, liberty:

> Liberty, let others despair of thee,
> But I will never despair of thee:
> Is the house shut? Is the master away?
> Nevertheless, be ready, be not weary of watching,
> He will surely return; his messengers come anon.[47]

"Resurgemus" was the last of the four-poem cluster Whitman published in March and June of 1850 and the last poem he would publish before the 1855 *Leaves*. All four in the cluster are political; all four express anger. In them we see Whitman breaking the shackles of poetic convention and devising new ways to express his strong feelings. The first poem of the group, "Song for Certain Congressmen," parodies, using conventional meter and rhyme, doughfaced politicians who have yielded to pressures from the slavocracy; the second, "Blood-Money," denounces Webster's speech in favor of compromise with the South, and it contains not only biblical references but biblical parallelism and cadences that represent Whitman's first experiment in free verse. The third poem, "The House of Friends," an angry response to a congressional committee set up to deal with the Compromise Bill, again experiments with free verse but awkwardly. It was with "Resurgemus" that Whitman first succeeded to his satisfaction in creating the revolutionary new poetry that would become distinctively his own.

In "Resurgemus" one sees the characteristically rhythmical lines without regular meter or rhyme yet controlled by selected poetic devices, including the parallelisms, repetitions, and rhythms of the King James Bible. Here one has Whitman's use of catalogues: "Hangman, priest, and taxgatherer, / Soldier, lawyer, and sycophant" (he would later add Jailer to the list); his use of midline caesuras, especially effective in the last stanza: "Is the house shut? // Is the master away?"; and of course, his parallelisms and repetitions, probably most felicitously used in the following stanza (italics added):

> *Those* corpses of young men,
> *Those* martyrs that hang from the gibbets,
> *Those* hearts pierced by the grey lead,
> Cold and motionless as they seem,
> Live elsewhere with undying vitality;
> *They live* in other young men, O, kings,
> *They live* in brothers, again ready to defy you;
> *They were* purified by death,
> *They were* taught and exalted.

Scansion of the stanza reveals that by the sixth and seventh lines, the meter has expanded to four stresses per line, and that in the final two lines, the meter is shortened to two stresses per line, bringing the stanza to a dramatic close. This stanzaic form, with rhythmical lines growing and receding in wavelike fashion, has been called an "envelope of parallelism,"[48] and although here it exists in relative isolation, it would proliferate in Whitman's poetry and shape his greatest poems.

Even though "Resurgemus" contains the beginnings of Whitman's major themes, imagery, and prosody, there is much, admittedly, that is derivative and awkward about it. The personification in the scarlet robes, for example, seems Gothic and sensational, like something out of Poe. "Lurid" and "bloated" Zweig calls it.[49] An allusion to Ahimoth, an obscure biblical figure, which Whitman later removed, is also too ornamental and literary, as he himself probably realized.[50] And the alliterations verge on the ostentatious—"front and form, in scarlet folds," for example. The final word of the poem, "anon," also jars because of its lack of freshness, although the biblical allusion to Matthew 25:13 in the last lines is subtly made.[51]

Over the course of time, Whitman would revise "Resurgemus." He changed a few words and phrases, unfortunately removing the bold word "delicious" in the second stanza, where he had celebrated the "grip upon the throats of kings." He also lengthened the lines by combining them when he republished the poem in the first *Leaves*. And he changed the title several times, making it more general and less tied to events in Italy. Although entitled "Resurgemus" in the *Tribune*, in the first edition it was, like all the other poems there, untitled. In the 1856 edition, it became "Poem of The Dead Young Men of Europe, the 72nd and 73rd Years of These States," and in the 1860 and later editions, it was "Europe, The 72d and 73d Years of These States." These changes in emphases from "We" to "Young Men" to "Europe" indicate the distancing that took place in Whitman's point of view as he grew older; nevertheless, at midcentury, as his transformation from conventional journalist to poetic genius was occurring, he identified with the young revolutionaries of Europe.

In his notebook entries of the late forties and early fifties, Whitman's almost mystical apprehension of his quotidian world appears. By observing, by being attentive to the sights, sounds, and smells of New York City and Brooklyn and Long Island, he acquired an acute awareness that informed the resolutions, reflections, aphorisms, and experimental lines of verse he was putting onto paper. It was the European revolutions and revolutionaries, however, that showed him how to go beyond his personal experiences, that allowed him to discover two of his major themes: liberty and rebirth. Around these many of his observations could be ordered. About these he could speak. With "Resurgemus" Whitman discovered the purpose of America's great poet: to create beauty by writing not about Spanish maidens, midnight reveries, the picturesque landscape, or even the death of a beautiful woman, but instead about liberty and the heroic struggle for it. "Like the French Romantics," as Betsy Erkkila has said, "he attempted to carry on the tradition of the social and political 'engagement' of the artist, an engagement which had its roots in the revolutionary period in France and America."[52] In 1860, Whitman himself described the stages of his becoming a poet:

> Long I thought that knowledge alone would suffice me—O if I could but
> obtain knowledge!
> Then my lands engrossed me—Lands of the prairies, Ohio's land, the
> southern savannas, engrossed me—For them I would live—I would be
> their orator;
> Then I met the examples of old and new heroes—I heard of warriors, sailors,
> and all dauntless persons—And it seemed to me that I too had it in me to
> be as dauntless as any—and would be so.
>
> [*Leaves*, 595]

Whitman's writing of his revolutionary new poetry became his way of demonstrating his heroism: "to enclose all, it came to me to strike up the songs of the New World—And then I believed my life must be spent in singing" (595). Student, Traveler, Observer of Heroes, Poet: these are stages in

Whitman's early development, and many of the heroes were provided by the revolutions in Europe.

From "Resurgemus" to *Leaves of Grass* (1855)

After writing "Resurgemus," Whitman continued to develop his interest in Europe and its revolutionary heroes and martyrs. During the early 1850s, he became acquainted with a group of young artists that gathered at the studio of Henry Kirke Brown, a Brooklyn sculptor, and at Brown's he listened and learned. "There I would meet all sorts," he recalled, "—young fellows from abroad stopped here in their swoopings: they would tell us of students, studios, the teachers, they had just left in Paris, Rome, Florence." From one of these students, a "sparkling fellow," Whitman learned about the great French songwriter Pierre-Jean de Béranger, who had twice been imprisoned, in 1821 and 1828, for his songs celebrating the spirit of the first revolution. "He spoke of Beranger," Whitman related. "—I was greatly interested; he either knew Beranger or knew a heap about him. In this crowd I was myself called Beranger."[53] Several years previously, Fuller had met Béranger in Paris and informed her *Tribune* readers that "the great national lyrist of France . . . lives in the hearts of the people. . . . His wit, his pathos, his exquisite lyric grace, have made the most delicate strings vibrate, and I can feel, as well as see, what he is in his nation and his place."[54] After the 1848 French revolution, Béranger was elected to the Constituent Assembly, and like Lamartine, he represented for Whitman the great poet engaged in the struggle for liberty. Writing of Béranger in 1858, Whitman called him "the French Poet of Freedom," who "wrote the great lyric of his, calling upon the nations to 'join hands' in amity and with prophetic vision told them of the day when international quarrels should cease."[55] It may have been Béranger's chansons that encouraged Whitman to think of himself as a singer and of his poems as songs, and it may have been Béranger's internationalism that encouraged Whitman to conceive of himself as an international poet.[56] "I had more than my own native land in view when I was composing Leaves of Grass," Whitman later explained. "I wished to take the first step toward calling into existence a cycle of international poems."[57]

Little is known about Whitman's life between 1851 and 1855, when he was writing *Leaves of Grass*, other than that he built houses, read, thought, and lectured. He also stopped dressing as a stylish gentleman and started dressing as a worker, perhaps owing to the influence of George Sand, as Esther Shephard has argued,[58] but more likely, in my opinion, because of his sympathy with workers, especially the workers of Paris who were prominent revolutionaries and martyrs of 1848–49. The persona of "Song of Myself" seems less than the typical American in his attitude toward work as he loafs at his ease, and according to Whitman's brother George, Walt adopted the same attitude. George recalled, "I was in Brooklyn in the early fifties, when Walt came back from New Orleans. We all lived together. No change seemed to come over him: he was the same man he had been, grown older and wiser. He made a living now—wrote a little, worked a little, loafed a little. He had an idea that money was of no consequence. He was not very practical—the others of us could give him points in this direction—but as for the rest, we could not understand him—we gave him up. I guess it was about those years he had an idea he could lecture. He wrote what mother called 'barrels' of lectures."[59]

One of Whitman's lectures, which his artist friends invited him to give at the first awards ceremony of the Brooklyn Art Union, shows how the revolutions of 1848–49 had shaped, or were shaping, his conception of himself as an artist. Whitman delivered his remarks on the evening of 31 March 1851, and in comparison with his editorials of several years earlier, they evince considerable development in the depth and precision of his thought. After praising the beauty and simplicity of Grecian art and criticizing the "frippery, cant, and vulgar selfishness" of the present age, Whitman turns to "heroic actions" and their relationship to "the artistical impulse":

> He who does great deeds, does them from his sensitiveness to moral beauty. Such men are not merely artists, they are artistic material. Washington in some great crisis, Lawrence in the bloody deck of the *Chesapeake*, Mary Stewart at the block, Kossuth in captivity and Mazzini in exile,—all great rebels and innovators, especially if their intellectual majesty bears itself out with calmness amid popular odium or circumstances of cruelty and an infliction of suffering, exhibit the highest phases of the artistic spirit. A sublime moral beauty is present to them, and they realize them. It may be almost said to emanate from them. The painter, the sculptor, the poet express heroic beauty better in description; for description is their trade, and they have learned it. But the others *are* heroic beauty, the best beloved of art.[60]

This passage reveals clearly how Whitman's conception of art at the time centered upon the fact and appeal of political martyrdom. Revolutionaries such as Kossuth and Mazzini are living poetry; they exhibit the heroic beauty the artist describes. If the artist, however, becomes a great innovator, his stature can equal that of his subject. Through rebellion and innovation, the artist, the poet, can *be* heroic beauty too. The latter idea is conventionally romantic, of course, but the way Whitman acted upon it was original. Unlike Byron, whose love of liberty he shared, Whitman avoided linking himself with his literary predecessors.

In a later section of his Art Union address, Whitman gives his audience, and perhaps himself, further advice about achieving distinction: they should not dwell upon the "great old masters," but study "a still better, higher school, . . . the school of all grand actions and grand virtues, of heroism, of the death of captives and martyrs—of all the mighty deeds written in the

pages of history—deeds of daring, and enthusiasm, and devotion, and fortitude." They must, he says, "read how slaves have battled against their
oppressors—how the bullets of tyrants have, since the first king ruled,
never been able to put down the unquenchable thirst of man for his rights."
In this mention of kings and the rights of man, we can hear echoes of
Thomas Paine, one of Whitman's old heroes, but his immediate context is
revolution in Europe and the struggles of his new heroes. This becomes
clear when he refers to recent events in Italy: "In Naples, in Rome, in Venice, that ardor for liberty which is a constituent part of all well developed
artists and without which a man cannot be such, has had a struggle—a hot
and baffled one. The inexplicable destinies have shaped it so. The dead lie
in their graves; but their august and beautiful enthusiasm is not dead:—"
He then concludes with eighteen lines from "Resurgemus," further establishing the contemporary context of his remarks.[61]

    The ideas found in Whitman's lecture resemble those in Emerson's *Na-
ture*, which had recently been republished.[62] Emerson, too, speaks of the
beauty of heroic action, yet, of course, he professed not to see any in the
European revolutionary scene. For him, "revolutions of violence . . . are
scrambles merely,"[63] or so he wrote in a London journal. Concurrently and
contrastingly, Whitman in the notebook where "Song of Myself" was finding
initial expression revealed how deeply rooted that poem was in the concept
of heroic martyrdom:

    The Poet
    All the large hearts of heroes
    All the courage of olden time and new

    . . . .

    I am the man; I suffered, I was there:
    All the beautiful disdain and calmness of martyrs
    The old woman that was chained and burnt with dry wood, and her children
       looking on.
    The great queens that walked serenely to the block,
    The hunted slave who flags in the race at last, and leans up by the fence,
       blowing and covered with sweat,
    And the twinges that sting like needles his breast and neck
    The murderous buck-shot and the bullets.
    All this I not only feel and see but am.[64]

Ironically, it was not Whitman, but Emerson, who eventually became an
ardent abolitionist and even championed the cause of John Brown, the most
famous martyr of the day. Whitman, as I have said, maintained his distance
from abolitionism, expressed disdain for blacks, and when asked why he had
not responded strongly to John Brown's execution, replied, "I am never convinced by the formal martyrdoms alone: I see martyrdoms wherever I go: it
is an average factor in life: why should I go off emotionally half-cocked only

about the ostentatious cases?"[65] Essential to Whitman's ideal poet were "serenity" and "calmness," which for him were a part of heroic martyrdom. Also, his identifications, it must be said, tended to be narcisstic. That is, in visualizing himself as a foiled revolutionary or a hunted slave, what he saw was himself, not the revolutionary or slave. As D. H. Lawrence unkindly pointed out years ago, Whitman's identifications often ring false because of their self-regard, because the "merging" often denies "sympathy."[66]

Within nine months of his lecture at the Brooklyn Art Union, Whitman had the opportunity to see in the United States one of the most famous of the foiled European revolutionaries, Kossuth, and one wonders whether he welcomed it. In so many ways Whitman, as poet, dealt with the general, with the type, and even though he loaded his lines with concrete examples, their importance seems to reside in their representativeness. Also, he seems to have needed distance to best appreciate and respond to other people. In fact, what interested him most as a poet was not particular people or things or ideas, but rather the general interactions between them, the dynamics of meaning flowing between subjects and objects. Much like a biologist, he was fascinated with life at those meadow-forest areas of transition, where species, though perhaps not individuals, change most noticeably due to the environment; the title of his greatest poem, "Crossing Brooklyn Ferry," tells us much about the subordination of individuals to process and flux in his scheme of values. The poem itself, of course, does the same.

When Kossuth began his famous tour of the United States, which lasted from December 1851 to July 1852, Whitman saw him. During his visit to Brooklyn, Kossuth was escorted to the armory and to Plymouth Church by a troop of horse guards, and there he spoke to large crowds. In the opinion of Joseph Jay Rubin, "Whitman gave his sympathy . . . to the living symbol of freedom, crushed by emperors and czars, when Kossuth came to America that December in search of means to reverse the calamity in Hungary."[67] In his notebook, Whitman merely recorded that "I saw him make his entree in N Y latter part of 1851 riding up Broadway."[68] Rubin is probably right, though, for indeed Kossuth as symbol would have stimulated Whitman's growing sympathy for revolutionary heroes and martyrs. In the *Crescent* in the spring of 1848, Whitman had expressed reservations about the Hungarian revolution, for he saw the Magyar nobles, of whom Kossuth was the leader, fighting against Austria for a freedom they themselves would not grant to the Croats and Slavonians of southern Hungary.[69] The more he learned about the Hungarians, though, through a detailed study of their political and social history, the more he sympathized with them.

In the early 1850s, Whitman educated himself by clipping articles of interest from newspapers and journals, reading them, and annotating them. His primary interest was in literature, but history and geography were a close second.[70] Two articles he studied dealt favorably with the Hungarian

Kossuth's Entrance into Central Park, New York. (Courtesy of Louis Szathmary Family Ar-
chives, Chicago.)

revolution and Kossuth's role in it: "Hungary," which appeared in the *Westminster Review* in July 1849, and "The Slavonians and Eastern Europe,"
which appeared in the *North British Review* in August 1849. He probably
read these articles in the early 1850s. The first is a twenty-six-page account
of the social and political history of Hungary, emphasizing the heroic role
Kossuth had recently played in it. There Whitman read about Kossuth's
"large powers of mind, fervid eloquence, skilful debating talent, and thorough knowledge of public affairs," traits that Americans witnessed during his
visit to the United States. In the second article, at the top of which Whitman
wrote "valuable resumé," Kossuth is described as "gifted with a power of
speech quite miraculous, and uniting a marvellous sagacity and genius for
organization, with an oriental depth and fervour of soul." Of particular interest to Whitman, indicated by his markings, was the recent perseverance of
the Hungarians in their struggle against Austria. Whitman underlined the
passage as follows: "All that title to freedom . . . that arises from lion-like
courage, from fierce hard obstinacy, from perfect soundness of head joined
to strength of heart, from unwearied and successful perseverance in a course
once begun . . . this the Hungarians showed themselves most unmistakably
to possess."[71] Whitman's own stubbornness, a trait noted by several ac-

quaintances, no doubt made him appreciate the perseverance of the Hungarians. In addition, the fight for liberty, described in both articles, coincided with the matter of "Resurgemus" and with the course Whitman had set himself for becoming a great prophet–poet.

When Whitman wrote the now-famous preface for the first edition of *Leaves of Grass*, he focused upon the need for an American poet as great as its geography and people. His opening assertions that "Americans of all nations at any time upon the earth have probably the fullest poetical nature," and "the United States themselves are essentially the greatest poem" (709) seem to support the view that the preface expresses "a rather bumptious American nationalism."[72] Actually, however, the preface is much more international, more "kosmopolitan," in spirit than most readers realize. It becomes so in part because of Whitman's insistence that America "is not merely a nation but a teeming nation of nations" (709). Like the speaker of "Song of Myself" (who calls himself "a kosmos"), its role is representative. The United States, he declares, is the "race of races," and he explains, "I know that what answers for me an American must answer for any individual or nation that serves for a part of my materials" (728). The materials he draws upon indeed come from Europe as well as America, although knowledge of European history is often necessary to appreciate this.

In the preface, Whitman defines his ideal poet as a revolutionary hero; however, like Lamartine, this hero is defiant, not aggressive: "A heroic person walks at his ease through and out of that custom or precedent or authority that suits him not. . . . Nothing is finer than silent defiance advancing from new free forms" (717). For Whitman "the great poet is the equable man" (712); however, this does not keep the poet from serving Mars if the occasion demands: he can "arouse" the time; "he can make every word he speaks draw blood" (713). The political activism of Whitman's poet remains primarily verbal and literary, not physical. He sees, he loves, he speaks, but, ideally, he judges not, argues not, moralizes not.

After describing the traits of the great poet, Whitman turns to "the grand idea" the poet "must sustain": liberty. In his lecture of 1851, Whitman had concluded, "As there can be no true Artist, without a glowing thought for freedom, so freedom pays the artist back again many fold, and under her umbrage Art must sooner or later tower to its loftiest and most perfect proportions."[73] In the preface, he makes the same point, and as he does he treats first international, then national issues—tyranny in Europe, then slavery in the United States—a progression that parallels his political-poetical development between 1848 and 1850. "Liberty takes the adherence of heroes wherever men and women exist," he asserts, "but never takes any adherence or welcome from the rest more than from poets. . . . The attitude of great poets is to cheer up slaves and horrify despots." In order to indicate how enduring liberty is, he gives several scenarios. The first refers

to Europe after the revolutions, and what we see is the material of "Resurgemus." "The battle rages with many a loud alarm and frequent advance and
retreat . . . . the enemy triumphs . . . . the prison, the handcuffs, the iron
necklace and anklet, the scaffold, garrotte and leadballs do their work . . . .
the cause is asleep . . . . the strong throats are choked with their own blood
. . . . the young men drop their eyelashes toward the ground when they
pass each other . . . . and is liberty gone out of that place? No. never" (Whitman's ellipses). This treatment of oppression in Europe leads him naturally
into commentary upon slavery in the United States, with the Fugitive Slave
Act receiving much attention. Whitman explains how to determine that liberty has disappeared. It is "when the memories of the old martyrs are faded
utterly away [. . .] when the laws of the free are grudgingly permitted and
laws for informers and bloodmoney are sweet to the taste of the people
[. . .] when we are elated with noble joy at the sight of slaves . . . . when
the soul [. . .] has much extasy over the word and deed that put back a
helpless innocent person into the gripe of the gripers or into any cruel in-
feriority [. . .] when the swarms of cringers, suckers, doughfaces, lice of
politics, [. . .] obtain a response of love and natural deference from the
people" (720–21) (my ellipses bracketed). Throughout these passages, then,
Whitman reveals that the political passion he felt (and expressed) at midcentury has not only been kept alive during the past half decade, but has been
nurtured and pruned into a mature conception of America's great poet and
that poet's role.

The relationship between the European revolutions and Whitman's
great American poet described in the preface becomes even more apparent
after one reads "To a Foil'd European Revolutionaire," which appeared in
the 1856 edition. Here one encounters lines from the 1855 preface being
reused to identify Whitman's persona and the purpose of his poetry:

> Courage yet, my brother or my sister! . . .
> (Not songs of loyalty alone are these,
> But songs of insurrection also,
> For I am the sworn poet of every dauntless rebel the world over, . . .)
> The battle rages with many a loud alarm and frequent advance and retreat,
> The infidel triumphs, or supposes he triumphs,
> The prison, scaffold, garrote, handcuffs, iron necklace and leadballs do their
>   work,
> The named and unnamed heroes pass to other spheres,
> The great speakers and writers are exiled, they lie sick in distant lands,
> The cause is asleep, the strongest throats are choked with their own blood,
> The young men droop their eyelashes toward the ground when they meet;
> But for all this Liberty has not gone out of the place, nor the infidel
>   enter'd into full possession.   [370–71]

Knowing that the appeal of defeat and martyrdom would not be obvious to many of his readers, Whitman in the 1855 preface attempted to explain his emphasis by citing "prudence," which closely resembles Emerson's notion of "compensation." For Whitman, as for Emerson, transcendence of the time-bound world of individuals allows one to perceive that physical loss corresponds to spiritual gain. This is what Fuller too came to believe in Italy, or rather asserted as a belief after the fall of the Roman Republic. And within Whitman's expanded definition of "prudence," he seems to refer obliquely to Fuller, whose death at sea off Fire Island in the summer of 1850 affected him greatly; she perished clinging to her child as others abandoned ship and tried to make it to shore through the surf. "All will come round," he claims. "All the self-denial that stood steady and aloof on wrecks and saw others take the seats of the boats . . . all offering of substance or life for the good old cause, or for a friend's sake or opinion's sake . . . all pains of enthusiasts scoffed at by their neighbors [. . .] all that was ever manfully begun, whether it succeeded or no [. . .] these singly and wholly inured at their time and inure now and will inure always to the identities from which they spring or shall spring" (725).

Although it should be clear by now that Whitman's response to the revolutions of 1848–49 abundantly informed "Resurgemus" and the 1855 preface, the question remains, did it inform his greatest early poem, "Song of Myself." In several lines he does claim to "beat the gong of revolt, and stop with fugitives and them that plot and conspire" (52); however, these sentiments remain submerged. Malcolm Cowley's remark that in the poem Whitman "is not advocating rebellion or even reform" has validity.[74] The themes of brotherhood and equality are more central to "Song of Myself" than is the theme of liberty, and overall the poem is more religious than political. Nevertheless, we do see in it a development of the rhythms and poetic devices that first appeared in "Resurgemus." We see also the image of grass growing from the graves of young men, signifying "there is really no death, / And if ever there was it led forward life" (34). And we see the theme of liberty developed, especially in the sections treating the "hounded slave," the massacre of the Texans at Goliad, and the battle of the *BonHomme Richard* and the *Serapis*. A few lines of "Song of Myself" seem to contradict the idea that revolution is central to Whitman's ideal poet: "Battles, the horrors of fratricidal war, the fever of doubtful news, the fitful events; / These come to me days and nights and go from me again, / But they are not the Me myself" (32). These lines, however, were added in 1867,[75] when Whitman's persona was undergoing the metamorphosis from one of the turbulent roughs to the good gray poet. They thus are a misleading indicator of the political passion behind the early poetry.

The evolution in Whitman's persona was gradual and, in fact, only partial. The emphasis upon liberty, revolution, and martyrdom remained a distinctive feature of almost all his editions. Several poems of 1856, in addition to "To a Foil'd European Revolutionaire," contain the spirit of "Resurgemus." In "Song of the Open Road," he informs his reader, with the rhetoric of Garibaldi,

> My call is the call of battle, I nourish active rebellion,
> He going with me must go well arm'd,
> He going with me goes often with spare diet, poverty, angry enemies, desertions.
>
> [158]

In "Song of the Broad-Axe," he envisions the axe in Europe being used by the headsman for good and ill:

> I see the clear sunset of the martyrs,
> I see from the scaffolds the descending ghosts,
> Ghosts of dead lords, uncrown'd ladies, impeach'd ministers, rejected kings,
> Rivals, traitors, poisoners, disgraced chieftains and the rest.
>
> I see those who in any land have died for the good cause,
> The seed is spare, nevertheless the crop shall never run out,
> (Mind you O foreign kings, O priests, the crop shall never run out.)
>
> [191–92]

And in his "Poem of Salutation" (later "Salut Au Monde!") and "Poem of the Sayers of the Words of the Earth" (later "A Song of the Rolling Earth"), he expresses an exuberant internationalism, which features French words and French liberty.[76]

In the third edition of 1860, revolutionary sentiments pervade several poems, such as "Poem of Joys" (later "A Song of Joys") and "To a Certain Cantatrice," where he alludes to "One who should serve the good old cause, the great idea, the progress and freedom of the race, / Some brave confronter of despots, some daring rebel" (11). While the European revolutions of 1848–49 inspired Whitman to become the American poet of liberty and to write poems attacking despotism and slavery, the great French Revolution remained a source of imagery for his attacks, and near the end of "France, the Eighteenth Year of these States," published in 1860, he turns to the United States and the imminent Civil War, envisioning a French revolution on American soil:

> O Liberty! O mate for me!
> Here too the blaze, the grape-shot and the axe, in reserve, to fetch them out
> in case of need,
> Here too, though long represt, can never be destroy'd,
> Here too could rise at last murdering and ecstatic,
> Here too demanding full arrears of vengeance.
>
> [236]

(The subject of the last lines, Negro slaves, is omitted, perhaps to keep the poem acceptably general, perhaps to give it a frightening "sublime murkiness.")

For Whitman, the approaching civil war was another example of the People battling the Aristocracy. In his *Eagle* editorials, written while he was anticipating revolutionary upheavals abroad and observing the Free-Soil debate at home, he had declared that the claims of slavery were being advanced by a little band of southerners, whose "chivalric bearing (sometimes a sort of impudence)" resembled "the dauntless conduct of kings and nobles when arraigned for punishment before an outraged and too long-suffering people."[77] When the civil war loomed even more ominously in the late 1850s, Whitman continued to draw upon the French Revolution for imagery to conceptualize and treat the conflict. He wrote in one of his notebooks,

> (How will it do for figure?)
> *Get a perfect account of the attack and taking of the Bastille*
>   (fire, blood, smoke, death, shouts, attack, desperation)
>   symbol of the attack on slavery in These States—
> The masses of the north, stern and muscular
> The enthusiasts not only of these lands, but of all lands.
> The determined purpose—death does not stop it—it is filled up by others—
>   and their death by others still.—[78]

Of course, once the Civil War actually began and Whitman witnessed the "blood, smoke, death" at first hand, he temporarily lost his lust for revolutionary revenge.

In Whitman's fourth edition of *Leaves* (1867), there is a noticeable change in his attitude toward the European scene and in his intended purpose for *Leaves*. In this edition, he forsakes his stance as a poet of all nations and becomes blatantly chauvinistic. "[My ambition is] to give something to our literature which will be our own;" he wrote, "with neither foreign spirit, nor imagery nor form, but adapted to our case, grown out of our associations, boldly portraying the West, strengthening and intensifying the national soul, and finding the entire foundations of its birth and growth in our own country."[79] The cause of this change, according to Whitman's two most eminent critics, Allen and Asselineau, can be traced to the Civil War. Allen has speculated that Whitman's nationalism became "over-stimulated," because of "the hostility of England and other European nations to the North during the Civil War." Asselineau has likewise observed that "the Civil War seems to have exacerbated Whitman's nationalism. The fervor with which he celebrated the Union made him unjust to other nations. He had fits of xenophobia."[80] This xenophobia can be seen in hostile lines about Europe in "By Blue Ontario's Shore" (which were later removed) and in "Turn O Libertad."

In Whitman's poems of the 1870s he returned to international themes and praise of the European revolutionary tradition. He grouped a number of his poems of the 1871 edition under the title "Songs of Insurrection," introducing them with the exclamation: "O latent right of insurrection! / O quenchless, indispensable fire!" Asselineau thinks that these "unusually violent lines," as he calls them, can be explained by a new concern on Whitman's part for the social problems of the Gilded Age.[81] Whitman, however, would never have supported popular violence in the cities and streets of the United States, given his conservative temperament. It was revolution in distant Europe that stirred his literary imagination at this time as it had in the past. During the French revolution of 1871, the communists took over Paris for two months after Louis Napoleon and his troops were defeated by the Prussians. Before and after government troops regained the city, thousands of French people were killed, including women and children who had fought with the communists. The poem "O Star of France" reveals Whitman's considerable ambivalence about these events; it also shows, however, that he stuck with his admiration of France and her insurrectionary ways:

> Dim smitten star,
> Orb not of France alone, pale symbol of my soul, its dearest hopes,
> The struggle and the daring, rage divine for liberty,
> Of aspirations toward the far ideal, enthusiast's dreams of brotherhood,
> Of terror to the tyrant and the priest.
>
> Star crucified—by traitors sold,
> Star panting o'er a land of death, heroic land,
> Strange, passionate, mocking, frivolous land.
> Miserable! yet for thy errors, vanities, sins, I will not now rebuke thee,
> Thy unexampled woes and pangs have quell'd them all,
> And left thee sacred.

[396]

At the end of the poem, Whitman insists that France will again shine bright and clear and "high o'er the European world" (397), but his rhetoric seems inflated and strained. He had reached the age of fifty-two, and revolution in France no longer evoked fresh, "delicious" poetry, but labored occasional verse. As a poet he had ceased to be, in word and in mood, "one of the roughs"; the "original pent fury" linking *Leaves of Grass* with the spirit of revolution remains most deeply and earnestly embedded in the earlier poems.

8

Kossuth "Fever" and the Serenity of *Walden*

> I look down from my height on nations,
> And they become ashes before me;
> Calm is my dwelling in the clouds;
> Pleasant are the great fields of my rest.
>
> —THOREAU, "The Spirit of Lodin" (Journal Entry, 1 May 1851)

When Walt Whitman saw Kossuth on 6 December 1851, the famous Hungarian revolutionary had just arrived in the United States and was receiving an enthusiastic, thunderous welcome. Cannon and gun salutes in New York harbor, a grand parade down Broadway, and torchlight processions in front of Irving House, where he and his entourage enjoyed luxurious rooms as guests of the city, were just some of the tributes. He had come to the United States to obtain money, arms, and, if possible, a promise of official intervention to support a new Hungarian revolution against Austria and Russia. He received much attention and praise, but little support. In fact, the excitement evoked by his visit was the flare of a dying ember, and it signaled the approaching end of American interest in the revolutions of 1848–49. Nevertheless, like the earlier fervor, it did affect a number of writers, in addition to Whitman. Stowe, in *Uncle Tom's Cabin*, linked her antislavery themes to what she called "the great, last QUESTION of the age," the "great controversy now going on in the world between the despotic and the republican principle,"[1] and she drew upon contemporary interest in Kossuth and the Hungarian cause to add unity and force to her novel. Emerson played host to Kossuth and wrote an address praising him, while Melville and Hawthorne alluded to him satirically in their works. Most significantly, Thoreau, stirred by Kossuth's visit and news of European affairs, returned to the manuscript of *Walden* and revised and expanded it throughout 1852. Although engaged by current events, Thoreau fought a spiritual battle to remain aloof, "to preserve the mind's chastity" by reading "not the Times" but "the Eternities."[2] Imagining that he had won, he celebrated his victory in *Walden*.

The Hungarian Revolution and *Uncle Tom's Cabin*

Before coming to America, Kossuth earned his reputation as a hero by the role he played in the Hungarian revolution of 1848–49. His fiery speech against Austrian hegemony delivered in the Hungarian Diet on 3 March 1848 inflamed the students' demonstrations in Vienna and inspired their demand for a constitution from Emperor Ferdinand I. In October 1848, Kossuth then successfully defended Hungary from Austrian invasion, as his peoples' army drove the imperial troops out of the country and pursued them to the gates of Vienna. As Horace Greeley colorfully put it in his introduction to Kossuth's biography, "The Austrian legions were hurled from the heart of Hungary back across the frontier to the vicinity of their own capital, tracking their flight by the lavish effusion of their blood. Never was a revolutionary government more promptly or more formidably subjected to the stern ordeal of the sword, and never was one more completely successful."[3] Once Czar Nicholas chose to intervene on behalf of Austria, however, Kossuth could not preserve the independence of his nation. Elected governor of the newly proclaimed Hungarian Republic in April 1849, Kossuth fought with his countrymen against overwhelming military odds, but the inevitable occurred in August 1849 when the republican forces were defeated by the combined imperial and Russian armies. Fleeing to Turkey to escape certain execution, Kossuth and twelve hundred followers were arrested and confined by the sultan. Two years later, in September 1851, the United States government, responding to public sentiment, arranged for Kossuth's release.

Throughout 1851 and 1852 American interest in the European political scene focused upon Hungary, where the republican revolutionaries were suffering reprisals as a result of their defeat at the hands of Austria and Russia. The *National Era*, among other periodicals, kept track of Hungarian refugees and exiles and on 2 October 1851 announced that the Turkish sultan had put an end to the "unjust confinement" of Kossuth, who now was on his way to the United States by way of London. On 5 June 1851 the *National Era* had begun the serial publication of *Uncle Tom's Cabin*, and before the final chapter appeared on 1 April 1852, Stowe had responded to current events by incorporating the revolutionary scene into her novel. First, as I pointed out in chapter 3, she used revolution in Europe as an ominous backdrop for the novel, one portending the possible apocalyptic uprising of the oppressed masses at home as well as abroad. Second, she used the fight for freedom in Hungary as a unifying link between the heroism of her main characters.

As many readers notice, *Uncle Tom's Cabin* has two plots that appear almost unconnected: George and Eliza's flight to Canada and freedom, and Tom's journey to New Orleans to live with the benevolent St. Clare and then with the vicious Legree. Examined closely, however, the two plots can be seen to be joined by their common reference to the Hungarian revolutionary cause. In the climax to the first plot, George Harris and his family,

The Hungarian War. (From *Illustrated London News*, 15 (28 July 1849), 57.)

assisted by Phineas, climb to the top of a large rock to confront their pursuers. In this scene, entitled "The Freeman's Defence," George atop the
rock makes his "declaration of independence" to the pursuers, who would
put him and his wife and child back into slavery. As he makes his stand,
Stowe thus addresses her readers:

> If it had been only a Hungarian youth, now bravely defending in some
> mountain fastness the retreat of fugitives escaping from Austria into America,
> this would have been sublime heroism; but as it was a youth of African descent,
> defending the retreat of fugitives through America into Canada, of course we
> are too well instructed and patriotic to see any heroism in it; and if any of our
> readers do, they must do it on their own private responsibility. When despair-
> ing Hungarian fugitives make their way, against all the search-warrants and
> authorities of their lawful government, to America, press and political cabinet
> ring with applause and welcome. When despairing African fugitives do the
> same thing,—it is—what *is* it? [253]

The Freeman's Defence. Illustration by George Cruikshank in *Uncle Tom's Cabin*. London, 1890.

Certainly we are to see that it is heroism just the same; by her comparison, Stowe strikes a responsive chord within her contemporary readers and thus expands their sympathy for George and his family.

When Stowe constructed the main climax to her second plot, she again turned to the Hungarians to tie St. Clare's heroism to George's and both to historic international events. Just as George is made to resemble the Hungarian freedom fighters as he makes his stand on the rock, St. Clare emulates the Hungarian nobles when, after the death of Eva, he decides to free all his slaves. As he is making his decision, St. Clare's cousin Ophelia asks him, "Do you suppose it possible that a nation ever will voluntarily emancipate?" and he replies: "I don't know. This is a day of great deeds. Heroism and disinterestedness are rising up, here and there, in the earth. The Hungarian nobles set free millions of serfs, at an immense pecuniary loss; and, perhaps, among us may be found generous spirits, who do not estimate honor and justice by dollars and cents" (372). St. Clare's oblique reference is, of course, to himself, for he has decided to act upon his beliefs and perform a "great deed." He has decided, in the spirit of the Hungarians, to free his slaves. Unfortunately, his intention has to serve as his deed, for he loses the opportunity to act; minutes later he is fatally stabbed as he tries to separate two men fighting in a café. Stowe, while allowing him his moment of heroism, sacrifices him to show that even a slave owner with good intentions can inflict misery upon his slaves by dying prematurely. The sale, suffering, and death of Uncle Tom in the chapters that follow illustrate the point.

Kossuth "Fever"

As the last chapters of *Uncle Tom's Cabin* were appearing in the *Era*, Kossuth arrived in the United States. Despite the opposition to him mounted by Catholics (who knew of his collusion with Mazzini against Pope Pius IX), by Abolitionists (who resented his refusal to speak out against American slavery), and by southerners (who sold millions of dollars of cotton a year to Austria and Russia), he nevertheless enjoyed the enthusiastic admiration of most Americans during his seven-month stay in the country, and the high emotions that attended his appearance in a number of cities led observers to talk about the "Kossuth fever" sweeping the nation. Handsome, colorful, charismatic, this martyred rebel inspired adulation in almost all Americans who saw or heard him. His aristocratic manners and fashionable dress (especially his high plumed hat and black velvet coat) made a memorable first impression, and when he spoke he enthralled his listeners. Having supposedly taught himself English during an earlier imprisonment using only a grammar book, Johnson's dictionary, and a volume of Shakespeare, his speeches soared with poetic eloquence as he asked for money, arms, and men to reliberate his nation. In the eyes of most Americans Kossuth seemed a legitimate revolutionary hero, one resembling their own George Washington, and they outdid themselves paying their respects.

   During his stay in New York, the city gave a lavish banquet in his honor at Irving House, to which four hundred distinguished guests were invited. Likewise, the New York editors honored him with a banquet at Astor House, with William Cullen Bryant presiding. After visiting Philadelphia, Kossuth traveled to Washington, D.C., and received invitations from the White House, the Senate, and the House, all of which he accepted. After lobbying unsuccessfully for the adoption of an interventionist policy by the government, he toured the western states, raising funds for his cause. In response to his visit, some 250 poems, dozens of books, hundreds of pamphlets, and thousands of editorials were written about him.[4] A few of the poems, such as those by Garrison and William Ellery Channing, took him to task for maintaining a politic silence about black slavery, as did a number of the editorials. Panegyrics, however, predominated.

Portrait of Louis Kossuth. (From *Illustrated London News*, 19 (11 October 1851), 44.)

Sympathy for intervention on behalf of republicanism in Europe was greatest in the frontier states, where the expansionist spirit flourished, and there—in Ohio, Indiana, Missouri—Kossuth was warmly received. In Springfield, Illinois, Abraham Lincoln, although against intervention, drafted resolutions expressing sympathy for Kossuth, "the most worthy and distinguished representative of the cause of civil and religious liberty on the continent of Europe," and in Columbus, Ohio, a fifteen-year-old William Dean Howells listened with rapt attention as Kossuth spoke on the steps of the statehouse. At age eighty, Howells recalled, "I hung on the words of the picturesque black-bearded, black-haired, black-eyed man, in the braided coat of the Magyars, and the hat with an ostrich plume up the side which set a fashion among us, and I believed with all my soul that in a certain event we might find the despotisms of the Old World banded against us, and 'would yet see Cossacks,' as I thrilled to hear Kossuth say."[5]

Howells, like so many of his countrymen, bought himself a Kossuth hat, complete with the ostrich plume, to demonstrate his sympathy. Meanwhile, Kossuth marches, Kossuth dances, Kossuth oysters, Kossuth restaurants, Kossuth buttons, flags, and photographs became signs of the times. As Donald S. Spencer has found, even a manufacturer of rat poison capitalized on the revolutionary's popularity:

> Kossuth's coming, so they say;
> He's a lion in his way
> And made tyranny his prey;
> But for bugs and such as they
> Our old Lyon is O.K.
> Rats and mice, too, he can slay.[6]

After making his way through the Midwest and the South (where he was coolly received), Kossuth visited a number of cities and towns in New England, where the people were eager to see him. The major writers in the region of course noticed his presence.

Melville, when Kossuth first arrived in the country, had been deeply engrossed in finishing *Pierre* and struggling to get out of debt. His vivacious Berkshire neighbor Sarah Morewood informed their mutual friend George Duyckinck that Melville responded to her charge of being reclusive by saying that "if he left home to look after Hungary the cause in hunger would suffer."[7] He later paid attention to Kossuth, though, and in "I and My Chimney" he observes satirically that the grass around his house which grows every spring "is like Kossuth's rising of what he calls the peoples."[8] It is actually Melville's narrator who says this, and although this character seems almost a self-parody as he voices an exaggerated aristocratic conservatism, most of the story's humor seems directed at revolutionaries like Kossuth who would topple existing governments to establish new ones of their own. The narrator's chimney, we are told many times, dominates the house he shares with his wife and daughters; "it stands, solitary and alone—not a council of ten flues, but, like his sacred majesty of Russia, a unit of an autocrat" (1305). Through a series of such allusions, it becomes not only Czar Nicholas but also Henry VIII, Louis XIV, and Charles V. Moreover, like Charles I and Louis XVI, it has suffered decapitation. A previous owner "sliced" fifteen feet from its top, "actually beheading my royal old chimney—" says the narrator; "a regicidal act" (1302). Because he identifies with his chimney (obviously a symbol of his manhood and sovereignty), the narrator resists his wife's attempts to have it torn down. She, of course, is a reformer, who has the Swedenborgian credentials to show her modernity. Thwarted in her efforts to destroy the chimney, she enlists the aid of Mr. Scribe, a mathematically minded planner (reminiscent of Fourier and other utopian reformers) who measures the chimney and decides it can be divided into "many thousand and odd valuable bricks" (1314).

The narrator foils the plans of Scribe, and at the end of the story he recalls several other "narrow escapes," especially the time he returned home to find "three savages, in blue jean overalls," tearing his chimney down. At the time, he "narrowly escaped three brickbats which fell, from high aloft, at [his] feet" (1326). This occurred seven years in the past, and since the story was written in the spring of 1855,[9] these falling brickbats seem linked to the upheavals of 1848 and the toppling of Louis Philippe, Metternich, and Pius IX. As for the savages in blue jeans, they could be any group of revolutionaries specializing in leveling, but their clothes tie them more closely to the workers of Paris than to the Hungarian nobility. In any case, the narrator takes pride in their defeat and in the maintenance of his autocratic independence. In this respect he resembles the courageous perceiver of "visable truth" whom Melville described in a letter to Hawthorne, "the man who, like Russia or the British Empire, declares himself a sovereign nature (in himself) amid the powers of heaven, hell, and earth" (*Letters*, 124). We know that in some moods Melville conceived of himself as such a man, so the degree of self-satire in "I And My Chimney" is probably less than a liberal reader would wish. Much of the defiant conservatism in the work reflects that of its author.

Melville's friend and former neighbor Hawthorne, who in 1852 now lived in West Newton, also had little sympathy for the Hungarian revolutionary who spoke of the rising of "the peoples." In a letter to E. P. Whipple, Hawthorne asked, "Are you a Kossuthian? I am about as enthusiastic as a lump of frozen mud, but am going to hear him at Charlestown, tomorrow, in hope of warming up a little."[10] Young Julian Hawthorne, we know, was stunned to see the great Kossuth,[11] but his father remained cool. In *The Blithedale Romance*, which he was then completing, Hawthorne revealed his sense of aloofness from political enthusiasms, or rather his halfhearted interest in them; poking fun at himself, he has Coverdale say, "Were there any cause, in this whole chaos of human struggle, worth a sane man's dying for, and which my death would benefit, then—provided, however, the effort did not involve an unreasonable amount of trouble—methinks I might be bold to offer up my life. If Kossuth, for example, would pitch the battle-field of Hungarian rights within an easy ride of my abode, and choose a mild, sunny morning, after breakfast, for the conflict, Miles Coverdale would gladly be his man, for one brave rush upon the levelled bayonets. Farther than that, I should be loth to pledge myself" (246–47).

In Hawthorne's eyes, there was something foolish about the mad rush to support Kossuth's cause and in the hyperbolic praise heaped upon him. He told Emerson that "you have said the only word that has yet been worthily spoken to Kossuth,"[12] and his reference was to Emerson's "Address to Kossuth," delivered at Concord on 11 May 1852. Kossuth came to Concord in May because of its historical importance as the site of the beginning of the American Revolution. Emerson was asked to give the welcoming address, and in it he tried to praise Kossuth without flattery and to reassure him that the debate he had inspired in the country about America's role in European affairs did not imply a lack of sympathy. After saying that Concord had "been hungry to see the man whose extraordinary eloquence is seconded by the splendor and the solidity of his actions," Emerson told him that they had "watched with attention" his progress through the country and seen how sympathy for him had stood "the test of party." With dubious logic and false divination, Emerson asserted, "As you see, the love you win is worth something; for it has been argued through; its foundations searched . . . it will last, and it will draw all opinion to itself." Calling Kossuth an "angel of freedom" who would overcome "whatever obstruction from selfishness, indifference, or from property" he might encounter, Emerson closed by claiming that Americans had all been instructed by him "in the rights and wrongs of Hungary" and were "parties already to her freedom."[13] All in all the address was appropriately complimentary, vacuous, and vague.

Kossuth's response, on the other hand, made it pointedly clear that men and arms, not sunny forecasts, were what he sought. With a worldliness that would have irritated Thoreau if he had attended the ceremony, Kossuth declared:

> I have met distinguished men trusting so much to the operative power of your institutions and of your example, that they really believe they will make their way throughout the world merely by their moral influence. But there is one thing those gentlemen have disregarded in their philanthropic reliance; and that is, that the sun never yet made its way by itself through well closed shutters and doors; they must be drawn open, that the blessed rays of the sun may get in. I have never yet heard of a despot who had yielded to the moral influence of liberty. The ground of Concord itself is an evidence of it. The doors and shutters of oppression must be opened by bayonets, that the blessed rays of your institutions may penetrate into the dark dwelling-house of oppressed humanity.[14]

After Kossuth's speech, Emerson hosted a reception for him at his house, and in later years, he referred to him as one of the great men of the age. Thoreau, disappointed by Emerson and the proceedings, wrote in his journal, "The best men that I know are not serene, a world in themselves. They dwell in form. They flatter and study effect, only more finely than the rest. . . . I accuse my finest acquaintances of an immense frivolity."[15]

The Serenity of *Walden*

Kossuth's visit to the United States and Concord brought to a head a struggle Thoreau had been engaged in for some time. During the years following the European revolutions of 1848–49, Thoreau struggled to develop his spiritual side and rid himself of what he considered a degrading interest in current events. He also tried to communicate to Emerson and the world his own capacity for heroism. After the disappointing reception of *A Week on the Concord and Merrimack Rivers* in the summer of 1849, Thoreau had become uncertain about how to proceed with his life. Setting the third draft of *Walden* aside as unpublishable, he studied Hinduism, visited Cape Cod several times, took a trip to Canada, and began his Indian book project. The next year, 1851, he started to focus his energies, and, as Lewis Leary has said, these twelve months were a watershed in his life, a time of consolidation, of self-discovery, of preparation for some important new effort.[16] "I find myself uncommonly prepared for *some* literary work . . . ," he wrote in his journal on 7 September 1851. "I am prepared not so much for contemplation, as for forceful expression" (2:467). Subsequently, 1852 became Thoreau's annus mirabilis, the year his months of living deliberately yielded a magnificent harvest. Realizing that his journal possessed an integrity and value of its own, he lavished upon it the care and craft that turned it into his richest literary achievement; he also wrote at this time most of his essay "Life Without Principle," which, as Walter Harding has observed, "contains virtually all the fundamental principles upon which he based his life";[17] and, more important, he radically revised and reshaped *Walden*, changing it from a factual account of his life in the woods into the embryo of a profound spiritual autobiography, illuminated by the idea of spiritual renewal, shaped and informed by the cycle of the seasons.[18]

The catalyst for the metamorphosis of *Walden* was Thoreau's desire to resolve, in writing if not in fact, the conflict he felt between the spiritual and the animal in himself. On the one hand, his recent communion with nature had yielded, as it had in his youth, transcendence—not of the world of material fact, but rather of the world of trivial fact. At times he achieved a state of pure spirituality in the woods. On 17 August 1851, for example, he recorded in his journal, "My heart leaps into my mouth at the sound of the wind in the woods. I, whose life was but yesterday so desultory and shallow, suddenly recover my spirits, my spirituality, through my hearing. . . . I did not despair of worthier moods, and now I have occasion to be grateful for the flood of life that is flowing over me" (2:391–92). At such times, he reexperienced the ecstasy of his youth, when, as he put it, "the morning and the evening were sweet to me, and I led a life aloof from society of men" (2:307). Despite these experiences, which he valued greatly, another aspect of Thoreau's personality cared about society, cared passionately about justice, about the actions of governments, about the fate of actual men in the nineteenth century. This part of him, however, he associated with his impure animal nature, and he sought to purge it. "I do not think much of the actual," he wrote himself. "It is something which we have long since done with. It is a sort of vomit in which the unclean love to wallow"

(*Jo*, 2:44). During the writing of the fourth version of *Walden*, which coincided with Kossuth's tour of the country, Thoreau created a myth about himself as someone who had risen above the affairs of men, someone who felt the animal dying out in him and the spiritual being established.

In *Walden*, the European revolutions of 1848–49, the reaction and reprisals that followed, all the attention given in the newspapers to Kossuth's visit, to Louis Napoleon's coup d'état, to a possible war between France and Great Britain, all these go unmentioned, and their absence reveals how earnestly, perhaps even how desperately, Thoreau sought to diminish their importance to his life. In his journals we see his fascination with and antagonism toward the news of national and international affairs. He devotes half of his essay "Life Without Principle," moreover, to a castigation of the news, telling the reader about its danger, its foulness, its profanity—even mentioning Kossuth by name and ridiculing the "stir" about him: "That excitement about Kossuth, consider how characteristic, but superficial, it was! . . . For all fruit of that stir we have the Kossuth hat."[19] In *Walden*, however, he purifies his book and his persona by ignoring contemporary world affairs. Characterizing himself (untruthfully) as one "who rarely looks into the newspapers," he claims that "nothing new does ever happen in foreign parts, a French revolution not excepted."[20]

Thoreau's struggle to achieve an oriental aloofness from the affairs of men seems to have first become a serious endeavor for him in the summer of 1850, when Emerson asked him to go to Fire Island to retrieve the body and possessions of Margaret Fuller. As Robert D. Richardson, Jr., has pointed out, "Death gave life a new imperative for Thoreau."[21] Despite Fuller's rejections of his *Dial* contributions in the early 1840s, Thoreau became her friend and admirer, and during her last summer in Concord, he took her boat riding at dawn on the river. The task he faced at Fire Island thus could not have been pleasant, yet in his journal and in letters to others, he strove to project a philosophical serenity about what he found. In a letter to his admirer H. G. O. Blake, he wrote that he had in his pocket a button torn from the coat of Count Ossoli: "Held up, it intercepts the light,—an actual button,—and yet all the life it is connected with is less substantial to me, and interests me less, than my faintest dream. Our thoughts are the epochs in our lives: all else is but as a journal of the winds that blew while we were here" (*Corr*, 265). Thoreau had not known Ossoli, so his aloof serenity here comes easily; he had known Fuller though, and his attempt to rise above the fact of her death shows strain.

When Thoreau arrived at the site of the wreck, Fuller's body had not been found, but he stayed in the area and a week later learned that something once human had washed ashore. As he approached it, he saw bones, and in the draft of his letter to Blake he asserted, "There was nothing at all remarkable about them. They were simply some bones lying on the beach.

They would not detain a walker there more than so much seaweed. I should think that the fates would not take the trouble to show me any bones again, I so slightly appreciate the favor" (*Jo*, 2:44). He recalled the experience in his journal some three months later, however, and there revealed the difficulty he had in dismissing what he had seen: "I once went in search of the relics of a human body . . . ," he wrote, "which had been cast up the day before on to the beach, though the sharks had stripped off the flesh. . . . It was as conspicuous on that sandy plain as if a generation had labored to pile up a cairn there. . . . It reigned over the shore. That dead body possessed the shore as no living one could. It showed a title to the sands which no living ruler could" (*Jo*, 2:80). Thoreau had no way of knowing whether the body was Fuller's or not, but she was surely on his mind, and her endeavor to convince others of the legitimacy of her "title" may have been as well. His description, which obviously contrasts with his earlier one, reveals the power and significance the facts possessed in his eyes. Here as always he cared too much about the human to dismiss its annihilation with convincing disdain.

During the last months of 1850 and all of 1851, Thoreau dedicated himself to living deliberately, to fronting what he called the essential. During these months, he spent many hours walking through the fields and woods of Concord, recording his observations in his journal. At the same time, he read the newspapers and found himself engaged by what he found. The political news from Europe focused upon the failure of the republican movement, the reaction and reprisals, the futile attempts by exiles such as Mazzini and Kossuth to enlist aid in the struggle for a new round of upheavals. Austria, meanwhile, charged that the United States, especially its new Secretary of State Webster, was encouraging anti-Austrian sentiment and intruding in the affairs of Europe. On 17 November 1850, Thoreau revealed both his disdain for the news of the day and his concern about its power to capture his attention: "It is a strange age of the world this, when empires, kingdoms, and republics come a-begging to our doors and utter their complaints at our elbows. I cannot take up a newspaper but I find that some wretched government or other, hard pushed and on its last legs, is interceding with me, the reader, to vote for it,—more importunate than an Italian beggar" (*Jo*, 2:101–02). At times the newspapers contributed to the problem he called "the village" (2:110), which kept him from getting to the woods in spirit, although he walked miles into it bodily. One way he tried to overcome this problem was through the process of diminution, which can be seen in the following outburst of 1 May 1851: "Nations! What are nations? Tartars! and Huns! and Chinamen! Like insects they swarm. The historian strives in vain to make them memorable. It is for want of a man that there are so many men." Quoting "The Spirit of Lodin," from which the epigraph of this chapter is taken, he claims to "look down from my height on nations, / And they become ashes before me" (*Jo*, 2:188). By adopting an Olympian point of view, Thoreau elevates himself and diminishes men both in size and importance. Like Emerson in the "Mind and Manners" lectures, he also reaffirms his belief that the regeneration of the self, the building up of the single solitary soul, is far more important than the activities of masses of men, be they parties, tribes, or nations.

Throughout 1851, as Thoreau continued to read the papers, he developed a loathing for them linked to that part of himself unable to ignore them. The news, he came to assert, could profane the "very *sanctum sanctorum*" of the mind:

> I find it so difficult to dispose of the few facts which to me are significant, that I hesitate to burden my mind with the most insignificant, which only a divine mind could illustrate. Such is, for the most part, the news,—in newspapers and conversation. It is important to preserve the mind's chastity in this respect. . . . By all manner of boards and traps, threatening the extreme penalty of the divine law, . . . it behooves us to preserve the purity and sanctity of the mind. . . . It is so hard to forget what it is worse than useless to remember. If I am to be a channel of thoroughfare, I prefer that it be of the mountain springs, and not the town sewers,—the Parnassian streams. [*Jo* 2:289–90]

In the winter of 1851–52, Thoreau's struggle to assure his own purity became obsessive. Sherman Paul has traced his dissatisfaction with himself to surveying, which Thoreau found trivial and coarsening.[22] Mary Elkins Moller has speculated that Thoreau was also having sexual fantasies about Lidian Emerson and felt ashamed of them.[23] Whatever the truth of these views (and I think the second takes Thoreau's references to chastity too literally), the fact remains that Thoreau at this time was also struggling to escape from his interest in current events. Surprisingly, this private denouncer of the press had become a subscriber to Greeley's *Weekly Tribune*, a fact that heightened the tension he felt about preserving his mind's chastity. On 20 January 1852, he wrote,

> I do not know but it is too much to read one newspaper in a week, for I now take the weekly *Tribune,* and for a few days past, it seems to me, I have not dwelt in Concord; the sun, the clouds, the snow, the trees say not so much to me. You cannot serve two masters. . . . To read the things distant and sounding betrays us into slighting these which are then apparently near and small. We learn to look abroad for our mind and spirit's daily nutriment, and what is this dull town to me? . . . All summer and far into the fall I unconsciously went by the newspapers and the news, and now I find it was because the morning and the evening were full of news to me. My walks were full of incidents. I attended not to the affairs of Europe, but to my own affairs in Concord fields. [*Jo*, 3:208]

Thoreau's quest for purity and serenity had become particularly difficult because of the excitement surrounding Kossuth's visit and the new interest

Emerson had taken in things Thoreau considered trivial, including Kossuth. The gradual estrangement of the two men may have begun while Emerson was in England in 1847–48, writing letters home for Lidian and Thoreau which were little more than catalogues of the great people he had met. Although we know this was his way of providing himself a record of his activities, it probably disappointed. After his return from Europe, Emerson had lectured throughout the country, praising England and its people, but when he engaged Thoreau in a conversation on the topic, Henry, not surprisingly, said that the English were "mere soldiers" and their business was "winding up."[24] In the summer of 1851, Emerson, unaware of the new scope and grandeur of Thoreau's journal, unaware of the growth in his spiritual development, wrote off his friend as one who "will not stick." "He is a boy," Emerson added, "& will be an old boy. Pounding beans is good to the end of pounding Empires, but not, if at the end of years, it is only beans."[25]

In a like manner, Thoreau at about this time began to see that his friend would continue to disappoint him. He bristled at Emerson's patronizing attitude; he disagreed with his treatment of Fuller in the *Memoirs;* and most of all he resented his new worldliness. In *English Traits* (1856) Emerson, drawing upon his lectures of 1848–50, would celebrate the manners of the British aristocracy and assert that "whatever tends to form manners or to finish men, has a great value. Every one who has tasted the delight of friendship will respect every social guard which our manners can establish" (187). For Thoreau, there was "something devilish in manners" (*Jo,* 3:256) that could come between friends, and writing of Emerson in the winter of 1851, he complained, "One of the best men I know often offends me by uttering made words—the very best words, of course, or dinner speeches, most smooth and gracious and fluent repartees. . . . O would you but be simple and downright! Would you but cease your palaver! It is the misfortune of being a gentleman and famous" (*Jo,* 3:141). As Joel Porte has observed, the failure of *A Week* and Emerson's "manifest success" had probably contributed to Thoreau's bitterness.[26]

In "Life Without Principle," Thoreau controverted his friend's high regard for English manners by attacking the "good breeding" of members of Parliament. "The finest manners in the world," he declared, "are awkwardness and fatuity, when contrasted with a finer intelligence. . . . It is the vice, but not the excellence of manners, that they are continually being deserted by the character." His caustic allusion to the London *Times* in "Life Without Principle" also addressed Emerson's new enthusiasms. "Read not the Times," Thoreau told his readers. "Read the Eternities. Conventionalities are at length as bad as impurities."[27] And despite the pun, he considered the matter of utmost importance.

In the early months of 1852, Kossuth's visit to Concord widened the separation between Thoreau and Emerson into a permanent gulf. As Thoreau spent more and more time communing with nature, trying to cleanse himself of what he called the "news," Emerson saw fit to criticize him for these efforts. Frustrated, Thoreau declared in his journal, "I have got to that pass with my friend that our words do not pass with each other for what they are worth. We speak in vain; there is none to hear. He finds fault with me that I walk alone, when I pine for want of a companion; that I commit my thoughts to a diary even on my walks, instead of seeking to share them generously with a friend; curses my practice even" (3:389–90). Emerson, who would soon lecture on the "Conduct of Life" in Canada and then deliver his "Address to Kossuth" in Concord, could not see the heroism in Thoreau's aloofness. Thoreau, meanwhile, who sought to become a better man through his solitary walks, felt unappreciated and frustrated. On 4 May, in an entry both defensive and immodest, he dismissed the great Kossuth and those like Emerson who honored him:

> This excitement about Kossuth is not interesting to me, it is so superficial. It is only another kind of dancing or of politics. Men are making speeches to him all over the country, but each expresses only the thought, or the want of thought, of the multitude. No man stands on truth. . . . You can pass your hand under the largest mob, a nation in revolution even, and, however solid a bulk they may make, like a hail-cloud in the atmosphere, you may not meet so much as a cobweb of support. They may not rest, even by a point, on eternal foundations. But an individual standing on truth you cannot pass your hand under, for his foundations reach to the centre of the universe. So superficial these men and their doings, it is life on a leaf or a chip which has nothing but air or water beneath. [4:15–16]

The length and tone of this entry reveals the importance of the matter to him; obviously, he considers himself the "individual standing on truth," whose depth far exceeds that of any "nation in revolution" or military hero. And one week later, during the excitement surrounding Kossuth's visit to Concord, during the afternoon of Emerson's speech and reception, Thoreau, in order to show how little he thought of these matters, entered only the following in his journal: "P.M.—*Kossuth here*" (4:45).

All of Thoreau's struggle with current events, with Kossuth's visit, with Emerson's worldliness and disesteem lay behind the important fourth version of *Walden*. As he revised and expanded his manuscript throughout 1852, Thoreau endowed his persona with a serene aloofness, creating a hero interested in eternal truths, not bayonets, a hero celebrating moral revolutions, not pointless political ones. Having discovered that "a sane and growing man revolutionizes every day" and that no "institutions of man can survive a morning experience" (*Jo*, 2:213–14), he fashioned an answer to his best friend, who thought Kossuth a great man and Henry Thoreau an unsociable boy.

As he revised *Walden*, Thoreau made major additions to the chapters

"Where I Lived and What I Lived For," "Solitude," "Visitors," "Ponds," "Baker Farm," "Higher Laws," "Brute Neighbors," "Spring," and "Conclusion."[28] The thrust of almost all of these additions is to show how nature, which is holy and heroic, can bestow those virtues on one who practices chastity. His central statement on chastity was added, of course, to "Higher Laws" and asserts that "we are conscious of an animal in us, which awakens in proportion as our higher nature slumbers. . . . Chastity is the flowering of man; and what are called Genius, Heroism, Holiness, and the like, are but various fruits which succeed it. Man flows at once to God when the channel of purity is open. . . . He is blessed who is assured that the animal is dying out in him day by day, and the divine being established" (219–20). Not surprisingly, Thoreau presents himself as having achieved this assuredness. He is among the blessed.

The chastity Thoreau has in mind is as much intellectual as physical, and to attain it one must abstain not merely from sexual intercourse but also from trivial thoughts and interests. In his addition to "Solitude" he explains the process it involves: "By a conscious effort of the mind we can stand aloof from actions and their consequences; and all things, good and bad, go by us like a torrent." The result is a feeling of doubleness, whereby a person "may be either a drift-wood in the stream, or Indra in the sky looking down on it." He admits that "this doubleness may easily make us poor neighbors and friends sometimes" (134–35), but he makes it clear that it is worth the price. In "The Ponds" he adds paragraphs stressing the "serenity and purity" of Walden and suggests a correspondence between it and himself. "Many men have been likened to it," he writes, "but few deserve that honor" (192). That he has earned the honor through his way of life is a point made repeatedly. In his addition to "Baker Farm," Thoreau highlights the blessedness which communion with nature has accorded him. Like Whitman's persona in "Crossing Brooklyn Ferry," or more recently Loren Eisley's star thrower, Thoreau's hero becomes literally illuminated by nature. He stands one day at the base "of a rainbow's arch, which filled the lower stratum of the atmosphere, tinging the grass and leaves around, and dazzling [him] as if [he] looked through colored crystal." To emphasize the religious implications of the experience, he adds, "As I walked on the railroad causeway, I used to wonder at the halo of light around my shadow, and would fain fancy myself one of the elect" (202). In the additions to the "Conclusion," Thoreau makes explicit the successful effort to achieve spiritual renewal through aloofness. "I delight to come to my bearings,—" he declares, "not walk in procession with pomp and parade, in a conspicuous place, but to walk even with the Builder of the universe, if I may,—not to live in this restless, nervous, bustling, trivial Nineteenth Century, but stand or sit thoughtfully while it goes by" (329–30).

The place he would sit, of course, is far above men and their doings, which diminishes them in his eyes. And this particular view is the one dramatized in his most famous addition, the classic battle of the ants in "Brute Neighbors." The episode comes from an entry made in his journal on 22 January 1852, while Kossuth was visiting Washington and while Greeley in his *Tribune* and James Watson Webb in his *Courier and Enquirer* were debating the nature of the Hungarian War. Thoreau, like most of his contemporaries, found himself engaged (against his will, however) by what Stowe called "the great controversy now going on in the world between the despotic and the republican principle," and this is why he associates the two tribes of warring ants with the European revolutionary scene and calls them "the red republicans and the black despots or imperialists" (*Jo*, 3:210). His description of their war has become famous because of its frequent use in anthologies, and Raymond Adams is surely right when he says that one reason for its selection is that it is "easily taken from its context." Adams errs though in adding that "it is an episode that hardly has so much as a context."[29] By virtue of both its hidden connection to revolutionary Europe and its subtle connection to the theme of spiritual serenity, the episode is part of larger contexts that shaped its features.

As Thoreau describes the battle of the ants, he reveals that side of his personality engaged by physical heroism in the actual world. The ferocity and resolve of the combatants, the mutilation and gore that attend their life-and-death struggle thoroughly engage him. "I felt for the rest of that day," he admits, "as if I had had my feelings excited and harrowed by witnessing the struggle, the ferocity and carnage, of a human battle before my door" (231). On the other hand, through the use of the mock-heroic, Thoreau generates an irony that allows him to stress once more the spiritual side of his persona, the side that dismisses politics, revolutions, and wars as trivial. The mother of a single red ant, we are told, had charged her son "to return with his shield or upon it," and the fighting ants, the narrator speculates, could, not to his surprise, have "had their respective musical bands stationed on some eminent chip, and playing their national airs the while, to excite the slow and cheer the dying combatants" (230). With such irony Thoreau diminishes the importance, not of the ants, but of the men they resemble.[30] Just as he claimed that Kossuth and his American admirers were involved in "life on a leaf or a chip," he here brings the metaphor to life and makes the same statement about warring nations. The purpose of this addition, and of his others, is to show that true heroism is associated with aloof serenity, not brutal warfare.

When Thoreau revised his journal entry for inclusion in *Walden*, he claimed the ant battle occurred "in the Presidency of Polk, five years before the passage of Webster's Fugitive-Slave Bill" (232), thus making it contemporaneous with his stay at the pond and registering his criticism, as he had in "Civil Disobedience," of the Mexican War. Ultimately, the issue of slavery disturbed him far more than revolution in Europe, and he found it difficult to resist the temptation to speak out against it. In later versions of *Walden*, Thoreau expanded upon the ideas he introduced in 1852, extending his treatment of the triumph of the spiritual over the animal and filling out his account of the progress of the seasons, which, of course, complements the theme of renewal.[31] Meanwhile, paradoxically, he remained a deeply passionate man, more engaged than others of his acquaintance by the "trivial Nineteenth Century." When the slave Anthony Burns was arrested in 1854, Thoreau, burning with rage, publicly denounced the Massachusetts authorities in his inflammatory "Slavery in Massachusetts": "I walk toward one of our ponds," he thundered, "but what signifies the beauty of nature when men are base? . . . Who can be serene in a country where both the rulers and the ruled are without principle? The remembrance of my country spoils my walk. My thoughts are murder to the State, and involuntarily go plotting against her."[32] Five years later, of course, he stepped forward to defend John Brown more ardently and persuasively than anyone else in the country. Clearly then, in 1852, when Thoreau endowed the persona of *Walden* with remarkable purity and serenity, he was mythologizing himself; he was, in response to the "*tintinnabulum* from without" (*Walden*, 329), creating a new kind of hero for a revolutionary age.

Epilogue

> It seems an inconsistency to assert unconditional democracy in all things, and yet confess a dislike to all mankind—in the mass. But not so.
>
> —MELVILLE, Letter to Hawthorne (June 1851)

Political issues and events have an inherent power to excite the emotions and stir the imagination, and, as the preceding eight chapters have attempted to show, the revolutions of 1848–49 did both. Emerson, though at first and last disdainful of the revolutions, could not resist their impact; they challenged the individualism he held so dear, made him rethink his growing attachment to men of status and power, and inspired him to articulate in new form the idealism at the center of his spiritual life. Fuller, under the influence of the revolutions, indeed in the midst of one, achieved her greatest success as a writer. Her *Tribune* dispatches, written in the polemical tradition of Jefferson and Paine, show an insight, control, and passion that make them a remarkable record of a failed revolution. Hawthorne and Melville, while regarding the revolutions skeptically, were moved to incorporate into their masterpieces the imagery, issues, and characters gaining public attention around them. Whitman, inspired by the heroic fight for liberty he covered as editor, celebrated the martyred revolutionaries in his poetry and reconceived himself as a poet of insurrection and revolt. Finally, Thoreau, as we have just seen, responded to the residual excitement about the revolutions by redefining heroism for his age and showing the praise due an oriental hero in the midst of a tumultuous Western world.

Of all the writers discussed in this study, Fuller alone had the opportunity, the inclination, and ultimately the resolve to align herself wholeheartedly with European democratic liberalism. Although F. O. Matthiessen has declared that "the one common denominator" of the five major writers of the American renaissance was "their devotion to the possibilities of democracy,"[1] this study makes clear that at midcentury these writers shared a personal conservatism that made them far from devoted to the struggle for freedom and equality in Europe in 1848–49. Emerson's conservatism and Thoreau's took the form of commitment to spiritual elitism, which encouraged them to remain aloof from the political affairs of men. Emerson relented only when it came to what he considered great men.

Whitman, although radical certainly as a poet, maintained a hostile attitude toward actual, as opposed to imaginary, radicalism. Although the idea of revolution fascinated him, when it translated into new governments, new laws, new social programs, he recoiled from it. As Asselineau has shown, there was in Whitman's character the conservatism of his roots: "Much as he approved of Rousseau's declarations on the fundamental equality of all men beyond racial differences, he nevertheless continued to behave and to react like a Long Island peasant whose grandparents had owned slaves."[2] Melville and Hawthorne likewise inherited the conservatism of their families, but it was the patrician strain that made them value hierarchical order and distrust democratic leveling. Moreover, their "Calvinistic sense of Innate Depravity,"[3] as Melville called it, made them skeptical of any attempts to reform society through radical action.

Having said the above, I must now add that in their literary works all of these writers go far beyond any political label such as "conservative" that one would attach to their personal views. Just as Whitman became that marvelous persona who declares himself "the sworn poet of every dauntless rebel the world over," so too did Hawthorne and Melville in the act of creating revolutionary characters on the order of Hester and Ahab reveal their unconscious attraction to heroic insurrection and revolt. Once they entered their fictional worlds, they transcended their quotidian beliefs and opinions and evidenced a loving empathy for their creations. No one can read *The Scarlet Letter* without sensing Hawthorne's deep admiration for Hester, which runs counter to his judgment of her. No one can read *Moby-Dick* without understanding what Melville meant when he said he had written a wicked book yet felt spotless as a lamb. Ahab's rebellion against the kingdom of whatever god rules the universe was surely Melville's as he wrote, just as it becomes ours as we read. With Thoreau and *Walden*, we have a similar process moving in the opposite direction. Thoreau not only appreciated angry, defiant rebellion; he practiced it. And yet this latent anarchist, this ardent defender of an insane murderer, became the serene and detached narrator of *Walden*. As Albert Rothenberg has documented, the creative process, practiced at the highest levels, involves not only conscious intent but also unconscious anxieties and desires. These are uncovered during the act of creation as the artist struggles toward psychological freedom.[4]

The literary radicalism of American renaissance writers, which often runs counter to their personal conservatism, has been discussed by a number of critics, many of whom have taken a doctrinaire approach and interpreted the literature to advance Marxist political agendas. Obviously, many of the findings of this study call into question the historical validity of such supposedly historicist studies.[5] Certainly the works of Emerson, Hawthorne, Melville, Whitman, and Thoreau can be viewed as representing radical resistance to the "hegemonic forces" of American industrial capitalism; nevertheless, they also reflect, much more than has been acknowledged, the middle-class values of nineteenth-century American society, especially as they react to authentic, life-and-death radicalism in action. As Raymond Williams has brilliantly explained, the hegemonic is an inescapable system of meanings and values that saturates the whole process of living, which for artists, of course, includes their creative efforts. "The most interesting and difficult part of any cultural analysis, in complex societies," Williams has also pointed out, "is that which seeks to grasp the hegemonic in its active and formative but also its transformational processes. Works of art, by their substantial and general character, are often especially important as sources of this complex evidence."[6] The critic who has best grasped the transformational effects of the hegemonic as evidenced in the works of the American renaissance is Sacvan Bercovitch, whose theoretical model featuring the American "ritual of consensus" accords well with my own particular findings. Bercovitch has shown how the writers of the American renaissance were both radical and conservative as they drew upon the American ideology to "redefine radicalism as an affirmation of cultural values."[7] As he explains in his "Epilogue" to *The American Jeremiad* (1978),

> To be American for our classic writers was by definition to be radical—to turn against the past, to defy the status quo and become an agent of change. And at the same time to be radical as an American was to transmute the revolutionary impulse in some basic sense: by spiritualizing it (as in *Walden*), by diffusing or deflecting it (as in *Leaves of Grass*), by translating it into a choice between blasphemy and regeneration (as in *Moby-Dick*), or most generally by accommodating it to society. . . . In every case, "America" resolved a conflict of values by reconciling personal, national, and cultural ideals.[8]

Although Bercovitch's work emphasizes the national and cultural features of the transmuting process, the results of the present study suggest that the writers of the American renaissance, at least as they reacted and responded to radicalism abroad, were primarily involved in elaborate processes of personal self-justification. Emerson, returning to the idealism of his early career, reemphasized the aloof seer as the true revolutionist in order to assert his superiority to the potent revolutionary activists of the times. "Archimedes buried himself in his geometry," he reminded himself, "when Marcellus or Demetrius were battering down their walls."[9] Thoreau essentially strove for the same position, but in his case he felt himself and his values in competition with a particular revolutionary hero, whose acclaim precipitated the "spiritualizing" in *Walden*. Fuller, caught up in a desperate political situation, assumed in her writing the role of Liberty leading the People to ennoble herself and her cause, while Hawthorne, on the other hand, after his ouster from the custom house, represented himself, with encouragement from the times, as a victim of a revolutionary mob and created in Hester a beautiful and heroic counterpart who remained sympathetic until her latent subversiveness emerged. Melville, too, while responding to the spirit of the times with the sky-assaulting Ahab, showed his personal opposition to, and power over, this spirit by detailing the sweeping destruction accompanying his protagonist's rebellion. Finally, Whitman, like Hawthorne, discovered that the role of martyr, suggested by events in Europe, not only suited his strongest feelings but allowed him to triumph morally and vicariously over the absolutism he hated. Although certainly the American past, particularly its revolutionary tradition, suggested to these writers how "the revolutionary impulse" could be "co-opted" to elevate the self and affirm American cultural values, it is important to notice that at midcentury the impulse itself surfaced in full, life-threatening force in Europe not America, and that while it stirred and provoked the American literary mind, its origins were foreign and social, not native and personal. Moreover, in the cases of all but Fuller, the personal took precedence over the social in the process of "co-optation" that resulted. A glorification of the undervalued individual, not of the American way, remained primary as these authors fashioned their artful representations.

Notes

Preface

1   F. O. Matthiessen, *American Renaissance: Art and Expression in the Age of Emerson and Whitman* (New York: Oxford, 1941), p. vii.
2   Larry J. Reynolds, "*The Scarlet Letter* and Revolutions Abroad," *American Literature* 57 (March 1985): 44–67 and "1848 and the Origins of *Leaves of Grass*," *American Transcendental Quarterly* 1 (December 1987): 291–99.

Chapter 1. Revolution and Response

1   Henry David Thoreau, *Reform Papers*, ed. Wendell Glick (Princeton: Princeton Univ. Press, 1973), p. 67.
2   Margaret Fuller, *Life Without and Life Within*, ed. Arthur B. Fuller (1860; rpt. Upper Saddle River, N.J.: Literature House/Gregg Press, 1970), p. 212; Friedrich Engels, *Brusseler Zeitung*, 23 January 1848, quoted in *Birth of the Communist "Manifesto": With Full Text of the "Manifesto," All Prefaces by Marx and Engels, Early Drafts by Engels and Other Supplementary Material*, ed. Dirk J. Struik (New York: International, 1971), p. 49.
3   Karl Marx, *Manifesto of the Communist Party*, trans. Samuel Moore, rev. and ed. Friedrich Engels, 1888; rpt. *Birth of the Communist "Manifesto*," p. 125.
4   R. B. Rose, "Louis Blanc: The Collapse of a Hero," in *Intellectuals and Revolution: Socialism and the Experience of 1848*, ed. Eugene Kamenka and F. B. Smith (1979; rpt. New York: St. Martin's Press, 1980), pp. 35–38.
5   Alexis de Tocqueville, *Recollections*, trans. George Lawrence, ed. J. P. Mayer and A. P. Kerr (1893; Garden City, N.Y.: Doubleday, 1970), pp. 13–14.
6   Useful summaries of European events can be found in: *The Opening of an Era: 1848*, ed. François Fejtö (New York: Howard Fertig, 1966); Peter N. Stearns, *1848: The Revolutionary Tide in Europe* (New York: Norton, 1974); Maurice

Agulhon, *The Republican Experiment, 1848–1852*, trans. Janet Lloyd (1973; Cambridge: Cambridge Univ. Press, 1983); and Charles Breunig, *The Age of Revolution and Reaction, 1789–1850* (New York: Norton, 1970).

7   New York *Tribune*, 13 March 1848, p. 1.

8   Thoreau, *Reform Papers*, p. 77.

9   *The Letters of Queen Victoria*, ed. Arthur Christopher Benson and Viscount Esher, 3 vols. (London: John Murray, 1907), 2:196.

10 Maurice Chazin discusses Emerson's influence upon Quinet, Michelet, and Mickiewicz in "Quinet, an Early Discoverer of Emerson," *PMLA* 48 (1933): 147–63.

11 Daniel Stern, *Histoire de la Révolution de 1848* (1850; 3d ed., Paris: Librarie Internationale, 1853), pp. 52–53.

12 According to Stearns, *1848*, pp. 20–28, the key urban protest group came from the ranks of the artisans.

13 See William Cullen Bryant, *Letters of a Traveller, or Notes of Things Seen in Europe and America* (New York: Putnam, 1851); Caroline Kirkland, *Holidays Abroad; or Europe from the West*, 2 vols. (New York: Baker and Scribner, 1849).

14 See Christopher Pearse Cranch, "The Bird and the Bell," in *Collected Poems*, ed. Joseph M. DeFalco (Gainesville, Fl.: Scholars' Facsimiles & Reprints, 1971), pp. 1–22; William Wetmore Story, "Giannone," in *Poems* (1856; enlarged ed., 2 vols., Boston: Houghton, Mifflin, 1886), 2:78–104.

15 See James Freeman Clarke, *Eleven Weeks in Europe; and What May Be Seen in that Time* (Boston: Ticknor, Reed and Fields, 1852); William Ware, *Sketches of European Capitals* (Boston: Phillips, Sampson, and Company, 1851).

16 Gordon Milne, *George William Curtis & the Genteel Tradition* (Bloomington: Indiana Univ. Press, 1956), p. 41.

17 Elizabeth Robins Pennell, *Charles Godfrey Leland: A Biography* (1906; rpt. Freeport, N.Y.: Books for Libraries Press, 1970), pp. 135–36.

18 Nathalia Wright discusses this novel in *American Novelists in Italy* (Philadelphia: Univ. of Pennsylvania Press, 1965), pp. 78–82.

19 New York *Herald*, 3 April 1848, p. 1. Goodrich reprinted this letter in his *Recollections of a Lifetime; or Men and Things I Have Seen* (1857; rpt. Detroit: Gale Research, 1967), pp. 451–71.

20 New York *Herald*, 3 April 1848, p. 1.

21 Ibid.

22 Letter to Evert Duyckinck, 5 March 1848, Duyckinck Family Papers; Rare Books and Manuscripts Division; New York Public Library; Astor, Lenox and Tilden Foundations.

23 This scene is described in Priscilla Robertson, *Revolutions of 1848* (Princeton: Princeton Univ. Press, 1952), p. 36.

24 *The Life and Letters of George Bancroft*, ed. Mark Anthony DeWolfe Howe (1908; rpt. New York: Da Capo Press, 1970), 2:31.

25 Letter to Evert Duyckinck, 5 March 1848.

26 Ibid.

27 Ibid.

28 Evert Duyckinck, Letter to George Duyckinck, 18 March 1848, Duyckinck Family Papers; New York Public Library.

29 New York *Herald*, 19 March, 1848; see also, New York *Tribune*, 20 March 1848; Richmond *Enquirer*, 31 March, 7 April 1848; Washington, *National Intelligencer*, 27 March 1848; Portland *Transcript*, 1 April, 29 April, 1848; New Orleans *Crescent*, 1 April 1848; Boston *Post*, 3 April 1848; Scioto *Gazette*, 5 April 1848; *American Quarterly Register and Magazine*, May 1848; *American Review*, June 1848; *Brownson's Quarterly Review*, July 1848.

30 Quoted in *Stryker's American Quarterly Register and Magazine* 1 (September 1848): 517.

31 New York *Evening Post*, 29 March 1848, p. 2; New York *Tribune*, 21 March 1848, p. 2.

32 Quoted in H. T. Tuckerman, *The Life of John Pendleton Kennedy* (New York: G. P. Putnam, 1871), pp. 407–08.

33 Letter to George Duyckinck, 3 April 1848, Duyckinck Family Papers, New York Public Library.

34 *Life and Letters of Bayard Taylor*, ed. Marie Hansen-Taylor and Horace E. Scudder, 2 vols (Boston: Houghton Mifflin, 1884), 1:123–24.

35 Tuckerman, *Life of Kennedy*, p. 407.

36 *America in the Forties: The Letters of Ole Munch Raeder*, trans. and ed. Gunnar J. Malmin (Minneapolis: Univ. of Minnesota Press, 1929), p. 169.

37 Merrell R. Davis, *Melville's "Mardi": A Chartless Voyage* (1952; rpt. Hamden, Conn: Archon Books, 1967), pp. 79–99, discusses the growth of this stage of the book. See also, Watson Branch, "The Etiology of *Mardi*," *Philological Quarterly* 64 (1985):2–19.

38 Herman Melville, *Mardi: And a Voyage Thither*, ed. Harrison Hayford, Hershel Parker, and G. Thomas Tanselle (Evanston, Ill.: Northwestern Univ. Press, 1970), p. 524. Hereafter cited parenthetically.

39 See R. T. Clark, "The German Liberals in New Orleans, 1840–1860," *Louisiana Historical Quarterly* (January 1927):137–38.

40 New Orleans *Crescent*, 31 March 1848, p. 2.

41 New Orleans *Crescent*, 17 April 1848, p. 3.

42 Joseph Jay Rubin, *The Historic Whitman* (University Park: Pennsylvania State Univ. Press, 1973), pp. 197–201, discusses Whitman's response to the news from abroad in the spring of 1848.

43 Boston *Post*, 27 May 1848, p. 2; *Literary World* 3 (15 April 1848): 206.

44 *The Letters of Henry Wadsworth Longfellow*, ed. Andrew Hilen, vol. 3, 1844–1856 (Cambridge, Mass.: Belknap Press of Harvard Univ. Press, 1972), 171, 168.

45 *The Life and Letters of George Bancroft*, 2:31, 33.

46 *The Letters of John Greenleaf Whittier*, ed. John B. Pickard, vol. 3, 1846–1860 (Cambridge: Belknap Press of Harvard Univ. Press, 1975), 102; *The Complete Poetical Works of Whittier*, Cambridge Edition (Boston: Houghton Mifflin, 1894), p. 309.

47 *The Poetical Works of James Russell Lowell*, Cambridge Edition (Boston: Houghton Mifflin, 1978), pp. 92, 94.

48 See Leon Howard, *Victorian Knight-Errant: A Study of the Early Literary Career of James Russell Lowell* (Berkeley: Univ. of California Press, 1952), pp. 244–49.

49 See Eugene N. Curtis, "American Opinion of French Nineteenth Century Rev-
    olutions," *American Historical Review* 29 (October 1923–July 1924): 249–70.
50 *The Works of John C. Calhoun*, ed. Richard K. Cralle, vol. 4, *Speeches* (1851–
    56; rpt. New York: Russell & Russell, 1968), p. 452; New Orleans *Crescent*, 11
    April 1848, p. 2.
51 *The Letters of James Kirke Paulding*, ed. Ralph M. Aderman (Madison: Univ.
    of Wisconsin Press, 1962), pp. 476–77.
52 "The French Republic," *Southern Quarterly Review* 14 (July 1848): 233. See
    also, Savannah *Republican*, 4 April, 1848.
53 Lowell, *Poetical Works*, pp. 201, 199.
54 *The Writings and Speeches of Daniel Webster*, 18 vols. (Boston: Little Brown,
    1903), 18:280.
55 Edward L. Pierce, *Memoirs and Letters of Charles Sumner*, vol. 3, 1845–1860
    (Boston: Robert Bros., 1893), p. 37.
56 See esp. "The Revolutions in Europe," *North American Review* 67 (July 1848):
    194–240; "The Revolution in Prussia," *North American Review* 68 (January
    1849): 220–60; "French Ideas of Democracy and a Community of Goods," *North
    American Review* 69 (October 1849): 277–325; "Foreign Miscellany," *American
    Whig Review* 1 (May 1848): 537–41; "Societary Theories," *American Whig Re-
    view* 1 (June 1848): 632–46; and "French Revolution: M Louis Blanc," *American
    Whig Review* 2 (July 1848): 90–100.
57 Among the European nobility, the usage was the same. Prince John of Saxony,
    for example, who would endure a revolution in his own country in May of 1849,
    defined for his American friend George Ticknor one cause for the "crisis" in
    Europe: "The anarchical party, or party of the red republicans, composed of a
    great part of the proletaires, of some men of broken fortunes, who like revolu-
    tions for revolutions sake, and of the disciples of communism and socialism."
    Life, Letters, and Journals of George Ticknor, vol. 2 (Boston: Osgood, 1876), p.
    237.
58 See Oscar Hammen, *The Red '48ers: Karl Marx and Friedrich Engels* (New
    York: Scribner, 1969), pp. 200–05.
59 Robertson, *Revolutions of 1848*, pp. 61–64.
60 New York *Courier and Enquirer*, 1 April 1848, p. 2; *The Life of George Ban-
    croft*, 2:87–88.
61 New York *Herald*, 29 March 1849, p. 1; Eugene Lies, "Lamartine," *Sartain's
    Union Magazine* 5 (July 1849): 25–30; Park Benjamin, "Lamartine's Thoughts on
    Poetry," *Southern Literary Messenger* 14 (October 1848): 605–06; "Alphonse de
    Lamartine," New York *Tribune*, 6 April 1848, p. 2; New York *Evening Post*, 23
    June 1849, p. 1; *The Knickerbocker Magazine* 33 (June 1849): 557; *The Diary of
    George Templeton Strong*, 2 vols., ed. Allan Nevins and Milton Halsey Thomas
    (New York: Macmillan, 1952), 1:344.
62 17 May 1848, p. 2.
63 Brooklyn *Daily Eagle*, 10 August 1847, quoted in Floyd Stovall, *The Fore-
    ground of "Leaves of Grass"* (Charlottesville: Univ. of Virginia Press, 1974), p.
    123; New Orleans *Crescent*, 16 March 1848, p. 2; *Crescent*, 18 May 1848, p. 2.
64 *The Life and Letters of George Bancroft*, 2:57–58, 2:94–95; Tocqueville, *Rec-
    ollections*, p. 111.

65 Alphonse de Lamartine, *History of the French Revolution of 1848*, trans. Francis A. Durivage and William S. Chase, 2 vols. (1854; New York: AMS Press, 1973), 1:111, 113.
66 *Sartain's Union Magazine* 4 (January 1849): 4.
67 New Orleans *Crescent*, 27 April 1848, p. 1.
68 *Blackwood's* 63 (June 1848): 767.
69 For an able discussion of the influence of the 1848 revolution upon the contemporary visual arts in France, see T. J. Clark, *The Absolute Bourgeois: Artists and Politics in France 1848–1851* (Greenwich, Conn: New York Graphic Society, 1973).

Chapter 2. Emerson and "The Movement"

1   Townsend Scudder III, "A Chronological List of Emerson's Lectures on His British Lecture Tour of 1847–1848," *PMLA* 51 (1936): 243.
2   *The Journals and Miscellaneous Notebooks of Ralph Waldo Emerson* (hereafter abbreviated *JMN*), vol 10, 1847–1848, ed. Merton M. Sealts, Jr. (Cambridge, Mass: Belknap Press of Harvard Univ. Press, 1973), p. 154.
3   John C. Gerber, "Emerson and the Political Economists," *New England Quarterly* 22 (September 1949): 352.
4   See *The Early Lectures of Ralph Waldo Emerson*, vol. 3, 1838–1842, ed. Robert E. Spiller and Wallace E. Williams (Cambridge, Mass: Belknap Press of Harvard Univ. Press, 1972), pp. 186–87, 199.
5   *The Letters of Ralph Waldo Emerson*, ed. Ralph L. Rusk, vol. 4, 1848–1855 (New York: Columbia Univ. Press, 1939), p. 15.
6   Houghton Library lectures MS, 200 (1), leaves 3, 38A, 34. See also, *The Complete Works of Ralph Waldo Emerson*, ed. Edward Waldo Emerson, 12 vols. (1903–04; rpt. New York: AMS Press, 1968), vol. 10, *Lectures and Biographical Sketches*, pp. 31, 35.
7   *Letters of Emerson*, 4:27.
8   *JMN*, 10:296, 310.
9   *JMN*, 10:312, 318. He would later incorporate this latter entry into "Natural Aristocracy"; see Emerson, *Complete Works*, 10:47.
10 *JMN*, 10:310.
11 Carlyle, who was Emerson's unofficial host during his stay in London, took a perverse delight in how the French revolution of 1848 was frightening the British aristocracy. At this point in his life, however, Carlyle was no friend of democracy. As an ultraconservative, he viewed 1848 as "one of the most singular, disastrous, amazing, and on the whole humiliating years the European world ever saw. Not since the irruption of the Northern Barbarians has there been the like. Everywhere immeasurable Democracy rose monstrous, loud, blatant, inarticulate as the voice of Chaos" ("The Present Time," in *Latter-Day Pamphlets*, ed. Thomas Carlyle [1853; rpt. Freeport, New York: Books for Libraries Press, 1972], p. 32).
12 *JMN*, 10:239.
13 Houghton Library MS, 201 (7), leaf 2.
14 *Letters of Emerson*, 4:38, 31.

180 NOTES TO PAGES 28–37

15 Emerson, *Complete Works,* vol. 5, *English Traits,* p. 270.
16 *Letters of Emerson,* 4:39, 31.
17 Rpt. New York *Herald,* 30 April 1848, p. 1.
18 Emerson, *Complete Works,* 5:264.
19 *Harbinger,* rpt. New York *Tribune,* 8 May 1849, p. 1.
20 New Orleans *Crescent,* 9 May 1848, p. 2; New York *Tribune,* 24 July 1849, p. 1.
21 London *Times,* 22 July 1849, p. 5.
22 While in Liverpool in 1839, Melville probably heard a Chartist harangue a crowd (William H. Gilman, *Melville's Early Life and "Redburn"* [1951; rpt. New York: Russell & Russell, 1972], p. 7). He apparently drew upon this experience in *Redburn* as he has his protagonist listen to the speech of a "pale, hollow-eyed" young Chartist who he speculates is "some despairing elder son, supporting by hard toil his mother and his sisters; for of such many political desperadoes are made" (*Redburn,* ed. Harrison Hayford, Hershel Parker, and G. Thomas Tanselle [Evanston, Ill.: Northwestern Univ. Press, 1969], p. 206). As Gilman points out, Melville's comment "is interesting for its mingling of human sympathy and political conservatism" (p. 141). The comment is probably more indicative of Melville's current (1849) outlook than of his past (1839) one.
23 An excellent recent study of this uprising is David J. V. Jones's *The Last Rising: The Newport Insurrection of 1839* (Oxford: Clarendon Press, 1985).
24 Houghton Library lecture MS, 201 (7), leaf 3; *JMN,* 10:325.
25 "What is life but the angle of vision?" he would ask in his lecture "Powers and Laws of Thought" (Emerson, *Complete Works,* vol. 12, *Natural History of Intellect,* p. 10).
26 *Letters of Emerson,* 4:74.
27 Rpt. New York *Tribune,* 8 May 1848, p. 1.
28 T. Wemyss Reid, *Life of the Right Honourable William Edward Forster,* 2d ed., 2 vols. (London: Chapman and Hall, 1888), 1:236–37.
29 *Letters of Emerson,* 4:73, 73–74.
30 *Letters of Emerson,* 4:73; *JMN,* 10:323.
31 *JMN,* 10:319.
32 Houghton Library lecture MS, 200 (8), leaves 77–78.
33 *JMN,* 10:327, 324; *Letters of Emerson,* 4:76–77.
34 *JMN,* 10:325–26.
35 *Letters of Emerson,* 4:63; *JMN,* 10:310.
36 *Letters of Emerson,* 4:78, 80.
37 He later revised these three lectures for a course in philosophy at Harvard in 1870–71. As Sherman Paul has pointed out, Emerson's stated desire to teach students "to appreciate *the miracle of the mind*" was "an aim that had absorbed the full span of his life" (*Emerson's Angle of Vision* [Cambridge: Harvard Univ. Press, 1952], p. 87).
38 Townsend Scudder III discusses the context and reception of these lectures in "Emerson in London and the London Lectures," *American Literature* 8 (March 1936): 22–36.
39 *JMN,* 10:328.
40 Stephen E. Whicher has emphasized the "unusually large gap, even a contradiction, between [Emerson's] teachings and his experience. He taught self-

reliance and felt self-distrust, worshipped reality and knew illusion, proclaimed freedom and submitted to fate. No one has expected more of man; few have found him less competent" ("Emerson's Tragic Sense," 1953; rpt. *Emerson: A Collection of Critical Essays,* ed. Milton Konvitz and Stephen E. Whicher [Englewood Cliffs, N.J.: Prentice-Hall, 1962], p. 39).

41   Phyllis Cole "Emerson, England, and Fate," in *Emerson: Prophecy, Metamorphosis, and Influence,* ed. David Levin (New York: Columbia Univ. Press, 1975), pp. 83–105.

42   Quoted in Ralph L. Rusk, *The Life of Ralph Waldo Emerson* (New York: Columbia Univ. Press, 1949), p. 358.

43   *Letters of Emerson,* 4:48.

44   *The Complete Prose Works of Matthew Arnold,* ed. R. H. Super, vol. 10, *Philistinism in England and America* (Ann Arbor: Univ. of Michigan Press, 1974), p. 167.

45   David Robinson has labeled and discussed this voice in *Apostle of Culture: Emerson as Preacher and Lecturer* (Philadelphia: Univ. of Pennsylvania Press, 1982), pp. 176–79.

46   Gay Wilson Allen points out that Emerson's "lectures on England, London, and the manners of his contemporary world might seem to indicate that he had turned from Neoplatonic speculation to the realities of his everyday world, and he was moving in that direction as he struggled ever harder to earn money to pay his taxes and support his family. But his continued ambition to anatomize the mind shows that he had not become a *nominalist* in any philosophical sense" (*Waldo Emerson* [New York: Viking, 1981], p. 523).

47   Ibid., p. 509.

48   Emerson, "Notes," *Complete Works,* 5:380.

49   Quoted in James Elliot Cabot, *A Memoir of Ralph Waldo Emerson,* 2 vols. (Boston: Houghton Mifflin, 1887), 2:558.

50   Houghton Library MS, 200 (3), leaves 39–40, 33, 46.

51   A reporter for *Jerrold's Newspaper* summarized this and the other lectures in the series; his 1848 article is reprinted in Kenneth Walter Cameron, *Emerson among His Contemporaries; A Harvest of Estimates, Insights, and Anecdotes from the Victorian Literary World* (Hartford: Transcendental Books, 1967), pp. 20–24.

52   Houghton Library MS, 200 (9), leaves 19, 45.

53   Houghton Library MS, 200 (8), leaf 81.

54   Scudder, "Emerson in London," p. 30.

55   Houghton Library MS, 200 (2), leaf 15; see also, *The Complete Works,* 10:52.

56   Emerson, "Notes," *Complete Works,* 5:367.

57   See the early and late versions of the lecture, Houghton Library MSS, 200 (2) and 200 (1).

58   *JMN,* 10:310. Because of complaints about the high admission price for the Portman Square lectures (one guinea for the series), Emerson gave an additional three lectures, at moderate prices, in Exeter Hall before the "Metropolitan Early Closing Association." On 26 June, he also delivered a seventh discourse at Portman Square on "The Superlative in Manners and Literature."

59   *Letters of Emerson,* 4:80.

60 Quoted in Scudder, "Emerson in London," pp. 29-30.
61 See Scudder's "Emerson in London," pp. 35-36, and his *The Lonely Wayfaring Man: Emerson and Some Englishmen* (London: Oxford Univ. Press, 1936), pp. 154-67. William J. Sowder makes the same point in *Emerson's Impact on the British Isles and Canada* (Charlottesville: Univ. Press of Virginia, 1966), pp. 63, 67-68.
62 Quoted in Scudder, "Emerson in London," p. 35.
63 *Letters of Emerson*, 4:75; Houghton Library MS, 200 (8), leaves 95, 101; Thoreau, *Reform Papers*, p. 72.
64 Emerson, "Notes," *Complete Works*, 5:397-98.
65 Emerson, *Complete Works*, 5:287; *JMN*, 10:255.
66 Emerson, *Complete Works*, 5:82.

Chapter 3. The "Red Revolution"

1   See Stearns, *1848*, p. 92.
2   Georges Bourgin, "France and the Revolution of 1848," in Fejtö, *The Opening of an Era*, pp. 92-93.
3   New York *Courier and Enquirer*, 14 July 1848, p. 1.
4   Ik Marvel, *The Battle Summer: Being Transcripts from Personal Observation in Paris, During the Year 1848* (New York: Charles Scribner, 1849), pp. v-vi. Despite the book's title and subtitle, it deals only with events in France prior to Mitchell's arrival there in June 1848. A planned second volume was never written because of the harsh reviews the first received.
5   Quoted in James Harrison Wilson, *The Life of Charles A. Dana* (New York: Harper & Bros., 1907), p. 62.
6   See New York *Tribune*, 14 July 1848, p. 2. My guess is that Dana got in touch with the staff of *Démocratie Pacifique*, the Fourierist Paris newspaper. At the newspaper office he would have run into his American friend and supporter Albert Brisbane, who arrived in Paris on the evening of 23 June. For an account of Brisbane's adventures during the June Days, see Redelia Brisbane, *Albert Brisbane: A Mental Biography* (1893; rpt. New York: Burt Franklin, 1969), pp. 267-72.
7   New York *Courier and Enquirer*, 14 July 1848, pp. 1-2.
8   See esp. P. H. Amann, *Revolution and Mass Democracy: The Paris Club Movement in 1848* (Princeton: Princeton Univ. Press, 1975).
9   New York *Tribune*, 14 July 1848, p. 2.
10 New York *Evening Post*, 13 July 1848, p. 2.
11 *JMN*, vol. 9, 1848-1851, ed. A. W. Plumstead and William H. Gilman (Cambridge, Mass: Belknap Press of Harvard Univ. Press, 1975), p. 74.
12 Emerson, *Complete Works*, vol. 10, *Lectures and Biographical Sketches*, p. 63.
13 See Merton M. Sealts, Jr., "Melville and Emerson's Rainbow," *ESQ* 26 (1980): 59-61.
14 *The Letters of Herman Melville*, ed. Merrell R. Davis and William H. Gilman (New Haven: Yale Univ. Press, 1960), p. 77.

15 Hans Keller, *Emerson in Frankreich: Wirkungen und Parallelen* (Giessen: Universitat zu Griessen, 1932), pp. 91, 94.

16 Cameron, *Transcendental Log*, p. 50; *The Diary of George Templeton Strong*, 1:332; *The Letters of Elizabeth Barrett Browning to Mary Russell Mitford, 1836–1854*, ed. Meredith B. Raymond and Mary Rose Sullivan, 3 vols. (Winfield, Kan., Wedgestone Press, 1983), 3:285; quoted in F. O. Matthiessen, *The James Family: Including Selections from the Writings of Henry James, Senior, William, Henry, & Alice James* (1947; rpt. New York: Vintage Books, 1980), p. 45.

17 Thomas L. Brasher, *Whitman as Editor of the "Brooklyn Daily Eagle"* (Detroit: Wayne State University Press, 1971), pp. 138–39; New Orleans *Crescent*, 18 April 1848, p. 2.

18 Quoted in Gay Wilson Allen, *The Solitary Singer: A Critical Biography of Walt Whitman* (1955; rev. New York: New York Univ. Press, 1967), p. 212.

19 Letter of 29 May 1902 to J. H. Johnston, Washington, D.C., Berg Collection, New York Public Library. In 1888 Whitman told Horace Traubel, "My leanings are all towards the radicals: but I am not in any proper sense of the word a *revolutionnaire:* . . . I was in early life very bigoted in my anti-slavery, anti-capital-punishment and so on, so on, but I have always had a latent toleration for the people who choose the reactionary course" (Horace Traubel, *With Walt Whitman in Camden*, 6 vols. [1906–82], vols. 1–3 [rpt. New York: Rowman and Littlefield, 1961]; 1:193).

20 *Brownson's Quarterly Review* 4 (April 1850): 242; ibid. 6 (October 1852): 564.

21 *Uncle Tom's Cabin, or, Life among the Lowly* (1852; rpt. New York: Collier Macmillan, 1962), p. 289. Hereafter cited in text.

22 Noticing Stowe's treatment of the uprisings of the European masses, Charles H. Foster, in *The Rungless Ladder: Harriet Beecher Stowe and New England Puritanism* (Durham, N.C.: Duke University Press, 1954), asks, "How did Harriet Beecher Stowe ever come to express such views? Had she read Brownson's essay ["The Laboring Classes" (1840)] or heard in some devious fashion of the *Communist Manifesto?* Some forgotten letter of Harriet's, reposing in an old desk, might tell us the answer" (53). The answer is quite simple: her views derive from discussions of the European revolutions in countless newspapers and magazines of the day.

Mary R. Davidson, "The Power of Satire: 1848 and *Uncle Tom's Cabin*," a paper read at the Modern Language Association Convention, Chicago, 1985, points out parallels between the novel and the *Manifesto* but recognizes that "they may be related to the spirit of the times and not to any direct influence." I am indebted to Professor Davidson for sending me a copy of her paper.

23 *The Key to Uncle Tom's Cabin, Presenting the Original Facts and Documents upon which the Story Is Founded* (1853; rpt. New York: Arno Press and the New York Times, 1968), p. 309. In the early 1870s Stowe became even more outspoken in her opposition to political radicalism; in her novel *My Wife and I* (1871), she described Audacia Dangereyes' paper on women's rights as "an exposition of all the wildest principles of modern French communism. It consisted of attacks directed about equally against Christianity, marriage, the family state, and

all human laws and standing order, whatsoever. It was much the same kind of writing with which the populace of France was indoctrinated and leavened in the era preceding the first Revolution, and which in time bore fruit in blood" (quoted in Foster, *The Rungless Ladder*, p. 231).

24 *North American Review* 69 (October 1849): 278, 279.

Chapter 4. The "Cause" and Fuller's *Tribune* Letters

1 *History of Woman Suffrage*, vol. 1, 1848–1861, ed. Elizabeth Cady Stanton, Susan B. Anthony and Matilda Joslyn Gage (1881; rpt. New York: Arno & the New York Times, 1969), p. 70.

2 Sacvan Bercovitch, "The Ideological Context of the American Renaissance," in *Forms and Functions of History in American Literature: Essays in Honor of Ursula Brumm*, ed. Winfried Flack, Jürgen Peper, Willi Paul Adams (Berlin: Erich Schmidt Verlag, 1981), pp. 6, 13. See also Bercovitch, *The American Jeremiad* (Madison: Univ. of Wisconsin Press, 1978), pp. 158–59.

3 Quoted in *History of Woman Suffrage*, p. 805.

4 Ibid.

5 *Memoirs of Margaret Fuller Ossoli*, 2 vols., ed. Ralph Waldo Emerson, William Henry Channing, and James Freeman Clarke (1852; rpt. New York: Burt Franklin, 1972), 2:314.

6 Raymond and Sullivan, eds., *Letters of Elizabeth Barrett Browning to Mary Russell Mitford, 1836–1854*, 3:285, 309.

7 Excellent discussions of Fuller's radicalization can be found in Margaret V. Allen, "The Political and Social Criticism of Margaret Fuller," *South Atlantic Quarterly* 72 (Autumn 1973): 560–73; Ann Douglas, "Margaret Fuller and the Search for History: A Biographical Study," *Womens Studies* 4 (1976): 37–86; and Bell Gale Chevigny, "Growing Out of New England: The Emergence of Margaret Fuller's Radicalism," *Womens Studies* 5 (1977): 65–100. See also Douglas, *The Feminization of American Culture* (New York: Knopf, 1977), pp. 313–48; and Chevigny, *The Woman and the Myth: Margaret Fuller's Life and Writings* (Old Westbury, N.Y.: Feminist Press, 1976), pp. 282–303 and 366–401.

8 About 1837 Fuller wrote Harriet Martineau that Emerson's "influence has been more beneficial to me than that of any American, and . . . from him I first learned what is meant by an inward life. . . . Several of his sermons stand apart in memory, like landmarks of my spiritual history. It would take a volume to tell what this one influence did for me" (*Memoirs*, 1:195).

9 Allen, "Political and Social Criticism of Margaret Fuller," p. 564.

10 *Letters of Emerson*, 4:27–28.

11 *Letters of Emerson*, 3:459.

12 *Letters of Emerson*, 4:35.

13 *Letters of Emerson*, 4:88–89.

14 Margaret Fuller, *At Home and Abroad, or Things and Thoughts in America and Europe*, ed. Arthur B. Fuller (1856; rpt. Port Washington, N.Y.: Kennikat Press, 1971), pp. 171, 150, 160, 170, 181. Mazzini was still in London when Emerson arrived, and in a December 1847 letter to Fuller, Mazzini wrote, "I

... feel fearful that he leads or will lead man too much to contemplation. His work, I think very greatly needed in America, but in our own world we stand in need of one who will like Peter the Hermit inflame us to the Holy Crusade and *appeal* to the collective influences and inspiring sources, more than to individual self-improvement" (Leona Rostenberg, "Mazzini to Margaret Fuller, 1847–1849," *American Historical Review* 47 [October 1941]: 77).

15 *Letters of Emerson,* 3:452–53.
16 Fuller, *At Home and Abroad,* p. 128.
17 Gay Wilson Allen has pointed out that "in all the three months Emerson spent in traveling, lecturing, and being entertained in the hospitable homes of industrial England, he saw very little of the lives of the poor, though he read of their conditions. Unlike Margaret Fuller, he did not seek them out" (*Waldo Emerson,* p. 502).
18 Fuller, *At Home and Abroad,* p. 150.
19 *JMN,* 11:475.
20 See Chevigny, *The Woman and the Myth,* p. 296, and Robert N. Hudspeth, "Preface," *The Letters of Margaret Fuller,* 4 vols to date, (Ithaca, N.Y.: Cornell Univ. Press, 1983–), 4:12.
21 *Letters of Margaret Fuller,* 4:273.
22 Fuller, *At Home and Abroad,* p. 205.
23 *JMN,* 10:326.
24 *Letters of Emerson,* 4:33.
25 Fuller, *At Home and Abroad,* p. 215.
26 *Letters of Margaret Fuller,* 4:271.
27 Lawrence Buell, *Literary Transcendentalism: Style and Vision in the American Renaissance* (Ithaca, N.Y.: Cornell Univ. Press, 1973), pp. 147, 148.
28 Ernest Earnest, *Expatriates and Patriots: American Artists, Scholars, and Writers in Europe* (Durham: Duke Univ. Press, 1968), pp. 136–37.
29 New York *Tribune,* 11 September 1847, p. 1 [*At Home and Abroad,* p. 235]. Because Arthur Fuller revised his sister's *Tribune* letters before publishing them, the original texts of the Italian dispatches will be quoted and cited. Locations of the revised versions in *At Home and Abroad* are cited for reference and comparison.
30 New York *Tribune,* 25 December 1847, p. 3 [*At Home and Abroad,* pp. 239, 240].
31 New York *Tribune,* 1 January 1848, p. 1 [*At Home and Abroad,* p. 253].
32 New York *Tribune,* 1 January 1848, p. 1 [*At Home and Abroad,* pp. 254–55].
33 *Memoirs,* 2:235; New York *Tribune,* 4 May 1848, p. 1 [*At Home and Abroad,* p. 306].
34 New York *Tribune,* 15 June 1848, p. 1 [*At Home and Abroad,* p. 320]; quoted in Chevigny, *The Woman and the Myth,* p. 382.
35 For the plans, see New York *Tribune,* 10 November 1849, p. 1 and 22 January 1850, p. 4. Considérant, who became an American citizen, founded a short-lived colony at Reunion, Texas (near Dallas); Pierre Leroux, with his brother Jules, founded the Cloverdale colony in the Sonoma Valley of California; see *Socialism and American Life,* ed. Donald Drew Egbert and Stow Persons, vol. 1 (Princeton: Princeton Univ. Press, 1952), pp. 636, 188–90.

36 Joseph Jay Deiss, *The Roman Years of Margaret Fuller* (New York: Crowell, 1969), p. 120.
37 New York *Tribune*, 23 June 1849, p. 1 [*At Home and Abroad*, pp. 384–85].
38 H. Remsen Whitehouse, *A Revolutionary Princess: Christina Belgiojoso-Trivulzio, Her Life and Times, 1808–1871* (London: T. Fisher Unwin, 1906), pp. 137–39, 73.
39 New York *Tribune*, 9 January 1850, p. 1.
40 Chevigny, *The Woman and the Myth*, pp. 370, 371.
41 Douglas, "Margaret Fuller and the Search for History," p. 68.
42 *Poetical Works of James Russell Lowell*, p. 138.
43 Earnest, *Expatriates and Patriots*, p. 133.
44 *The Letters of James Freeman Clarke to Margaret Fuller*, ed. John Wesley Thomas (Hamburg: Cram, de Gruyter, 1957), p. 145.
45 New York *Tribune*, 29 January 1848, p. 1 [*At Home and Abroad*, p. 259].
46 New York *Tribune*, 24 July 1849, p. 1 [*At Home and Abroad*, p. 397].
47 New York *Tribune*, 23 July 1849, p. 1 [*At Home and Abroad*, p. 409].
48 New York *Tribune*, 11 August 1849, p. 2 [*At Home and Abroad*, p. 420].
49 New York *Tribune*, 24 July 1849, p. 1 [*At Home and Abroad*, p. 391].
50 New York *Weekly Tribune*, 6 October 1849, p. 2.
51 New York *Tribune*, 11 August 1849, p. 2 [*At Home and Abroad*, pp. 412–13].
52 New York *Weekly Tribune*, 6 October 1849, p. 2.
53 New York *Tribune, Supplement*, 13 February 1850, p. 1.
54 *Memoirs*, 2:239.
55 See Whitehouse, *A Revolutionary Princess*, pp. 168–69.
56 *The Poetical Works of James Russell Lowell*, pp. 94, 92.
57 New York *Tribune*, 23 June 1849, p. 1; 19 January 1849, p. 1; 26 January 1849, p. 1 [*At Home and Abroad*, pp. 380, 334, 338].
58 *Collected Poems of Christopher Pearse Cranch*, ed. Joseph M. DeFalco, pp. 167–68.
59 New York *Herald*, 27 June 1849, p. 2.
60 *Memoirs*, 2:247.
61 Leona Rostenberg, "Margaret Fuller's Roman Diary," *Journal of Modern History* 12 (June 1940): 218.
62 *Memoirs*, 2:268, 269–70. The addressee, William H. Channing, cited in the *Memoirs* for the first letter is incorrect; see Robert N. Hudspeth, "A Calendar of the Letters of Margaret Fuller," in *Studies in the American Renaissance, 1977*, ed. Joel Myerson (Boston: Twayne, 1978), p. 115.
63 Barbara Welter, *Dimity Convictions: The American Woman in the Nineteenth Century* (Athens, Oh.: Ohio Univ. Press, 1976), p. 159.
64 *Journal 2: 1842–1848*, ed. Robert Sattelmeyer (Princeton: Princeton Univ. Press, 1984), pp. 162–63.
65 *Margaret Fuller, American Romantic: A Selection from Her Writings and Correspondence*, ed. Perry Miller (Garden City, N.Y.: Anchor Books, Doubleday, 1963), pp. 247–48.
66 Ibid., p. 248.

Chapter 5. *The Scarlet Letter* and Revolutions Abroad

1 Nathaniel Hawthorne, *The Scarlet Letter*, ed. William Charvat, Roy Harvey
   Pearce, and Claude Simpson (Columbus: Ohio State Univ. Press, 1962), p. 263.
   Hereafter cited parenthetically in text.
2 In the spring of 1849 Caroline Sturgis Tappan was the first friend in America to
   whom Fuller confided her secret that she had had a baby and its father was an
   Italian marquis, Count Ossoli. Caroline was friends with the Hawthornes as well
   as with Fuller; she corresponded with Sophia in the summer of 1849, and Sophia visited her in the Berkshires 3–8 September 1849 shortly before Hawthorne began work in earnest on *The Scarlet Letter*. See Chevigny, *The Woman
   and the Myth*, p. 470, and Nathaniel Hawthorne, *The Letters, 1843–1853*, ed.
   Thomas Woodson, L. Neal Smith, and Norman Holmes Pearson (Columbus:
   Ohio State Univ. Press, 1985), p. 299n4.
3 Francis E. Kearns, "Margaret Fuller as a Model for Hester Prynne," *Jahrbuch
   für Amerikastudien* 10 (1965): 191–97.
4 Emerson, ed., *Memoirs of Margaret Fuller Ossoli*, 1:203.
5 Ibid., 1:56–57.
6 The most revealing information about the Hawthorne–Fuller relationship is
   contained in Margaret Fuller's journal of 1844, which deserves to be edited and
   published. The manuscript is on deposit by Mrs. Lewis F. Perry at the Massachusetts Historical Society.
7 Quoted in Julian Hawthorne, *Nathaniel Hawthorne and His Wife*, 2 vols. (1884;
   rpt. N.p.: Archon Books, 1968), 1:259–61.
8 Paula Blanchard, *Margaret Fuller: From Transcendentalism to Revolution* (New
   York: Delacorte Press, 1978), p. 195. Margaret Vanderhaar Allen, *The Achievement of Margaret Fuller* (University Park: Pennsylvania State Univ. Press,
   1979), has, I think, only slightly overstated the case with her assertion that
   "Hawthorne recognized Margaret's sexuality and passionate nature, responded
   to it, and was terrified of it and of his own passionate sexuality, actual or poten-
   tial" (p. 20).
9 In a letter of December 1848 to her mother, Sophia declared, "What good news
   from France! . . . There seems to be a fine fresh air in France just now. . . . It
   is very pretty when the people do not hurt the kings, but merely make them
   run. Since Prince Metternich has resigned, I conceive that monarchy is in its
   decline" (quoted in Julian Hawthorne, *Nathaniel Hawthorne and His Wife*,
   1:331).
10 See Celeste Loughman, "Hawthorne's Patriarchs and the American Revolution,"
   American Transcendental Quarterly 40 (1979): 340–41, and John P. Mc-
   Williams, Jr., "'Thorough-Going Democrat' and 'Modern Tory': Hawthorne and
   the Puritan Revolution of 1776," *Studies in Romanticism* 15 (1976): 551.
11 Hawthorne's reservations about the behavior of revolutionary mobs can also be
   seen in his sketches "The Old Tory" (1835) and "Liberty Tree" (1840). His manuscript "Septimius Felton" contains some of his final thoughts on the subject.
   "In times of Revolution and public disturbance," he writes, "all absurdities are
   more unrestrained; the measure of calm sense, the habits, the orderly decency,
   are in a measure lost. More people become insane, I should suppose; offenses

against public morality, female license, are more numerous; suicides, murders, all ungovernable outbreaks of men's thoughts, embodying themselves in wild acts, take place more frequently, and with less horror to the lookers-on" (*The Elixir of Life Manuscripts*, ed. Edward H. Davidson, Claude M. Simpson, and L. Neal Smith [Columbus: Ohio State Univ. Press, 1977], p. 67).

12 Nathaniel Hawthorne, "My Kinsman, Major Molineux," in *The Snow-Image and Uncollected Tales*, ed. J. Donald Crowley (Columbus: Ohio State Univ. Press, 1974), p. 230.

13 Letter to George Duyckinck, 18 April 1848; Duyckinck Family Papers, New York Public Library.

14 "Fall of the Throne of the Barricades," *Blackwood's* 63 (1848): 399.

15 Letter to Evert Duyckinck, 30 June 1848; Duyckinck Family Papers, New York Public Library.

16 See the review "Lamartine's Histoire des Girodins," *Southern Quarterly Review* 16 (1849): 58.

17 Arlin Turner, *Nathaniel Hawthorne: A Biography* (New York: Oxford Univ. Press, 1980), p. 181.

18 See Joseph B. Felt, *The Annals of Salem, from Its First Settlement* (Salem: W. & S. B. Ives, 1827), pp. 176, 317.

19 See Caleb H. Snow, *A History of Boston, the Metropolis of Massachusetts* (Boston: A Bowen, 1825), p. 169.

20 See John R. Byers, Jr., and James J. Owen, *A Concordance to the Five Novels of Nathaniel Hawthorne*, vol. 2 (New York: Garland, 1979), pp. 667, 579.

21 *Oxford English Dictionary*, vol. 9 (Oxford: Clarendon Press, 1933), p. 159. Beheading was not a common form of punishment in the Massachusetts Bay Colony. The only mention I have found of it involved the punishment of an Indian found guilty of theft and of striking a settler's wife in the head with a hammer, causing her to lose her senses. Neither a block nor a scaffold was used in his execution, however. "The executioner would strike off his head with a falchion," John Winthrop reported, "but he had eight blows at it before he could effect it, and the Indian sat upright and stirred not all the time" (*The History of New England from 1630 to 1649*, ed. James Savage, 2 vols. [1825–26; rpt. New York: Arno Press, 1972], 2:189).

22 Andrew Marvell, *The Complete English Poems*, ed. Elizabeth Story Donno (New York: St. Martin's Press, 1972), p. 56.

23 See Edward Dawson, *Hawthorne's Knowledge and Use of New England History: A Study of Sources* (Nashville: Joint Univ. Libraries, 1939), p. 17.

24 Marion L. Kesselring, *Hawthorne's Reading, 1828–1850* (1949; rpt. New York: Norwood, 1976), p. 52.

25 See Winthrop, *History of New England*, 2:85.

26 Felt, *Annals of Salem*, p. 175.

27 See Frederick Newberry, "Tradition and Disinheritance in *The Scarlet Letter*," *ESQ* 23, no. 1 (1977): 13.

28 The relationship between the French and English revolutions is one point emphasized in Lamartine's work; he points out that "Louis XVI had read much history, especially the history of England. . . . The portrait of Charles I., by Van Dyck, was constantly before his eyes in the closet in the Tuileries; his history

NOTES TO PAGES 88–96

continually open on his table. He had been struck by two circumstances; that James II. had lost his throne because he had left his kingdom, and that Charles I. had been beheaded for having made war against his parliament and his people" (Alphonse de Lamartine, *History of the Girondists* [New York: Harper, 1847–48], 1:52). This edition of Lamartine will hereafter be cited parenthetically in the text.

29 Kesselring, *Hawthorne's Reading*, p. 42.

30 Hawthorne and his wife spent much of the last half of August and the first part of September househunting, first on the Atlantic shore near Kittery Point and then in the Berkshires near Lenox. Hawthorne may have worked on *The Scarlet Letter* during the second week in September after Sophia returned from Lenox, but if he did, it was not with the commitment he later displayed, for on 17 September he set out with his friend Ephraim Miller on a leisurely three-day journey to Temple, New Hampshire. Assuming he rested on the twentieth, the day after his return, and knowing it was the twenty-seventh when Sophia first said he was writing "immensely" mornings and afternoons, it seems likely that between 21 September and 25 September he became absorbed in the writing of his romance.

31 Letter to Elizabeth P. Peabody (mother); Berg Collection; New York Public Library.

32 Nina Baym in her discussion of "The Custom-House" sketch posits that "like Hester, [Hawthorne] becomes a rebel because he is thrown out of society, by society. . . . The direct attack of 'The Custom-House' on some of the citizens of Salem adds a fillip of personal revenge to the theoretical rebellion that it dramatizes" (*The Shape of Hawthorne's Career* [Ithaca, N.Y.: Cornell Univ. Press, 1976], pp. 148–49). Hawthorne's attack, I think, can be more accurately termed a counterattack and seen as dramatizing not a rebellion but his reaction to a rebellion.

33 Leland Schubert, *Hawthorne the Artist* (Chapel Hill: Univ. of North Carolina Press, 1944), pp. 137–38.

34 Fuller, *At Home and Abroad*, p. 381.

35 Henry Nash Smith, *Democracy and the Novel: Popular Resistance to Classic American Writers* (New York: Oxford Univ. Press, 1978), p. 25.

36 For excellent discussions of Hawthorne's attitudes toward women activists, see Neal F. Doubleday, "Hawthorne's Hester and Feminism," *PMLA* 54 (1939): 825–28; Morton Cronin, "Hawthorne on Romantic Love and the Status of Women," *PMLA* 69 (1954): 89–98; and Darrel Abel, "Hawthorne on the Strong Dividing Lines of Nature," *American Transcendental Quarterly*, no. 14 (1972): 23–31.

37 Donald A. Ringe, "Hawthorne's Psychology of the Head and Heart," *PMLA* 65 (1950): 129.

38 Michael Davitt Bell, *Hawthorne and the Historical Romance of New England* (Princeton: Princeton Univ. Press, 1971), p. 140.

39 A number of critics have read this scene as ironic and seen Dimmesdale as deluded or damned; however, the Pietà tableau, Arthur's Christlike forgiveness of Chillingworth, and Hawthorne's own emotional response to the scene (when he read it to Sophia) make it difficult to agree with such a reading.

40 Michael J. Colacurcio, "Footsteps of Ann Hutchinson: The Context of *The Scar-*

let Letter," *ELH* 39 (1972): 459–94, and more recently, *The Province of Piety: Moral History in Hawthorne's Early Tales* (Cambridge: Harvard Univ. Press, 1984); Woodson, "Hawthorne's Interest in the Contemporary," *Nathaniel Hawthorne Society Newsletter* 7 (1981): 1.

Chapter 6. *Moby-Dick* and the Matter of France

1   See William Fortescue, *Alphonse de Lamartine: A Political Biography* (New York: St. Martin's, 1983), pp. 269–71.
2   *Democratic Review* 25 (August 1849): 137.
3   *The Poetical Works of James Russell Lowell*, p. 101.
4   Fortescue, *Alphonse de Lamartine*, p. 270.
5   *I Sit and Look Out: Editorials from the "Brooklyn Daily Times,"* ed. Emory Holloway and Vernolian Schwarz (New York: Columbia Univ. Press, 1932), p. 67.
6   Herman Melville, *Clarel: A Poem and Pilgrimage in the Holy Land*, ed. Walter E. Bezanson (New York: Hendricks House, 1960), p. 193. Hereafter cited parenthetically.
7   Cf. Fortescue's observation that Lamartine "was always a self-proclaimed man of peace: 'I have always been, and always will be, a partisan of peace,' he told the Chamber of Deputies on 27 January 1843; in the *Histoire des Girodins* he wrote that 'peace was the first of the Revolution's true principles'" (197–98). For Lamartine, "Napoleon's wars of aggression were a terrible perversion of the Revolutionary ideal" (198).
8   *Journal of a Visit to London & the Continent by Herman Melville, 1848–1850*, ed. Eleanor Melville Metcalf (Cambridge: Harvard Univ. Press, 1948), p. 53.
9   *Illustrated London News* 14 (March 21, 1849): 186.
10 *The Letters of William Cullen Bryant, Volume III, 1849–1857*, ed. William Cullen Bryant II and Thomas G. Voss (New York: Fordham Univ. Press, 1981), p. 95.
11 Herman Melville, *Typee: A Peep at Polynesian Life*, ed. Harrison Hayford, Hershel Parker, and G. Thomas Tanselle (Evanston, Ill.: Northwestern Univ. Press, 1968), p. 12.
12 Herman Melville, *Billy Budd, Sailor (An Inside Narrative)*, ed. Harrison Hayford and Merton M. Sealts, Jr. (Chicago: Univ. of Chicago Press, 1962), p. 129. Hereafter cited parenthetically.
13 Herman Melville, *Redburn*, p. 7.
14 Herman Melville, *Moby-Dick; or, The Whale*, ed. Harrison Hayford and Hershel Parker (New York: Norton, 1967), pp. 436–37. Hereafter cited parenthetically.
15 Herman Melville, *Israel Potter: His Fifty Years of Exile*, ed. Harrison Hayford, Hershel Parker, and G. Thomas Tanselle (Evanston, Ill.: Northwestern Univ. Press, 1982), p. 63.
16 Gilman, *Melville's Early Life and "Redburn,"* p. 7.
17 Letter of Allan Melvill to Thomas Melvill, Sr., June 13, 1818, Melville Family Papers; Gansevoort-Lansing Collection; Rare Books and Manuscripts Div.; New York Public Library; Astor, Lenox and Tilden Foundations.

18 Gilman, *Melville's Early Life*, p. 15.
19 Stanton Garner, "The Picaresque Career of Thomas Melvill, Junior," *Melville Society Extracts*, no. 60 (November 1984): 1.
20 Herman Melville, "Sketch of Major Thomas Melvill, Jr. By a Nephew," Melville Family Papers, Gansevoort-Lansing Collection, New York Public Library.
21 See R. R. Palmer, "Herman Melville et la Révolution Française," *Annales Historiques de la Révolution Française* 26 (July–September 1954): 254–56.
22 Letter of Thomas Melvill, Jr., to Thomas Melvill, Sr., June 13, 1802, copy, Melville Collection, Houghton Library, Harvard University.
23 Melville, "Sketch of Major Thomas Melvill."
24 Henry A. Murray discusses the many parallels between Priscilla and Isabel in his introduction to *Pierre* (Chicago: Hendricks House, 1949), p. lxv.
25 Melville, "Sketch of Major Thomas Melvill."
26 Letter of Julia Melvill to Augusta Melville, June 29, 1842, Melville Family Papers (Additions); Gansevoort-Lansing Collection; New York Public Library.
27 Letter of Thomas Melvill to Lemuel Shaw, September 6, 1843; Lemuel Shaw Papers; Massachusetts Historical Society.
28 Merton M. Sealts, Jr., "The Ghost of Major Melvill," *New England Quarterly* 30 (September 1957): 305.
29 J. E. A. Smith, "Herman Melville," 1891–92; rpt. in Merton M. Sealts, Jr., *The Early Lives of Melville: Nineteenth-Century Biographical Sketches and Their Authors* (Madison: Univ. of Wisconsin Press, 1974), p. 138.
30 Sealts, "The Ghost of Major Melvill," p. 305.
31 Letter of Priscilla Melvill to Augusta Melville, April 3, 1848; Melville Family Papers (Additions); Gansevoort-Lansing Collection; New York Public Library.
32 See Gilman, *Melville's Early Life*, pp. 68–69.
33 Letter of Priscilla Melvill to Augusta Melville, April 20, 1849; Melville Family Papers (Additions); Gansevoort-Lansing Collection; New York Public Library.
34 It was this lineage that Melville, like his father, Allan, seems to have been most proud of. During a visit to the Hawthorne's he told Sophia and she reported to her sister that he had bought an estate six miles from them "where he is really going to build a real towered house—an actual tower. He is married to a daughter of Judge Shaw Judge Lemuel Shaw, & has a child of year & half—Malcolm. He is of Scotch descent—of noble lineage—of the Lords of Melville & Leven, & Malcolm is a family name"; Jay Leyda, *The Melville Log: A Documentary Life of Herman Melville, 1819–1891*, 2 vols. (1951; rpt. with additional material, New York: Gordian Press, 1969), 2:296.
35 *Letters of Melville*, p. 29.
36 Eleanor Melville Metcalf, *Herman Melville: Cycle and Epicycle* (Cambridge: Harvard Univ. Press, 1953), p. 53.
37 *Letters of Melville*, p. 75.
38 Melville alluded to Burke's *Reflections on the Revolution in France* as early as 1839 in his "Lansingburgh Fragments" (Gilman, *Melville's Early Life*, p. 360), and in *Mardi* his narrator facetiously refers to "my late eloquent and prophetic friend and correspondent, Edmund Burke" (79). A number of critics, of course, have seen Burke's influence in *Billy Budd*.
39 See John Gerlach, "Messianic Nationalism in the Early Works of Herman Mel-

ville: Against Perry Miller," *Arizona Quarterly* 28 (Spring 1972): 5–26, for an able discussion of these passages. Melville's spread-eagle nationalism has been repeatedly examined; that it formed part of the American response to the European revolutions, however, has gone unnoticed. In fact, the two foremost studies of literary Young America (John Stafford, *The Literary Criticism of 'Young America': A Study in the Relationship of Politics and Literature, 1837–1850* [1952; rpt. New York: Russell and Russell, 1967], and Perry Miller, *The Raven and the Whale: The War of Words and Wits in the Era of Poe and Melville* [1956; rpt. Westport, Conn.: Greenwood Press, 1973]) have given the impression that Melville's contributions to the movement were embarrassingly belated, that he was a naïve enthusiast beating the drum after the band had stopped playing. In actuality, though, the country as a whole, in response to the revolutions of 1848–49, had become one large Young America, and Melville was merely contributing to the din sounding around him.

   For an example of the purple prose that came into fashion as a result of the revolutions, see Frederick Merk, *Manifest Destiny and Mission in American History, A Reinterpretation* (New York: Knopf, 1963), p. 199.

40 See my "Antidemocratic Emphasis in *White-Jacket,*" *American Literature* 48 (March 1976): 13–28.

41 See, for example, Willie T. Weathers, "*Moby Dick* and the Nineteenth-Century Scene," *Texas Studies in Language and Literature* 1 (Winter 1960): 477–501; Charles H. Foster, "Something in Emblems: A Reinterpretation of *Moby-Dick,*" *New England Quarterly* 34 (March 1961): 3–35; and Alan Heimert, "*Moby-Dick* and American Political Symbolism," *American Quarterly* 15 (Winter 1963): 498–534.

42 James Duban, *Melville's Major Fiction: Politics, Theology, and Imagination* (Dekalb, Ill.: Northern Illinois Univ. Press, 1983), p. 123; Michael Paul Rogin, *Subversive Genealogy: The Politics and Art of Herman Melville* (New York: Knopf, 1983), pp. 114, 130.

43 Lewis Mumford, *Herman Melville: A Study of His Life and Vision* (1929; rev. ed. New York: Harbinger Books, 1962), p. 124; Henry A. Murray, "'In Nomine Diaboli,'" *New England Quarterly* 24 (December 1951): 435–52; rpt. in *Melville: A Collection of Critical Essays,* ed. Richard Chase (Englewood Cliffs, N.J.: Prentice-Hall, 1962), p. 63.

44 The *Eroica,* as students of music know, was originally dedicated to Napoleon, but when he crowned himself emperor in May 1804, Beethoven, outraged, changed the title of the work to "Heroic Symphony, composed to celebrate the memory of a great man."

45 Thomas Carlyle, *On Heroes, Hero-Worship and the Heroic in History* (1897; rpt. New York: AMS Press, 1969), p. 204.

46 "A volume should be written on the image of Napoleon in democratic America," Perry Miller declared over thirty years ago (*The Raven and the Whale,* p. 189), and his statement is still true.

47 For an extended discussion of the war and battle imagery of *Moby-Dick,* see Joyce Sparer Adler, *War in Melville's Imagination* (New York: New York Univ. Press, 1981), pp. 58–61.

48   Leon Howard, *Herman Melville: A Biography* (Berkeley: Univ. of California Press, 1967), p. 110.

49   Leyda, *The Melville Log*, 1:xxvi.

50   Augustus Kinsley Gardner, *Old Wine in New Bottles* (New York: Francis, 1848), pp. 180, 181.

51   Leyda, *The Melville Log*, 1:xxvi.

52   Letter of Allan Melvill to Maria Melvill, June 11, 1818. Melville Family Papers; Gansevoort-Lansing Collection; New York Public Library. (I am indebted to Jay Leyda for helping me transcribe this quotation.)

53   H. Melville, "Sketch of Major Thomas Melvill."

54   Letter of Thomas Melville to Helen Melville, May 3, 1846, Melville Family Papers (Additions); Gansevoort-Lansing Collection; New York Public Library. The spelling errors are Thomas's.

55   Merton M. Sealts, Jr., "Melville and Emerson's Rainbow," *ESQ* 26 (1980): 67.

56   Ralph Waldo Emerson, *Complete Works*, vol. 4, *Representative Men*, pp. 224, 223.

57   Luther S. Mansfield and Howard P. Vincent point out this latter echo in their "Explanatory Notes," *Moby-Dick* (New York: Hendricks House, 1952), p. 823. Sealts, "Melville and Emerson's Rainbow," p.76n57, notes several other passages in Melville's writings that echo sentences in *Representative Men*.

58   See Merton M. Sealts, Jr., *Melville's Reading: A Check-List of Books Owned and Borrowed* (Madison: Univ. of Wisconsin Press, 1966), p. 48.

59   Although this specific indebtedness has not received critical attention, Carlyle's pervasive influence on *Moby-Dick* has not gone unnoticed. The influence of Carlyle's style, of his ideas about the emblematic nature of the visible world, of his characterization of Teufelsdröckh, of his dark view of industrialism and technology are treated, respectively, in Matthiessen, *American Renaissance*, pp. 384–85; Tyrus Hillway, *Herman Melville* (New York: Twayne, 1963), pp. 83–86; Howard, *Herman Melville: A Biography*, pp. 171–72, 178; Leo Marx, *The Machine in the Garden* (New York: Oxford, 1967), pp. 286, 297–99. The fullest discussion of the influence of *Heroes and Hero-Worship* upon Melville's creation of the heroic character of Ahab is Jonathan Arac, *Commissioned Spirits: The Shaping of Social Motion in Dickens, Carlyle, Melville, and Hawthorne* (New Brunswick, N.J.: Rutgers Univ. Press, 1979), pp. 148–63. For Arac, "Cromwell is the Carlylean hero who most resembles Ahab" (149).

60   The chapter "The Whiteness of the Whale" treats many more ideas than this one, of course; furthermore, there are a number of subtle differences between Ahab's perception of the visible world and Ishmael's. For the most sustained and informative comparison of the Ahabian and Ishmaelian epistemologies, see Robert Zoellner, *The Salt-Sea Mastodon: A Reading of Moby-Dick* (Berkeley: Univ. of Calif. Press, 1973).

61   For a discussion of the importance of Solomon and Ecclesiastes to Melville's thought and art, see Nathalia Wright, *Melville's Use of the Bible* (Durham, N.C.: Duke Univ. Press, 1949), pp. 95–101.

62   See my "Kings and Commoners in *Moby-Dick*," *Studies in the Novel* 12 (Summer 1980): 101–13.

63 See Josef and Shizuko Muller-Brockmann, *History of the Poster* (Zurich: ABC Verlag Zurich, 1971), p. 28; Morris B. Schnapper, *American Labor: A Pictorial Social History* (Washington, D.C.: Public Affairs Press, 1972), pp. 18, 47.

64 See Sean Wilentz, *Chants Democratic: New York City and the Rise of the American Working Class* (New York: Oxford Univ. Press, 1985), pp. 343-46.

65 Marx, *Manifesto of the Communist Party*, trans. Samuel Moore, p. 87.

66 Rpt. *Panorama 1842-1865: The World of the Early Victorians As Seen through the Eyes of the Illustrated London News* (Boston: Houghton Mifflin, 1969), p. 62; New York *Herald*, 14 July 1848, p. 3.

67 A long line of Melville critics, beginning with F. O. Matthiessen and continuing through and past H. Bruce Franklin, have minimized Melville's conservatism and exaggerated his democratic sympathies. To believe that Melville was "an artist whose creative imagination was forged in the furnace of his labor and oppression, an artist who saw the world of nineteenth-century American society and its commercial empire through the eyes of its victims" is not so much false as it is half true. The quotation comes from H. Bruce Franklin, *The Victim as Criminal and Artist: Literature from the American Prison* (New York: Oxford, 1978), p. 34, but it represents a common perception, or more accurately misperception, of Melville found in studies too numerous to cite.

68 "Explanatory Notes," in *Clarel*, pp. 587, 588.

69 If one has accepted the thesis and demonstration of this chapter, some of the ways in which *Billy Budd* shows the continuing influence of the revolutions of 1848-49 on Melville's imagination should be apparent. At the center of the book, of course, is the issue of revolution versus order; and given Melville's consistent distrust of political radicalism, given the familiar ideology informing his description of the mutineers of the Nore "transmuting the flag of founded law and freedom defined, into the enemy's red meteor of unbridled and unbounded revolt" (54), given the political conservatism evident in all Melville wrote from 1848 on, it becomes very difficult to read the novel, as so many critics have insisted it be read, as an ironic condemnation of Vere and his use of measured forms. Admittedly Melville's human sympathies and his democratic values are a part of the work, but when he chose as his setting the years of the French Revolution during the period of the Directory, he most likely did so with Burkean sentiments consistent with those he had expressed, albeit subtly and indirectly, in *Mardi*, in *Moby-Dick*, and in *Clarel*. When Captain Vere claims "with mankind, forms, measured forms are everything," and applies this to "the disruption of forms going on across the Channel and the consequences thereof" (128), he voices one of Melville's deepest convictions. For the most thorough and valuable discussion of the conservative context and emphases of *Billy Budd*, see Milton Stern, introduction to *Billy Budd* (Indianapolis: Bobbs-Merrill, 1975), pp. vii–xliv.

Chapter 7. Revolution, Martyrdom, and *Leaves of Grass*

1 Betsy Erkkila, *Walt Whitman among the French: Poet and Myth* (Princeton: Princeton Univ. Press, 1980), pp. 3-50.

2 See, for example, Emory Holloway, *Whitman, An Interpretation in Narrative*

(New York: Knopf, 1926), pp. 65–71; Maurice Bucke, "Walt Whitman and the Cosmic Sense," in *In Re Walt Whitman* (Philadelphia: David McKay, 1893), pp. 329–47; and Roger Asselineau, *The Evolution of Walt Whitman*, 2 vols. (Cambridge, Mass: Belknap Press of Harvard Univ. Press, 1960, 1962).

3   See, for example, F. O. Matthiessen, *American Renaissance*, pp. 522–24; Esther Shephard, *Walt Whitman's Pose* (New York: Harcourt, Brace, 1936); Gay Wilson Allen, "Walt Whitman and Jules Michelet," *Etudes Anglaises* 1 (May 1937): 230–37; and Fred Manning Smith, "Whitman's Poet-Prophet and Carlyle's Hero," *PMLA* 55 (1940): 1146–64.

4   Maurice Mendelson, *Life and Work of Walt Whitman: A Soviet View*, trans. Andrew Bromfield (Moscow: Progress Publishers, 1976), p. 146.

5   Mistaking cause for effect, Mendelson concludes that "the high passion of abolitionism . . . gave him a greater awareness of the grandeur of the revolutionary struggle in Europe" (p. 82).

6   See Brasher, *Whitman as Editor*, p. 162.

7   For an excellent discussion of Whitman and slavery, see Asselineau's chapter "Democracy and Racialism—Slavery," in *Evolution of Walt Whitman*, 2:179–91. Whitman's Free-Soil stance at midcentury resulted not from sympathy for slaves but from concern for white workingmen; he opposed the extension of slavery in the western territory, for he believed workers should be protected from the competition of slave labor. The question of whether slavery in the South should be abolished was of secondary importance to him at the time.

8   Walt Whitman, "To a Foil'd Revolutionaire," *Leaves of Grass: Comprehensive Reader's Edition*, ed. Harold W. Blodgett and Sculley Bradley (New York: Norton, 1965), p. 370. Hereafter cited parenthetically.

9   Justin Kaplan, *Walt Whitman: A Life* (New York: Simon and Schuster, 1980), p. 58.

10 *The Uncollected Poetry and Prose of Walt Whitman*, ed. Emory Holloway, 2 vols. (New York: Peter Smith, 1932), 2:286.

11 Allen, *The Solitary Singer*, p. 9.

12 Horace Traubel, *With Walt Whitman in Camden;* 1:467.

13 Erkkila, *Walt Whitman among the French*, pp. 12–24.

14 *The Gathering of the Forces, 1846–1847*, ed. Cleveland Rogers and John Black, 2 vols. (New York and London: Putnam's Sons, 1920), 1:109–10.

15 Ibid., 2:285–86.

16 Brooklyn *Daily Eagle*, 10 August 1847, p. 2.

17 Allen, *The Solitary Singer*, p. 44.

18 Ronald Paulson, *Representations of Revolution (1789–1820)* (New Haven and London: Yale Univ. Press, 1983), pp. 70–71, 76–78.

19 Traubel, *With Walt Whitman*, 117.

20 See Alexandra R. Murphy, *Jean-François Millet* (Boston: New York Graphic Society Books, Little Brown, 1984), p. 32.

21 Walt Whitman, *Prose Works 1892*, ed. Floyd Stovall, 2 vols. (New York: New York Univ. Press, 1963), 1:267–68.

22 Brasher, *Whitman as Editor*, p. 98.

23 Floyd Stovall, *The Foreground of "Leaves of Grass"* (Charlottesville: Univ. Press of Virginia, 1974), p. 123.

24 Brooklyn *Daily Eagle,* 10 August 1847, p. 2.
25 Allen, "Walt Whitman and Jules Michelet," p. 237.
26 *Gathering of the Forces,* 1:15–16.
27 Ibid., 1:12, 28.
28 Ibid., 1:23, 37, 38.
29 Ibid., 1:29, 30.
30 Ibid., 2:286–87.
31 *Uncollected Poetry and Prose,* 2:78.
32 Paul Zweig, *Walt Whitman: The Making of the Poet* (New York: Basic Books, 1984), p. 74.
33 New Orleans *Crescent,* 31 March 1848, p. 2.
34 Ibid., 8 April 1848, p. 1; 16 March 1848, p. 2; 20 May 1848, p. 2.
35 Ibid., 7 April 1848, p. 2; 17 April 1848, p. 2.
36 New York *Daily Tribune,* 21 June 1850, p. 2; rpt. *The Early Poems and the Fiction,* ed. Thomas L. Brasher (New York: New York Univ. Press, 1963), p. 38. The first line contained three typographical errors that Whitman later corrected.
37 New Orleans *Crescent,* 27 April 1848, p. 1; 21 April 1848, p. 2; 3 May 1848, p. 2; 18 May 1848, p. 2.
38 Kaplan, *Walt Whitman,* p. 136.
39 Betsy Erkkila, "Walt Whitman: The Politics of Language," *American Studies* 24 (1983): 26.
40 Quoted in Joseph Jay Rubin, *The Historic Whitman* (University Park: Pennsylvania State Univ. Press, 1973), p. 206.
41 Ibid., p. 207; Traubel, *With Walt Whitman,* 3:536.
42 Rubin, *Historic Whitman,* p. 223.
43 Asselineau, *Evolution of Walt Whitman,* 2:260.
44 Stovall, *The Foreground,* pp. 114–16.
45 New York *Daily Tribune,* 9 January 1850, p. 1; *Daily Tribune, Supplement,* 13 February 1850, p. 1.
46 Kaplan, *Walt Whitman,* p. 164.
47 *Early Poems and Fiction,* pp. 38–40.
48 See Gay Wilson Allen, *The New Walt Whitman Handbook* (New York: New York Univ. Press, 1975), pp. 223, 226, 232–33.
49 Zweig, *Walt Whitman* pp. 74–75.
50 Shephard makes this point in *Walt Whitman's Pose,* p. 80.
51 Allen, *The Solitary Singer,* p. 168.
52 Erkkila, *Walt Whitman among the French,* p. 25.
53 Traubel, *With Walt Whitman,* 2:502.
54 Fuller, *At Home and Abroad,* p. 195.
55 *I Sit and Look Out,* p. 159.
56 Erkkila, *Walt Whitman among the French,* p. 33.
57 Quoted by Allen, *New Walt Whitman Handbook,* p. 253. For another version, see *The Correspondence,* ed. Edwin Haviland Miller, 6 vols. (New York: New York Univ. Press, 1961–77), 3:369.
58 Shephard, *Walt Whitman's Pose,* p. 141.
59 Bucke, *In Re Walt Whitman,* p. 35.

60 *Uncollected Poetry and Prose*, 1:245, 246.

61 Ibid., pp. 246–47.

62 Rubin, *Historic Whitman*, p. 266.

63 *JMN*, 10:312.

64 *Notebooks and Unpublished Prose Manuscripts*, ed. Edward F. Grier, 6 vols. (New York: New York Univ. Press, 1984), 1:108–09.

65 Traubel, *With Walt Whitman*, 2:486.

66 D. H. Lawrence, *Studies in Classic American Literature* (1923; rpt. Garden City, N.Y.: Doubleday, 1951), pp. 187–88.

67 Rubin, *Historic Whitman*, p. 269.

68 *Notebooks and Unpublished Prose Manuscripts*, 3:1065.

69 "More of Revolution," New Orleans *Crescent*, 14 April 1848, p. 2.

70 Stovall, *The Foreground*, p. 146. Stovall has also pointed out that "Whitman approached European history chiefly through two main interests: popular literature, especially poetry, and revolutions leading to a more democratic society" (p. 182).

71 "Hungary," 240 and "The Slavonians and Eastern Europe," 301, 305, Trent Collection, Perkins Library, Duke University.

72 Malcolm Cowley, ed., *Walt Whitman's "Leaves of Grass": The First (1855) Edition* (New York: Viking, 1959), pp. xxvii–xxviii.

73 *Uncollected Poetry and Prose*, 1:247.

74 *Walt Whitman's "Leaves of Grass*," p. xxiv.

75 See *Leaves of Grass: A Textual Variorum of the Printed Poems*, vol. 1: *Poems, 1855–1856*, ed. Sculley Bradley, Harold W. Blodgett, Arthur Golden, and William White (New York: New York Univ. Press, 1980), p. 5.

76 Erkkila, "Walt Whitman: The Politics of Language," p. 29, discusses these features.

77 *Gathering of the Forces*, 1:213–14.

78 *Notebooks and Unpublished Prose Manuscripts*, 4:1354.

79 *Correspondence*, 1:288.

80 Allen, *The Solitary Singer*, p. 374; Asselineau, *Evolution of Walt Whitman*, 2:141.

81 Asselineau, *Evolution of Walt Whitman*, 1:203–04.

Chapter 8. Kossuth "Fever" and the Serenity of *Walden*

1 Harriet Beecher Stowe, *The Key to Uncle Tom's Cabin; Presenting the Original Facts and Documents upon which the Story Is Founded* (1854; rpt. New York: Arno Press and the New York Times, 1968), pp. 238, 237.

2 Thoreau, "Life Without Principle," In *Reform Papers*, ed. Wendell Glick, pp. 171, 173.

3 Introduction, P. C. Headley, *The Life of Louis Kossuth, Governor of Hungary* (Auburn: Derby and Miller, 1852), p. viii.

4 Joseph Szeplaki, "Bibliography on Louis Kossuth, Governor of Hungary, with Special Reference to His Trip in the United States, December 4, 1851–July 14, 1852." Available in the Ohio Univ. Library, Athens, Ohio.

5 *The Collected Works of Abraham Lincoln*, vol. 2, ed. Roy P. Basler (New Bruns-

wick, N.J.: Rutgers Univ. Press, 1953), p. 116; William Dean Howells, *Years of My Youth* (New York: Harper, 1916), p. 67.

6 Donald S. Spencer, *Louis Kossuth and Young America: A Study of Sectionalism and Foreign Policy, 1848–1852* (Columbia: Univ. of Missouri Press, 1977), p. 62.

7 Leyda, *The Melville Log*, 1:441. A summary of the responses to Kossuth's visit by American writers is provided by Edward Stone, "Kossuth's Hat: Foreign Militants and the American Muse," *ESQ* 23 (1977): 36–40.

8 "I and My Chimney," in *Herman Melville: Pierre, Israel Potter, The Piazza Tales, The Confidence-Man, Uncollected Prose, Billy Budd, Sailor,* Library of America Edition (New York: Viking, 1984), p. 1301. Hereafter cited in text.

9 Merton M. Sealts, Jr., "The Chronology of Melville's Short Fiction, 1853–1856," *Harvard Library Bulletin* 28 (October 1980): 402–03.

10 Hawthorne, *Letters, 1843–1853*, p. 537.

11 See Julian Hawthorne, *Hawthorne and His Circle* (New York: Harper, 1903), pp. 47–50.

12 Hawthorne, *Letters, 1843–1853*, p. 542.

13 Emerson, *Complete Works*, vol. 11, *Miscellanies*, pp. 397–401.

14 Quoted in New York *Weekly Tribune*, 22 May 1852, p. 6.

15 Thoreau, *The Journal of Henry D. Thoreau*, ed. Bradford Torrey and Francis H. Allen, 14 vols. (Boston: Houghton Mifflin, 1906), 4:46. Hereafter cited parenthetically in the text.

16 Lewis Leary, "'Now I Adventured': 1851 as a Watershed Year in Thoreau's Career," *ESQ* 19 (1973): 141–48.

17 Walter Harding, *A Thoreau Handbook* (New York: New York Univ. Press, 1959), p. 72.

18 J. Lyndon Shanley, *The Making of "Walden"* (Chicago: Univ. of Chicago Press, 1957), pp. 30–31, 66–67.

19 Thoreau, *Reform Papers*, p. 169.

20 Henry David Thoreau, *Walden*, ed. J. Lyndon Shanley (Princeton: Princeton Univ. Press, 1971), p. 95. Hereafter cited parenthetically in text.

21 Robert D. Richardson, Jr., *Henry Thoreau: A Life of the Mind* (Berkeley: Univ. of California Press, 1986), p. 214.

22 Sherman Paul, *The Shores of America: Thoreau's Inward Exploration* (Urbana: Univ. of Illinois Press, 1972), pp. 268, 288.

23 Mary Elkins Moller, *Thoreau in the Human Community* (Amherst: Univ. of Massachusetts Press, 1980), pp. 28–29.

24 *JMN*, 11:284.

25 Ibid., 404.

26 Joel Porte, *Emerson and Thoreau: Transcendentalists in Conflict* (Middletown, Conn.: Wesleyan Univ. Press, 1965), p. 34.

27 Thoreau, *Reform Papers*, pp. 175, 173.

28 Shanley, *Making of "Walden,"* p. 72.

29 Raymond Adams, "Thoreau's Mock-Heroics and the American Natural History Writers," *Studies in Philology* 52 (1955); rpt. in *The Recognition of Henry David Thoreau: Selected Criticism since 1848*, ed. Wendell Glick (Ann Arbor: Univ. of Michigan Press, 1969), p. 301.

30 Raymond Adams makes this point in "Thoreau's Mock-Heroics," p. 306, but he adds, "Are the unyielding insects displaying the bravery of the greatest legendary heroes? Or do men in human battles behave like insects? It is not entirely clear, and it was not intended to be clear" (310). Thoreau's emphasis on aloofness and purity would seem to make it evident that the mock-heroics are intended to diminish the significance of human warfare.

31 Shanley, *Making of "Walden,"* pp. 66–67.

32 Thoreau, *Reform Papers*, p. 108.

Epilogue

1 Matthiessen, *American Renaissance*, p. ix.

2 Asselineau, *Evolution of Walt Whitman*, 2:190.

3 "Hawthorne and His Mosses," rpt. *Moby-Dick*, p. 540.

4 Albert Rothenberg, *The Emerging Goddess: The Creative Process in Art, Science, and Other Fields* (Chicago: Univ. of Chicago Press, 1979), pp. 346–47, 374.

5 I have in mind books such as Carolyn Karcher, *Shadow Over the Promised Land: Slavery, Race, and Violence in Melville's America* (Baton Rouge: Louisiana Univ. Press, 1980); Joyce Sparer Adler, *War in Melville's Imagination* (New York: New York Univ. Press, 1981); Rogin, *Subversive Genealogy* (1983); M. Wynn Thomas, *The Lunar Light of Whitman's Poetry* (Cambridge, Mass.: Harvard Univ. Press, 1987); and Robert Shulman, *Social Criticism & Nineteenth-Century American Fictions* (Columbia: Univ. of Missouri Press, 1987).

6 Raymond Williams, *Marxism and Literature* (Oxford: Oxford Univ. Press, 1977), pp. 110, 113–14.

7 Afterword, *Ideology and Classic American Literature*, ed. Sacvan Bercovitch and Myra Jehlen (New York: Cambridge Univ. Press, 1986), p. 434.

8 Sacvan Bercovitch, *The American Jeremiad*, p. 203.

9 *JMN*, 10:310.

Index

Abel, Darrel, 189n36
Abolitionism, 65, 126
Adams, Raymond, 169, 199n30
Adler, Joyce Sparer, 192n47, 199n5
Agnew, Mary, 12
Agoult, Comtesse d'. *See* Stern, Daniel
Agulhon, Maurice, 175–76n6
Albert, the worker, 18
Albert, Prince Consort, 29
Alboni, Marietta, 137
Alison, Archibald, 82
Allen, Gay Wilson, 38, 128, 131, 151,
    181n46, 185n17, 195n3, 196n48
Allen, Margaret V., 57, 184n7
Amann, P. H., 182n8
America, 10, 12, 65, 78, 109, 147, 174
American Whig Review, 18, 178n56
Anti-Slavery Standard, 16
Arac, Jonathan, 193n59
Arago, François, 15, 82
Arnold, Matthew, 38
Asselineau, Roger, 136, 151, 152, 172, 195n7

Bancroft, George, 5, 8, 15, 19, 21, 27
Barbès, Armand, 18–19, 33, 34–35
Barnum, P. T., 19
Barras, Paul Jean, 104
Baym, Nina, 189n32
Beethoven, Ludwig van, 68, 110; *Eroica*,
    109, 110, 192n4
Belgiojoso, Princess Christina, 66, 74, 75
Bell, Michael Davitt, 94
Bennett, James Gordon, 55
Béranger, Pierre-Jean de, 142

Bercovitch, Sacvan, 54, 173; *The American
    Jeremiad*, 173
Bezanson, Walter E., 100, 124
Bible, 109, 140
Blackwood's Magazine, 23, 82
Blake, H. G. O., 163
Blake, William, 58
Blanc, Louis, 18, 32, 67, 117, 134; *History of
    the Ten Years, 1830–1840*, 3, 67
Blanchard, Paula, 80
Blanqui, Louis Auguste, 18, 34–35, 42
Bloody June Days, 43, 44–48, 53, 54–55, 69,
    72, 82, 97, 101, 108, 119–20
Bonaparte. *See* Napoleon Bonaparte
Boston *Courier*, 6
Boston *Daily Advertiser*, 6, 81
Boston *Post*, 82, 83
Bourgin, George, 45
Bowen, Francis, 53
Bradford, George, 28
Brady, William, 11
Branch, Watson, 177n37
Breunig, Charles, 176n6
Brisbane, Albert, 50, 182n6
Brook Farm, 26, 31, 32, 48, 50
Brooklyn *Advertiser*, 136
Brooklyn *Daily Eagle*, 20, 51, 126, 127, 130–
    33, 151
Brooklyn *Daily Times*, 98
Brown, Henry Kirke, 142
Brown, John, 144, 170
Browning, Elizabeth Barrett, 50, 56
Brownson, Orestes, 51–52
Brownson's Quarterly Review, 51

Bryant, William Cullen, 5, 11, 49, 87, 101, 157; "Italian Patriot Song," 14
Buchanan, James, 15
Buell, Lawrence, 63
Burke, Edmund, 128, 191n38
Burns, Anthony, 170
Byron, George Gordon, Lord, 21, 109, 143

Cabet, Etienne, 2
Caesar, Julius, 75
Calhoun, John, 16–17, 109, 115
Carlyle, Thomas, 9, 28, 33, 37, 38, 41, 42, 58, 59, 63, 88, 109, 110, 116, 179n11; French Revolution, 88, 131; Heroes and Hero-Worship, 110, 116, 125
Cass, Lewis, 109, 115
Cavaignac, General Louis, 44, 45, 46, 82, 108
Champion of American Labor, 119
Channing, William Ellery (1818–1901), 157
Channing, William Henry, 60, 62, 65, 77
Charles I, 84, 85–86, 91, 159, 188–89n28
Charles V, 159
Charles Albert, king of Piedmont, 64, 75, 117
Chartists, 3, 25, 28, 30–31, 36, 40, 41, 121, 180n22
Chazin, Maurice, 176n10
Chevigny, Bell Gale, 67, 184n7
Chopin, Frederic, 44, 58
Christ, 52, 53, 61, 74, 98, 110
Civil War, American, 53, 126, 150–51
Civil War, English, 85–86
Clark, T. J., 179n69
Clarke, James Freeman, 5, 68
Cloots, Anacharsis, 111
Clough, Arthur Hugh, 38, 41
Clubs of Paris, 18, 33–35
Colacurcio, Michael J., 96
Cole, Phyllis, 37
Coleridge, Samuel Taylor, 41
Communism, 4, 18–19, 26, 42, 45, 50–51, 66, 119–23, 183n23
Communist League, 2
Communist Manifesto, 2, 119
Considérant, Victor, 60, 66, 185n35
Cook, Eliza, "To Alphonse de Lamartine," 14
Cowley, Malcolm, 149
Cranch, Christopher, 5, 75–76
Crane, Stephen, 71
Cromwell, Oliver, 84, 110
Cronin, Morton, 189n36
Cruikshank, George, 156
Curtis, Eugene N., 178n49
Curtis, George William, 5, 45

Dana, Charles A., 5, 45, 46–48, 51, 135, 182n6
Dante, Alighieri, 109; Inferno, 59
Darguad, Jean-Marie, 98
Davidson, Mary R., 183n22
Davis, Merrell R., 177n37
Dawson, Edward, 188n23
De Quincey, Thomas, 58
Deiss, Joseph Jay, 66
Delacroix, Eugène: Liberty Leading the People, 8
Democratic Review, 97, 132
Dial, 62, 163
Dickens, Charles, 37, 58
Doherty, Hugh, 31, 60, 66
Dostoyevski, Fyodor, 3
Doubleday, Neal F., 189n36
Douglas, Ann, 68, 184n7
Duban, James, 109
Duyckinck, Evert, 7, 10, 11–12, 13, 82
Duyckinck, George, 5, 7–10, 82, 159

Earnest, Ernest, 63
Eisley, Loren, 168
Eldridge, Charles W., 51
Emerson, Edward Waldo, 41
Emerson, Ellen Tucker, 57
Emerson, Lydia (Lidian) Jackson, 26, 28, 37, 41, 42, 58, 61, 165, 166
Emerson, Mary Moody ("Aunt Mary"), 37
Emerson, Ralph Waldo, 25–43, 57–62; and Carylye, 33, 41, 42–43; on Chartists, 28–29, 31, 36, 41; conservatism of, 27–29, 42, 54, 171; on the English, 35, 58–59; on the French, 35, 43; and Fuller, 57–62; idealism of, 37, 39–40, 173; influence in England, 41–42; influence in France, 4, 50; and Kossuth, 153, 160–61; on Lamartine, 39, 44; and London Times, 28–29; and Melville, 49, 114–15; radicalism of, 40, 42, 172–73; and socialism, 26–28, 33–36, 40–42; and Thoreau, 42, 43, 162, 165–67; on French revolution of 1848, 49, 61; and Whitman, 125, 149; mentioned, 1, 5, 53, 63, 77, 116, 144
—Works: "Address to Kossuth," 160–61, 167; "The American Scholar," 37; "Conduct of Life" (lecture), 167; Conduct of Life, 38, 54; "Divinity School Address," 37; English Traits, 25, 29, 35, 38, 42, 43, 166; "France, or Urbanity," 43; "Mind and Manners in the Nineteenth Century," 25, 36–43, 44, 60, 165; "Napoleon," 25; "Natural Aristocracy," 26, 27, 37, 40, 49; Natural History of Intellect, 38; "Natural History of the Intellect," 37, 38–40; Nature, 39, 144; "Po-

etry and Eloquence," 37, 40; "Politics and Socialism," 37, 40, 42; "Powers and Laws of Thought," 37, 39; "Relation of Intellect to Natural Science," 37, 40; *Representative Men*, 25, 38, 114–15; "The Spirit of the Age," 26; "The Spirit of the Times," 26; "The Superlative in Manners and Literature," 181*n*58; "Tendencies and Duties of Men of Thought," 37, 40; "The Uses of Great Men," 25
Engels, Friedrich, 1–2, 131
Erkkila, Betsy, 136, 141, 194*n*1, 197*n*76

Farady, Michael, 39
Fejtö, François, 175*n*6
Felt, Joseph B., 84, 188*n*18; *Annals of Salem*, 86
Ferdinand I, emperor of Austria, 154
Ferdinand II, king of Naples and Sicily, 2, 3, 15, 16–17, 63
Five Glorious Days of Milan, 66, 74
Flaubert, Gustave: *Education Sentimentale*, 45
Fleury, Marie des Douleurs, 104–05
Fleury, M. Lamé, 104
Forster, Reverend William Edward, 33, 35
Fortescue, William, 190*n*7
Foster, Charles H., 183*n*22, 192*n*41
Fourier, Charles, 2, 27, 50, 54, 60, 61, 66, 74, 159
Fourierism, 26, 50, 60–62, 65–67, 74
Franklin, H. Bruce, 194*n*67
Frederick William IV, king of Prussia, 3
Freeman, The, 136
French Revolution, of 1789, 4, 9, 16, 23, 81–82, 84, 87–88, 110, 124, 128–30, 150; of 1848, 3, 4, 5–12, 18–24, 86, 87, 99–100, 101, 110, 123–24, 134–35; of 1871, 124, 152
Froude, J. A., 41
Fruitlands, 26
Fugitive Slave Act, 148
Fuller, Arthur B., 72, 185*n*29
Fuller, Margaret (Ossoli), 55–78; and Emerson, 57–62; on England, 59; on French revolution of 1848, 61–62, 65, 68; and Hawthorne, 76, 79–80; influence on Whitman, 137–39; and Lamartine, 20; and Mazzini, 65–66, 72, 77; persona of, 74–78, 173; radicalism of, 50, 56, 72–73, 91, 171; radicalization of, 57–62, 65; and socialism, 60–62, 64–67, 74, 174; style, 67–74; writing versus conversation, 77–78; mentioned, 1, 2, 5, 25, 30, 36, 37, 53, 81, 125, 131, 132, 136, 142, 149, 163, 164
—Works: "American Literature," 137; "Con-versations," 55; "The First of January," 1; "History of the Roman Republic," 57, 62, 76; *At Home and Abroad*, 72, 137; *Memoirs*, 166; *Summer on the Lakes*, 63, 68; *Tribune* dispatches from Italy, 45, 57, 62–78, 137–38, 171; *Woman in the Nineteenth Century*, 56, 62
Fuller, Richard, 77

Gardner, Dr. Augustus Kinsley: *Old Wine in New Bottles*, 113
Garibaldi, Giuseppe, 67, 71–72, 73, 81, 150
Garneray, Ambroise Louis, 111–13
Garrison, William Lloyd, 157
Gerber, John C., 26
Gerlach, John, 191*n*39
Goethe, Johann Wolfgang von, 25, 38, 109
Goodrich, Samuel, 5, 6–7, 45
Greeley, Horace, 11, 12, 46, 50, 57, 60, 68, 76, 79, 80, 138, 154, 165, 169
Greenough, Horatio, 5
Greenough, Henry: *Ernest Carroll*, 5
Gregory XVI, Pope, 64
Guillotin, Dr., 84
Guizot, François, 6, 85–86, 87, 96, 119, 132; *History of the English Revolution of 1640*, 85, 131

Hammen, Oscar, 178*n*58
Harbinger, 31
Harding, Walter, 162
Harper's Magazine, 5
Hawthorne, Elizabeth (Ebe), 79
Hawthorne, Julian, 160
Hawthorne, Nathaniel, 79–96; conservatism of, 49, 81, 89, 96, 172, 173–74; and English Civil War, 84–86; and French Revolution of 1789, 86–89; and Fuller, 76, 79–80; and Kossuth, 153, 160; and Lamartine, 20, 87–89, 96; radicalism of, 172; and revolutions of 1848–49, 24, 53, 80–83; mentioned, 5, 10, 25, 97, 100, 101, 109, 114, 137, 171
—Works: *The Blithedale Romance*, 52, 160; "Earth's Holocaust," 49, 82; "Endicott and the Red Cross," 84; "My Kinsman, Major Molineaux," 81; *The Scarlet Letter*, 20, 53, 79–96, 97, 172, 173
Hawthorne, Sophia Peabody, 79, 80, 81, 88, 187*n*9
Hawthorne, Una, 80
Hazlitt, William: *Napoleon*, 127, 131
Headley, Joel T., 5
Hedge, Frederick, 5
Heimert, Alan, 192*n*41
Helps, Arthur, 42

Hemingway, Ernest, 71
Henry VIII, 159
Hillard, George S., 5, 15, 81
Hillway, Tyrus, 193n59
Hoar, Elizabeth, 58
Holloway, Emory, 194n2
Howard, Leon, 177n48
Howells, William Dean, 158–59
Hudspeth, Robert N., 185n20
Hughes, Bishop John, 76, 82
Hugo, Victor, 127
Hutchinson, Anne, 50, 79, 93
Hutchinson, Thomas, 84

Illustrated London News, 8, 9, 33, 47, 70,
    73, 100, 120, 155
Ireland, Alexander, 58
Irving, Washington, 59

James II, 189n28
James, Henry, Sr., 50
Jarves, James Jackson, 5
Jefferson, Thomas, 51, 54, 127
Jerrold's Newspaper, 181n51
John, prince of Saxony, 178n57
Johnson, Samuel, 157
Jones, David J. V., 180n23
Jones, John Paul, 103
Josephine, empress of France, 114

Kaplan, Justin, 127, 136, 139
Karcher, Carolyn, 199n5
Kearns, Francis E., 79
Kendall, George, 5
Kennedy, John Pendleton, 11, 12
Kent, Rockwell, 123
Kirkland, Caroline, 5, 45
Knickerbocker Magazine, 5
Kossuth, Louis, 3, 136, 143, 145–46, 153,
    154, 157–61, 163, 164, 165, 166, 167, 169

Lafayette, Marquis de, 104, 127
Lamartine, Alphonse de, 3, 15, 18–24, 27,
    32, 35, 39, 44, 48, 51, 67, 82, 87–89, 96,
    97–100, 120, 122, 128, 134–36, 142, 147,
    190n7; History of the Girondists, 3–4, 19–
    20, 21, 67, 87–89, 97, 131, 134
Lamennais, Félicité Robert de, 60
Lawrence, Amos, 53
Lawrence, D. H., 145
Leary, Lewis, 162
Ledru-Rollin, Alexandre Auguste, 18, 19
Legun, Count de, 104
Lejeune, L. F., 112
Leland, Charles G., 5, 6
Leopold, grand duke of Baden, 64
Leroux, Jules, 185n35

Leroux, Pierre, 61, 66, 185n35
Lincoln, Abraham, 158
London Chronicle, 30
London Phalanx, 60
London Times, 28, 29–31, 37, 49, 59, 69, 73,
    166
Longfellow, Henry Wadsworth, 15; Evange-
    line, 15
Loughman, Celeste, 187n10
Louis Napoleon, 50, 81, 82, 100–01, 117,
    136, 152, 163
Louis Philippe, king of France, 3, 4, 5, 8, 15,
    16, 22, 61, 67, 85, 117, 132, 134, 160
Louis XIV, king of France, 159
Louis XVI, king of France, 52, 79, 84, 86–
    88, 91, 105, 127, 128, 159, 188n28
Lowell, James Russell, 15, 17, 68, 74, 98;
    Biglow Papers, 16, 17; "The Debate in the
    Sennit," 17; Fable for Critics, 68; "To La-
    martine, 1848," 98; "Ode to France, " 16,
    74; "The Pious Editor's Creed," 17

Manchester Guardian, 41
Mansfield, Luther S., 193n57
Marat, Jean Paul, 82, 88
Marie Antoinette, 79, 128
Marseilles Hymn, 10, 11, 14, 21, 28
Martineau, Harriet, 58
Martineau, James, 58
Marvel, Ik. See Mitchell, Donald
Marvell, Andrew: "An Horatian Ode," 84
Marx, Karl, 2, 18, 32, 42, 48, 54, 66, 119
Marx, Leo, 193n59
Mather, Cotton, 84
Matthiessen, F. O., 171, 193n59, 195n3
Mazzini, Joseph, 3, 59, 60, 65–66, 72, 77,
    81, 136, 143, 157, 164, 184n14
McWilliams, John P., Jr., 187n10
Melvill, Allan (father), 102–04, 113, 124
Melvill, Julia, 105
Melvill, Napoleon, 114
Melvill, Priscilla, 11, 105, 106, 107
Melvill, Robert, 11
Melvill, Thomas, 103–06, 107, 113–14, 124
Melville, Augusta, 105
Melville, Elizabeth Shaw, 114
Melville, Gansevoort, 106
Melville, Helen, 114
Melville, Herman, 97–124; and Carlyle, 110,
    116, 193n59; on Chartists, 30–31; conserv-
    atism of, 49–50, 53, 105–07, 121–24, 172,
    173–74; and Emerson, 49, 114–15; and
    France, 100–08; and French Revolution of
    1789, 110, 124; and French revolution of
    1848, 10, 13–14, 24, 49–50, 53, 101, 107–
    08, 117–24; and Kossuth, 153, 159–60;

and Lamartine, 20, 97–100; and Napoleon, 103, 110–14; nationalism of, 12, 108, 191–92n39; radicalism of, 172; mentioned, 5, 7, 11, 25, 125, 131, 137, 171
—Works: *Billy Budd*, 97, 101, 102, 107, 124, 194n69; *Clarel*, 97–100, 123–24; "The House-Top," 123; "I and My Chimney," 159–60; *Israel Potter*, 103; "Jimmy Rose," 106; *Mardi*, 13–14, 30–31, 49–50, 99, 101, 106, 107, 117, 119, 121; *Moby-Dick*, 12, 53, 97, 98, 99, 103, 106, 108–23, 172, 173; *Omoo*, 107; *Pierre*, 105, 106, 159; *Redburn*, 12, 102, 108, 131; *Typee*, 101, 107; *White-Jacket*, 12, 108
Melville, Tom, 114
Mendelson, Maurice, 125–26, 195n5
Merk, Frederick, 192n39
Metternich, Prince Clemens, 3, 50, 66, 117, 119, 160
Mexican War, 169
Michelet, Jules, 4, 35, 127, 176n10; *History of France*, 131; *The People*, 125
Mickiewicz, Adam, 4, 60, 176n10
Miller, Perry, 192n39, 192n46
Miller, Ephraim, 189n30
Millet, Jean-François, 128–30; *The Sower*, 129
Milton, John, 109
Mitchell, Donald (Ik Marvel), 5, 45–48, 55, 120; *The Battle Summer*, 46, 182n4; "Marvel Letters from Abroad," 46; *Reveries of a Bachelor*, 46
Moller, Mary Elkins, 165
Montaigne, Michel de, 25
Montégut, Émile, 50
Morewood, Sarah, 159
Morpeth, Lord, 41
Mott, Lucretia, 54, 55
Mumford, Lewis, 109
Murray, Henry A., 109, 110, 191n24

Napoleon Bonaparte, 25, 103, 110–17, 127, 190n7, 192n46
National workshops, 32, 33, 44, 117
National Era, 154, 157
Nationalism, 3, 4, 12, 108, 132, 151, 192n39
New Orleans *Crescent*, 14, 15, 17, 20, 22, 51, 133–35, 145
New York *Courier and Enquirer*, 19, 20, 46, 169
New York *Evening Post*, 19, 87
New York *Herald*, 6, 19, 120
New York *Tribune*, 2, 11, 12, 19, 45, 46, 48, 50, 55, 57, 59, 61, 62–68, 137, 138, 142, 165, 169
Newberry, Frederick, 188n27
Newman, John Henry, 38

Newport Insurrection, 30
Nicholas I, czar of Russia, 3, 45, 154, 159
North American Phalanx, 60
North American Review, 18, 53, 178n56
North British Review, 146

O'Connor, Feargus, 29
Orleans, Duchess of, 21
Ossoli, Marchese Giovanni Angelo, 58, 69, 74, 76–77, 80, 163
Ossoli, Margaret. *See* Fuller, Margaret
Oudinot, General Charles, 71
Owen, Robert, 2, 27, 39, 51

Paine, Thomas, 96, 126, 127, 144
Pall Mall Gazette, 41
Palmer, R. R., 191n21
Pape, Eric, 90
Paris Commune of 1871, 124
Paris, Count of, 21
Paul, Sherman, 165, 180n37
Paulding, James Kirke, 17
Paulson, Ronald, 128
Peabody, Elizabeth, 55, 79
Peabody, Sophia. *See* Hawthorne, Sophia
People's Charter, 29
Peuple, Le (periodical), 82
Philadelphia *North American*, 6
Pitt, William, 104
Piux IX, Pope, 15, 50, 52, 64, 69, 81, 138, 157, 160
Plato, 25
Poe, Edgar Allan, 140
Polk, James K., 11, 169
Porte, Joel, 166
Prescott, William H., 5
Presse, La (periodical), 23
Proudhon, Pierre Joseph, 2, 42

Quincy, Josiah, Jr., 15
Quinet, Edgar, 4, 176n10

Rachel, Mlle., 32
Radetzky, Count Josef, 138
Raeder, Ole Munch, 12
Read, Thomas Buchanan: "France is Free," 10–11, 14
Red republicanism, 18, 50–53, 100, 120
Red Revolution, 44–53, 97, 119
Red Scare, 18, 50, 51, 53
Reign of Terror, 23, 71, 82, 88, 127
Revolutionary imagery, 23–24, 31, 81–85, 94, 107–08, 111, 119, 130, 151; arm and hammer, 24, 118–23; barricades, 24, 111; figure of liberty, 8, 9, 14, 16, 24, 74–76, 79, 94, 95, 173; guillotine, 24, 45, 82–84;

Revolutionary imagery (*continued*)
liberty cap, 24; red flag, 22–24, 111, 119–23; scaffold, 24, 82–85, 87–89
Révolution Démocratique et Sociale, La (periodical), 82
Revue Indépendente, La, 61
Richardson, Robert D., Jr., 163
Ringe, Donald A., 94
Ripley, George, 50
Risorgimento, 65, 138
Robertson, Priscilla, 176n23
Robespierre, Maximilien, 82, 104
Robinson, David, 181n45
Robinson, Henry Crabb, 41
Rochester *Democrat*, 55
Rogin, Paul Michael, 109, 199n5
Rossi, Count Pellegrino, 75, 76
Rotch, Mary, 61, 66
Rothenberg, Albert, 172
Rousseau, Jean-Jacques, 127, 172; *Confessions*, 127
Rubin, Joseph Jay, 145, 177n42

Saint-Simon, Claude Henri de, 2
Saint-Simonism, 66
Sand, George, 19, 60, 127, 137, 142; *Countess of Rudolstadt*, 125; *Journeyman Joiner*, 131
Sartain's Union Magazine, 19
Schubert, Leland, 90
Scott, Sir Walter, 9, 72
Scudder, Townsend, III, 41, 180n38, 182n61
Sealts, Merton M., Jr., 105, 182n13, 193n58
Shakespeare, William, 25, 109, 157
Shanley, J. Lyndon, 198n18
Shaw, Lemuel, 105, 109
Shelley, Percy Bysshe: *Masque of Anarchy*, 31; "Ozymandias," 117
Shephard, Esther, 142, 195n3, 196n50
Shulman, Robert, 199n5
Signourney, Lydia: "Too Late," 22
Simms, William Gilmore, 17
Smith, Fred Manning, 195n3
Smith, Henry Nash, 92
Smith, J. E. A., 105
Snow, Caleb H., 84, 188n19
Socialism, 4, 18–19, 25, 26–28, 32, 35–36, 42, 45, 48, 50–51, 53, 58, 60, 65, 76
Southern Quarterly Review, 17
Southern Literary Messenger, 19
Sowder, William J., 182n61
Spencer, Donald S., 159
Spring, Marcus, 60, 76, 136
Spring, Rebecca, 60, 76
Stafford, John, 192n39
Stanton, Elizabeth Cady, 54
Stearns, Peter N., 175n6, 176n12

Sterling, James Hutchinson, 41
Stern, Daniel (pseudonym of Marie de Flavigny, Comtesse d'Agoult), 4, 32; *Histoire de la Révolution de 1848*, 4, 7, 34, 121, 122
Stern, Milton R., 194n69
Stone, Edward, 198n7
Story, William Wetmore, 5
Stovall, Floyd, 197n70
Stowe, Harriet Beecher, 52–53, 153–57; 183n22, 183n23; *Key to Uncle Tom's Cabin*, 53; *Uncle Tom's Cabin*, 52–53, 153–57
Strong, George Templeton, 50
Sumner, Charles, 15, 18
Sumner, George, 6, 18
Swedenborg, Emanuel, 25

Tappan, Caroline Sturgis, 187n2
Taylor, Zachary, 82–83
Taylor, Bayard, 12; "A Voice from Piedmont," 12
Tennyson, Alfred, 31
Thomas, M. Wynn, 199n5
Thoreau, Henry David, 153–70; aloofness, 1, 68–70; conservatism of, 171, 172; and Emerson, 40, 42, 43; and Fuller, 163–64; interest in current events, 163–67, and Kossuth, 165–67, 169, 173; radicalism of, 1, 42, 170, 172; mentioned, 2, 25, 50, 53, 67, 78
—Works: "Civil Disobedience," 1, 42, 50, 169; "Life without Principle," 162, 163, 166; "Slavery in Massachusetts," 170; "Spirit of Lodin," 153, 164; *Walden*, 63, 153, 162–70, 172; *A Week on the Concord and Merrimack Rivers*, 63, 162, 166
Ticknor, George, 15, 178n57
Tocqueville, Alexis de, 2, 21, 48
Token, 6
Town and Country Club, 50
Traubel, Horace, 128
Turner, Arlin, 83
Twain, Mark, 22

Vanity Fair (periodical), 5
Victoria, Queen, 3, 29
Vigoureux, Clarisse, 60
Vincent, Howard P., 193n57
Volney, Constantin François, 127
Voltaire (François Marie Arouet), 127

Ware, William, 5
Washington, George, 126, 135, 143, 157
Weathers, Willie T., 192n41
Webb, James Watson, 46, 169
Webster, Daniel, 18, 109, 115, 139, 164, 169
Wellington, Duke of, 29

Welter, Barbara, 77
Westminster Review, 146
Whicher, Stephen E., 180–81*n*40
Whipple, E. P., 160
Whitman, Andrew, 137
Whitman, Eddie, 137
Whitman, George, 142–43
Whitman, Hannah, 137
Whitman, Jesse, 137
Whitman, Walt, 125–52; conservatism of, 51, 172, 183*n*19; and Emerson, 125, 149; and French revolution of 1848, 14, 133–36, 141; and Fuller, 137–39; interest in Europe, 130–33, 142–47; interest in revolution in France, 17, 50–51, 126–30, 150–51; and Kossuth, 143, 145–47, 153; and Lamartine, 20, 23, 51, 98, 128, 134–36; nationalism of, 132–33, 151–52; radicalism of, 30, 136, 171, 174; and socialism, 51; mentioned, 5, 22, 25, 168
—Works: "Art Union Speech," 143, 145; "Bervance," 128; "Blood-Money," 139; "By Blue Ontario's Shore," 151; "Crossing Brooklyn Ferry," 145, 168; "Europe in the 72d and 73d Years of These States," 126, 141; "France, the 18th Year of These States," 130, 150; "The House of Friends," 139; *Leaves of Grass,* 14, 20, 67, 125, 126, 128, 139, 142, 147, 151, 152; "O Star of France," 152; "Preface" to 1855 *Leaves,* 134, 147–49; "Poem of Joys," 150; "Poem of Salutation," 150; "Poem of the Dead Young Men of Europe," 141; "Poem of the Sayers of the Words of the Earth,"150; "Resurgemus," 67, 126, 134–35, 138–41, 142, 144, 148, 149, 150; "Salut Au Monde!" 150; "Song for Certain Congressmen," 139; "A Song of Joys," 125, 150; "Song of Myself," 137, 142, 144, 147, 149; "Song of the Broad-Axe," 150; "Song of the Open Road," 150; "A Song of the Rolling Earth," 150; "Songs of Insurrection," 152; *Specimen Days,* 129; "There Was A Child Went Forth," 128; "To a Certain Cantatrice," 150; "To a Foil'd European Revolutionaire," 137, 148, 150; "Turn O Libertad," 151; "Wild Frank's Return," 128
Whitman, Walter (Sr.), 126, 127
Whittier, John Greenleaf, 15, 19; "The Crisis," 16; *Song of Labor,* 15
Wilentz, Sean, 194*n*64
Wilkinson, Garth, 29, 31, 40, 42, 58
Williams, Raymond, 173
Winthrop, John, 84, 92, 188*n*21
Women's Rights Convention, 54–55
Woodson, Thomas, 96
Wordsworth, William, 44, 58, 63
Working Man's Advocate, 119, 120
Wright, Frances, 126, 127, 137
Wright, Martha C., 54
Wright, Nathalia, 176*n*18; 193*n*61

Young America, 10, 12, 108, 132, 192*n*39

Zoellner, Robert, 193*n*60
Zweig, Paul, 133, 140